D1478209

The Right to Food

Printing:
Meyer en Siegers

ISBN 90-247-3087-2

The Right to Food

P. Alston
K. Tomaševski
(editors)

International Studies in Human Rights

 Stichting Studie- en Informatiecentrum Mensenrechten - SIM

MARTINUS NIJHOFF PUBLISHERS

c1

Preface

To assert that everyone has the right to food seems easy. Many international documents contain authoritative statements to that effect, in particular article 11 of the International Covenant on Social, Economic and Cultural Rights. However, its development into an operational legal right for the existing diversity of national legal systems is extremely difficult. Even if the content of the right to food would be accepted at the minimum of "freedom from hunger", one has to admit that there are neither specific obligations for states to guarantee it, nor effective mechanisms to supervise the implementation of the right to food.

In the face of widespread and continuing hunger, numerous international organizations were created, starting with the FAO in 1945. The policies and practices of those entities are bound by law and produce legal norms themselves, but they all stay within general international (economic) law, rather than international human rights law. The latter developed quite independently in the human rights bodies of the United Nations, but concentrated on civil and political rights, while treating the right to food - amidst other economic, social and cultural rights - as mere aspirational rights or programmatic goals to be achieved through economic growth.

The question is whether human rights law and human rights activists have better ways to assist the deprived than the usual reference to the preamble of the Universal Declaration of Human Rights:

"Whereas it is essential, if man is not compelled to have recourse, as a last resort, to rebellion against tyranny and oppression, that human rights should be protected by the rule of law, ..."

The issue of the "realization" of the right to food, as the most fundamental of the social and economic rights, is the focus of the Right to Food project which the Netherlands Institute of Human Rights (SIM) started in November 1983.

The Netherlands Ministry of Development Cooperation through a special grant made it possible to hire the services of Dr. Katarina Tomaševski, from Zagreb University, and organize an international conference from 6 to 9 June 1984 in Utrecht. This conference, "The Right to Food from Soft to Hard Law", also benefitted from the financial support of the Ministry of Foreign Affairs of Norway and Oxfam. The keynote speaker at the conference was Mr. Philip Alston, who together with Katarina Tomaševski undertook to edit this book.

The timing of the project is not arbitrary: the Universal Declaration on the Eradication of Hunger and Malnutrition will be one decade old on 16 November 1984. In 1982 the UN Subcommission for the Prevention of Discrimination and the Protection of Minorities entrusted Mr. Asbjørn Eide with a study on the Right to Food, which is expected to be submitted in final version in August 1985. The International Law Association (ILA) approved in 1984 the creation of a Right to Food committee, which is investigating the possibilities for an international legal instrument on the right to food. There-

5

fore the ILA and SIM decided to work together and several meetings of members of the ILA Right to Food Committee were organized. The committee will report to the ILA conference in 1986.

The SIM conference and this book have in common the desire to provide a meeting point between lawyers and decision makers, between researchers and activists. In that sense the book is likely to have a more lasting effect. The main articles are written by the editors themselves. The first one by Philip Alston, provides an overview of the whole problematic from a legal viewpoint and the other one, by Katarina Tomaševski, looks at the crucial issue of indicators for the realization of the right to food. Other authors tackle the problem from different angles, but all have in common to approach to the problem of world hunger from a human rights perspective. The width of their knowledge and expertise, and the renewed interest which the right to food receives in international organizations, make this book another effort in the struggle which is neither easy, nor hopeless.

The book is an outcome of the accumulated knowledge and commitment of people working in the food field and the human rights field who over many years have been trying to apply both tested human rights techniques and new concepts to the unyieldy matter of social, economic and cultural rights.

It provides powerful ammunition to the "idealists" who believe that social, economic and cultural rights can and must be made to work by adopting appropriate policies.

Hans Thoolen

Director Netherlands Institute of Human Rights (SIM)

Utrecht, July 1984.

6

Editors Introduction

At the conclusion of the World Food Conference held in Rome 1974 the governments of the world proclaimed "that within a decade no child will go to bed hungry, that no family will fear for its next day's bread, and that no human being's future and capacities will be stunted by malnutrition".

As that decade comes to a close the tragic reality is that little, if any, progress has been made towards meeting those goals. During the target year of 1984, as during every other year since the Conference, literally millions of children have starved to death, tens of millions have gone to bed hungry and malnutrition continues to afflict hundreds of millions of people in all parts of the world. These statistics make hunger by far the most flagrant and widespread of all serious human rights abuses. Yet, for the most part, it is a problem which has to date been perceived by most (well-fed) policy-makers, academics, human rights activists and others as a painful but inevitable fact of "life", rather than as an abregation of all that the concept of human rights stands for.

The present book is an attempt, for the first time, to make hunger a prominent issue on the international human rights agenda and to put the right to food on the agenda of national and international food agencies.

In the first chapter Philip Alston provides an overview of the problem and examines the role of law - past, present and future - in promoting the eradication of hunger and malnutrition. The assumption underlying that analysis, and shared by most if not all other contributors, is that there are significant benefits to be derived from tackling hunger as a human rights issue within the framework of established norms of international law. The question of duties attaching to the right to food, which Alston considers from the standpoint of international law, is further developed from a philosophical perspective by Henry Shue.

In a chapter dealing with the broad philosophical aspects of the right to food Amartya Sen establishes its validity as a basic right. This perspective is reinforced by a wide-ranging historical review undertaken by Pierre Spitz in which he shows that even in ancient times both the legitimacy of governments and their hold on power were often dependent on their ability to manage the local food system in the interests of avoiding widespread hunger. He also demonstrates that historically the occurrence of widespread hunger has usually been the result of an abuse of economic or political power.

Roger Plant then traces the evolution in recent decades of Latin American policies relevant to the right to food. His analysis emphasizes the potentially explosive consequences of the institutionalized gap between political rhetoric and its legislative embodiment on the one hand and the harsh reality of widespread hunger on the other - a contradiction which has also characterized much of the approach of the international community.

Other contributions deal with different aspects of the challenge of giving substance to the right to food through the creative use of law. In addressing the local and national dimensions of that challenge Clarence Dias and

7

James Paul survey some of the practical means by which activist popular organizations can make effective use of available legal resources in order to assert the right to food of local communities.

In the chapters dealing with the international dimensions particular emphasis is placed on establishing, from a jurisprudential viewpoint, that economic, social and cultural rights are full-fledged human rights and are not merely vague aspiration of limited hortatory value. This fundamentally important issue is approached from different angles by Fried van Hoof and Guy Goodwin-Gill.

Finally, the chapters by Katarina Tomaševski and Gert Westerveen are devoted to the complex but eminently practical issues of how respect for the right to food might effectively be monitored through the use of social indicators and how the right to food-related obligations of states under international law could more effectively be supervised by the international community.

In the final analysis, the stakes involved in efforts to give substance to the right to food are immense. Success would mean that the eradication of hunger and malnutrition would become a serious priority concern for all governments for the first time in world history. Failure would mean the continued loss of millions of human lives every year, despite the existence in the world of ample food and other resources with which to avoid such a tragedy. Moreover, if the right to food, as perhaps one of the most basic economic rights is, as a number of critics have claimed, not susceptible of implementation as a human right, then the foundations on which the past - 1945 international consensus on human rights have been constructed are invalid - with all the consequences which that would imply. The present volume thus constitutes a modest first step towards the operationalization of economic human rights, beginning with the right to food.

The attemps of the authors to deliver their message has been substantively assisted by the possibility to include cartoons of Plantu, Honoré and Bellenger in the book. We are indebted to the three artists and to EIP for the permission ro reprint the cartoons.

Philip Alston

Katarina Tomaševski

Part I:
An overview

International Law and the Human Right to Food

by
Philip Alston

Part I The Setting

1. Introduction

It is paradoxical, but hardly surprising, that the right to food has been endorsed more often and with greater unanimity and urgency than most other
human rights, while at the same time being violated more comprehensively
and systematically than probably any other right. What is perhaps more surprising is that the widespread violation of the right to food in practice has
been accompanied and even facilitated by the almost total neglect, for all
practical intents and purposes, of its theoretical, normative and institutional
aspects.[1]

Since 1948 when the Universal Declaration of Human Rights was adopted by the General Assembly, the right to food has, at least in formal terms,
been accorded universal recognition as a human right and has been specially
incorporated into a variety of normative instruments, some of which are
binding on States which have ratified them. This recognition has repeatedly
been reaffirmed in declarations, resolutions, programmes of action and
manifestoes usually adopted unanimously by all members of the international community. However, despite the importance attached to the norm,
no international agency or organ, whether in the human rights or food field,
has ever endeavoured to analyze, develop or codify the specific normative
implications of the right to food. On the contrary, they have to a significant
extent permitted a devaluation of the actual international law norm - the
right to adequate food - by the use of surrogate terms purporting to affect international law but which are in fact devoid of any recognized normative
content. The primary effect of using these surrogate terms has been to trans-
form the issue into a vague ethical or moral one, thereby removing it from the
comparatively specific domain of international law and divesting it of its normative status.

Against this background, the objectives of the present chapter are: (1) to
situate the problem of world hunger within the framework of international
law; (2) to identify the legal standards which presently exist; (3) to survey the
extent to which efforts have been made to date to implement the right; and
(4) to identify some of the measures by which the right to food could be made
more meaningful in practical terms in the years ahead.

The Dimensions and Nature of World Hunger

It is generally accepted that, in any given year in recent times, several million people have died from hunger-related causes. UNICEF estimates that 40,000 young children die every day (i.e. 15 million per year) from malnutrition and related infection. In 1984, according to the UN, half of Africa's population is immediately threatened by severe hunger and malnutrition.[2]

However, despite widespread agreement as to the validity of these appalling statistics, precise estimates of the extent of the overall problem vary considerably according to the data base and the methods and criteria used. The most widely quoted estimate is that contained in the FAO's "Assessment of the World Food Situation prepared for the 1974 World Food Conference". While noting the potential for inaccuracy inherent in such estimates, the report concluded that up to 30 per cent of the population of the developing world, or even higher in some areas, were subject to food deficiencies. Thus, between 400 and 450 million people were estimated to be hungry and malnourished.[3] These figures have recently been re-affirmed by the FAO. Higher estimates on the basis of different criteria have been suggested by Reutlinger and Selowsky of the World Bank who calculated that 840 million people were malnourished in the mid-60's; for 1975 their estimate increased to 932 million.[4] It is possible, as some commentators have argued, that such figures overestimate the prevalence of malnutrition because for example farmers may under-report their food production, surveys may under-estimate actual food consumption[5], or for a variety of other reasons. It has even been suggested that the FAO has a vested interest in inflating the relevant figures in order to increase the importance of its work.[6]

But whatever the exact magnitude of the situation, it is clear that at least 100 million people, and probably hundreds of millions, continue to be chronically malnourished.[7] As the Sixth Report on the World Health Situation noted in 1980, "contrary to earlier expectations, the extent of the problem appears to be increasing in spite of a large number of measures taken by different sectors of the government that are directly or indirectly involved in ending malnutrition. The need for a new strategy to combat malnutrition has thus emerged".[8]

According to a recent World Bank report, "in developing societies, malnutrition plays a part in substantial numbers of death, and inadequate diet and related illness interfere with the learning ability, capacity to work, behaviour, and well-being of large segments of the population. The nutritional state of the populous both influences and reflects the level and pace of national development".[9] It is clear from these few indicators of the effects of malnutrition that enjoyment of the right to food is intimately linked to the enjoyment of a whole range of other human rights including the rights to health, to education, and to work, and the rights relating to participation. Conversely "malnutrition is one aspect of a whole way of life - part of a package wrapped up in the bonds of polity... (It) reinforces and is reinforced by, high rates of population growth, disease, lack of health care, inertia and - above all - oppressive polity".[10]

In the present analysis it is proposed to avoid, as far as possible, becoming involved in the technical debate over the causes and remedies of the problem of hunger. It is relevant however to note that there is a strong degree of consensus on at least two important issues. The first is that the existing level of food production would, if equitably distributed, be sufficient to satisfy the right to food of every person in the world. According to one estimate the present world agricultural output *per capita* of grain alone could supply everyone with more than 3000 calories and 65 grams of protein daily.[11] Such a level is well in excess of the minimal nutritional requirements estimated by FAO for each region of the world. The second point of consensus is that malnutrition is largely a reflection of poverty. Thus the gross disparities in income and wealth which exist both among and within nations are the basic cause of the world food problem. As Amartya Sen has demonstrated in an empirical study of major famines of the last 40 years, each of which killed vast numbers of people, the major problem was poverty, not lack of food, since in each case the total supply of food either did not decline or declined only slightly. [12] For example, the Great Bengal Famine of 1943 killed three million people, but food output in that year was only slightly below that of 1942 and substantially higher, both in total and *per capita*, than in 1941, which was certainly not a famine year. Similarly, the Bangladesh Famine of 1974 did not involve a decline in food availability. On the basis of these two points of consensus it is clear that increased food production, which is a necessary element in any long-term programme to eradicate hunger, is by itself no guarantee of diminished hunger. More equitable distribution of wealth and income and efforts to foster appropriate dietary patterns are at least equally necessary.

But if this is the case, a further technical question arises in the context of a consideration of measures required to promote realization of the right to food. If hunger is primarily a function of poverty, which in turn is a reflection of existing political, economic and social structures, is it necessary to wait until the most pressing development problems have been overcome before really trying to tackle hunger. In human rights terms, the question is whether we can usefully focus on the right to food *per se* without also addressing the whole range of rights. If the latter approach is taken, does the focus become so dissipated and blurred as to be of no avail? This is a controversial question, since, as Berg concedes:

"Efforts to improve nutrition are often regarded as a palliative rather than as a solution to basic needs - a repugnant form of government charity, or a political act to allay political unrest. They are attacked for distracting attention from the need to change a system that has failed and for diverting and wasting resources that could be used to bring about an equitable distribution of income and wealth and broader participation by the poor in policy making and decision making".[13]

It is clear, particularly from studies on the effects of food aid and other interventionary programmes that the result, if not sometimes the objective, of such programmes has often been to reinforce the dependence of the poor on local power structures and on external sources of assistance, thereby strengthening the hand of actual or potential oppression and undermining efforts to achieve a degree of individual, local and national self-reliance.[14]

While there are no definitive answers to such complex questions the

11

weight of professional opinion is that certain types of intervention to bring about nutrition and health improvements can make a substantial difference.[15] Given the time which will be required in most countries to effect an equitable redistribution of wealth and income it would therefore seem unjustifiable to defer efforts to promote realization of the right to food until some perhaps long distant future.

The Relevance of Law to World Hunger

1. From Philosophy to Law

For the most part, human rights has acquired its present significance not because of its innate moral force but because since World War II it has been transformed from a subject of philosophical speculation and occasional invocation in circumstances of extreme moral outrage into a relatively cohesive body of principles which form part of international law. Nevertheless, this transformation has not, and nor should it have, deterred philosophers from continuing to debate whether or not the existence of world hunger gives rise to a moral obligation on the part of the "haves" to assist the "have-nots".[16] It may come as a surprise to some that the question as to whether there should be a "right" to food is one on which responsible persons can differ. In fact, there is no shortage of philosophers who argue strenuously and with great conviction: that it is morally preferable to withhold aid to the starving in order to avoid even greater suffering later ("lifeboat ethics"); or that any compulsory redistribution of resources from the rich to the starving would unjustifiably violate the property and other human rights of the rich; or, on more pragmatic grounds, that aid to the hungry would do more damage than good to the nations receiving such aid.[17]

Even among those philosophers in whose view such a right clearly does exist there are great differences of opinion as to the consequences which should flow from it.

But what is at least equally as surprising as this diversity of views is the fact that very few philosophers have endeavoured to relate their array of arguments as to the moral obligations of nations and their citizens with respect to those suffering from starvation or malnutrition to the existing legal obligations which most states have acknowledged, particularly in the context of international human rights law. Even those philosophers who have sought to apply their thinking to the most basic practical issues confronting governments have, almost without exception, done so on the assumption that governments are not legally bound to take any particular measures and that, within the community of nations, they would theoretically be entitled to adopt a stance of neutrality or inaction in the face of massive hunger. Such is of course not the case.

The philosophers' response may be that they must ply their trade and leave the lawyers to ply theirs. But the drawbacks of such pigeon-holing are considerable and surely outweigh the arguments in favour of disciplinary

12

purity. In particular, such resistance to even limited inter-disciplinarity probably encourages comparable narrow-mindedness on the part of econo- mists, nutritionists, development planners and others who insist that moral or ethical considerations are well outside their professional brief. One com- mentator has even argued that we should face the fact that policy-makers are never going to be swayed by moral or nutritional considerations *per se* and will only take such factors into account when it is politically or economically opportune to do so.[18] This reasoning is in fact implicit in the efforts of institu- tions like the World Bank to justify or "sell" nutrition programmes largely, if not exclusively, on the basis of their overall contribution to economic growth. That such "economism" can go very largely unchallenged is a seri- ous indictment of human rights lawyers and of the groups and agencies through which they operate, since much of the value of transforming moral principles into human rights norms in international law results from the "compulsory relevance" which they are thereby supposed to assume in all areas of governmental and inter-governmental activity. Indeed, the fact that the right to adequate food, as a part of positive international law, is binding on at least half of the States in the world community represents a compelling reason to approach the matter primarily as a question of legal interpretation rather than of philosophical reflexion.

If full advantage is to be taken of this transformation from philosophy to law it is also essential that the correct normative terminology be used as far as possible. It is thus inappropriate and unhelpful, at least in the context of technical analyses, to use terms such as "the right to eat", "the right to nour- ishment", "the right to be saved from starvation", or other such formulations which have no standing *per se* as norms of international law and the content of which is inevitably highly subjective. In some circumstances the use of these formulations as though they may have some normative standing con- tributes to a devaluation of the genuine norm, encourages terminological confusion and tends to confine the right to food to the realms of abstract phi- losophy and moral rather than legal responsibility. It seems unlikely that those, in international organizations and elsewhere, who consistently prefer such vague formulations while eschewing use of the appropriate right to food norm, are wholly unaware of the consequences.

3.2 The Relevance of International Law

The right to adequate food is already an integral part of the existing struc- ture of contemporary international law, whether we approach it from the perspective of those principles dealing with food or of those relating to hu- man rights. It is important to note, however, that in practice the convergence between these two sets of principles is extremely limited.

In the area of international law dealing with food, the proposition that the continuation of widespread hunger in the world is unacceptable and the no- tion that individuals have a right not to die from hunger and not to suffer (either physically or mentally) from malnutrition (i.e. that they have a right

13

to food), have long been accepted by the international community. Whether in the context of global statements of policy such as the Universal Declaration on the Eradication of Hunger and Malnutrition or the strategy for the Third United Nations Development Decade or in specific instruments such as the Food Aid Convention or through institutional arrangements such as those relating to FAO, IFAD, or the WFC, all states have unambiguously committed themselves to these principles. As in all areas of law, the fact that their actions are not always consistent with the obligations thereby assumed does not in itself contradict the validity of the basic principles. Rather it points to the need to devise more effective means by which to increase the accountability of states to ensure the consistency of their rhetoric with their actions in this domain.

Since the FAO was established in 1945, international organizations in the food field have proliferated at an alarming rate. Nevertheless, through the policies and practices which they have legitimated these international agencies have contributed substantially to shaping the norms which govern the international food regime.[19] In doing so, strong reliance has been placed on the relevant principles of international law and a large variety of legal forms and techniques has been used, ranging from conventions and recommendations to codes of conduct, statements of principle, declarations, programmes of action etc. This constant resort to both the forms and substance of international law has inevitably contributed significantly to shaping the international food regime as it exists today.

In the area of international law dealing with human rights the right to food is equally firmly entrenched as a basic norm. Whether on the basis of treaty obligations, of customary international law principles, or of established practice, all states in the international community have recognized the existence of the right to adequate food. Indeed, in many respects, the human rights regime provides the essential ethical framework within which the policy governing specific issue areas in international law should evolve. But therein lies the problem.

International economic law in general, and that part of it dealing with food in particular, has not been shaped by reference to the human rights principles contained in the UN Charter and the International Bill of Human Rights, nor have its appropriateness or effectiveness been evaluated in terms of its impact on respect for those principles. By and large, international law dealing with food issues has succeeded in remaining hermetically sealed from human rights considerations.

The achievement of this artificial dichotomy has been greatly facilitated by the approaches adopted in each of the respective fields. In the field of human rights the exclusive preoccupation at the international level until recently has been with developing effective *post hoc* responses to violations of civil and political rights. Preventive rather than curative measures were rarely pursued, and economic rights such as the right to food were treated as mere "aspirational rights" (the explicit contradiction in terms notwithstanding). International economic law was a long way from the concerns of human rights lawyers and the major issues were in any event assumed to be well be-

14

yond their competence.

An equally restrictive approach to international economic law has succeeded in presenting it as primarily a system of constraining rules and of means by which to ensure the smooth functioning of international commerce through conflict avoidance or resolution. When thus viewed as a series of rules and regulations the exclusion of broad policy considerations of an ethical, humanitarian or moral nature is much more readily justified. The result is distinctly reminiscent of the much-criticized approach adopted in the International Court of Justice by Judges Fitzmaurice and Spender in their joint dissenting opinion in the 1962 South-West Africa Case: "We are not unmindful of, nor are we insensible to, various considerations of a non-juridical character, social, humanitarian and other, which underlie this case: but these are matters for the political rather than the legal arena".[20]

As a practical application of this purportedly watertight distinction between "political" and "technical" (whether legal or economic) issues, it has been argued for example that the inclusion of "fair labour standards" (i.e. labour rights) clauses in international commodity agreements is an undesirable encumbrance which only impedes the achievement of "a realistic commodity and development policy oriented to practical results".[21]

In other words, hard-nosed international economic negotiations are only made unnecessarily complicated if account has to be taken of such soft and extraneous matters as the rights of workers.

Similarly, while the terminology used in the context of international economic law often closely resembles that used in the human rights field, its meaning is dramatically different from one context to the other. Thus for example when international economic law speaks of discrimination, unfairness, and inequality, it refers to inter-State discrimination in the enjoyment of trade preferences, unfairness in competition and inequality in bargaining power. These are treated as legal matters, while their human rights counterparts are assumed to be political.

But, in practice, international law is not simply a series of specific rules and regulations. Rather it is more appropriately viewed as a continuing process in which choices must be made between competing norms and policy considerations according to the relevant context. Nor is law essentially an arbitral process. Legal decision-making is involved wherever decisions are made by authorized persons or organs, within the framework of established practices and norms.

With respect to food it is clear that the established norms must include (*inter alia*) those which have evolved in the human rights context. The artificial compartmentalization which in the past has ensured the separation of these norms from those governing the global food regime must be broken down.

In the final analysis the overall legitimacy of a system of law must be assessed by reference to the results in human terms which it sanctions. As long as international law sustains and fortifies a system which tolerates current levels of hunger and malnutrition in the world, its legitimacy must be open to question. The application of traditional international law approaches to the quest to resolve the crisis of world hunger has, to date, yielded little. Indeed,

15

discussions among international lawyers on this subject have rarely gone beyond a recitation of the relevant human rights provisions, the occasional reference to resolutions or declarations adopted in forums such as the World Food Conference, and simplistic (and often wholly inappropriate) proposals for the the additional expenditure of billions of dollars per year on investment in food.[22] In principle, however, there is no reason (other than a manifest lack of political will) why international law cannot contribute significantly to the realization of the right to food on a global scale. The challenge lies in the creative exploitation of its potential first by bringing together existing but separate streams of international law and second through the development of new and imaginative techniques designed to give practical effect to the international community's long-professed but equally long-neglected commitment to the promotion of economic human rights for all. Some of the means by which these aims might be pursued constitute the subject of much of the analysis in the remaining parts of this chapter.

3.3 The Role of Municipal Law in the Realization of the Right to Food

The most direct means by which municipal law can deal with the right to food is through the adoption of relevant constitutional provisions or of specific legislation. Although reference is made below to a range of such techniques which has been employed, it is clear that relatively few states have opted for this approach. Indeed, many appear to have carefully avoided proclaiming the right to food as such. Thus, for example, in a recent report to the Economic and Social Council the United Kingdom noted in a definitive fashion that "there are no laws, regulations or agreements, nor court decisions bearing on the right of everyone to adequate food in the United Kingdom..."[23] (E/1980/6/Add.16, p.21).

But in fact, whether or not specific right to food legislation exists, the legal framework of every society regulates, either directly or indirectly, the terms of access of individuals and groups to the resources and other means and entitlements which they may need in order to satisfy their right to food. The importance of law in facilitating or preventing the type of structural and other changes which may be essential for promotion of the right to food is all too often neglected. Revolutionaries are not interested in piecemeal changes or in what they see as structural tinkering, while some reformers are sceptical of the extent to which legislative measures can be useful in bringing about the changes which they believe can more easily be achieved through less formal means. It is true that the place of law in some states is little more than that of a formality or technical afterthought, but in others its role can be crucial. As Sen has noted, "starvation deaths can reflect legality with a vengeance".

In Latin America, for example, law and legal philosophy have often been at the heart of the development process especially in the context of legislation dealing with matters such as working conditions, freedom of association, particularly with respect to rural workers organizations, and agrarian reform. While the gap between the relevant laws and social reality has usual-

16

ly been great, the role of law has nevertheless been an important element in the evolution of societal perceptions, and in the establishment of certain parameters within which a particular debate or struggle can take place. As a recent study of law and agrarian reform in Costa Rica concluded, law may be viewed as:

"an instrument of political mobilization in certain areas where very strong interests clash; as providing the framework within which issues are formulated and decisions are made; as a means of allocating decision-making authority and selecting action-channels for implementation; and as providing a series of levers which if activated might speed the implementation of social change."[24]

A good indication of the role which law inevitably plays in the determination of the allocation of scarce resources such as food is provided by the following FAO-recommended list of activities which may need to be undertaken in a period of chronic food shortages and for which legislative authority would usually be required:

"(i) declaring a state of 'food emergency'; (ii) requisitioning food stocks held by producers, traders or millers; (iii) requisitioning packaging material held by traders or millers; (iv) mobilizing transport and storage facilities available in the private sector; (v) facilitating handling and storage at different points including ports, procurement centres and consuming centres; (vi) introducing and administering statutory rationing; (vii) enforcing terms and conditions under which the private trade may be associated with procurement and public distribution; (viii) fixing the procurement price and the price at which food may be sold through government controlled outlets; (ix) imposing price control; (x) regulating manufacture, movement, storage and distribution of food by private trade or millers; (xi) creating, on a stand-by basis, food disaster units."[25]

Given the importance of law in promoting the realization of the right to food, it may be asked why states have generally avoided giving normative expression to the right. Two major, albeit very different, reasons may be advanced. The first is that a strong policy commitment to promotion of the right to work and, as a backup, the right to social security, is seen as being adequate to deal with the problem of hunger and malnutrition.

In other words, if a person is employed, or, failing that, is supported by a social security scheme, the threat of hunger should not arise. There is thus no need to recognize the right to food separately when it is already covered indirectly. This reasoning is implicit in the relevant reports of many of the States Parties under the International Covenant on Economic, Social and Cultural Rights. It also appears to be the only reasonable explanation for the failure of otherwise comprehensive human rights instruments, such as the European Social Charter and the African Charter on Human and Peoples' Rights, to make any mention whatsoever of the right to food.

But despite the extent to which this reasoning appears to have been endorsed by States, it is unsatisfactory. In addition to its discounting the considerable symbolic importance of specifically recognizing the right to food, its validity is undermined by the plight of millions of people, spread across

17

most states, who are starving or suffering from malnutrition and who are clearly not protected by either employment or social security. Reports of a significant incidence of hunger in the United States at the present time clearly illustrate this reality. The result is that one of the most fundamental human rights - the right to food - is, for reasons which do not stand up to scrutiny, ignored in the legislation of the vast majority of States. As discussed below the difficulty of giving precise normative content to the right is also not an adequate reason for this neglect.

The second reason why states have generally avoided giving normative expression to the right concerns the potential of the concept for fuelling domestic unrest by underlining the often stark contrast between government rhetoric and reality. History is replete with examples of governments which have been overthrown by the starving masses in whose name (but not interests) they have ruled. Thus, as Pierre Spitz has noted, there are dangers for governments in recognizing the right to food:

"...It would imply for example, recognizing that the unemployed person without resources has the right to steal in order to eat. Few courts of justice would accept such logic. However, in condemning the thief to prison they ensure his right to food - a right that he had no right to exercise while at liberty. To recognize the right to food is to recognize, also, the right of peasants to organize themselves against the taking over of land by a few, the right of workers to organize themselves in defence of their livelihood, the right of the unemployed to organize themselves to loot food stores in order to survive. It is not unusual for these movements to meet the opposition of those who had, a little hastily, in the euphoria of some conference, recognized solemnly the right to food and the right to a livelihood... but suddenly decide to put the rights of ownership first."[26]

He is of course not the first to have recognized these dangers. In 1955 the Thai Government objected to the right to food provision contained in the then draft Covenant on the basis that "the intention of this article is very good but it is likely to justify those criminal cases in which some offenders have been acquitted because they had stolen bread or other food in order not to die of starvation".[27] In practice, the right to loot and steal was most recently invoked by large numbers of starving people during the 1983 Brazilian food riots. While such notions will be dismissed as needlessly provocative by many lawyers, they in fact raise the most fundamental of issues: that of the legitimacy of a legal system which does not provide for any positive response to massive denials of human rights. The point is best illustrated by Sen's example of the people who, during the Bengal famine of 1943, which killed 3 million, "died in front of well-stocked food shops protected by the State". On the basis of a survey of major recent famines he concludes that "most...seem to have taken place in societies with 'law and order', without anything 'illegal' about the processes leading to starvation".[28]

While a few strict "positivists" might still argue, from a jurisprudential perspective, that questions of legality can be divorced from questions of the morality of a particular law or legal system, most legal philosophers today would reject the concept of law as a value-free science. Certainly the issue

18

presents no dilemma in terms of international law.

Thus the Universal Declaration of Human Rights proclaims that "it is essential, if man is not to be compelled to have recourse, as a last resort, to rebellion against tyranny and oppression, that human rights should be protected by the rule of law". By definition, the rule of law is itself only legitimate if it is based upon respect for human rights. Thus a system which maintains law and order with respect to riot control, the protection of property, etc., while doing nothing either to prevent or respond to violations of other basic rights, such as the right to food, cannot claim to fulfil the requirements of the rule of law.

Part II Existing Standards

4. The Relationship Between the Right to Food and Other Human Rights

The issue of the relative weight and importance to be accorded to different human rights is one of the most fundamental, complex and ideologically fraught in the entire human rights field. Although the UN General Assembly has repeatedly affirmed the importance of the concept of indivisibility, there remains a tendency on the part of governments and commentators to seek to accord absolute priority to one particular right or to give overall priority to political rights over economic rights, or *vice-versa*.

The right to food has very often been identified as having such absolute priority. Indeed, in biological terms, such a narrow focus seems justified: "(N)o right has meaning or value once starvation strikes. It is an ultimate deprivation of rights, for without food, life ends, and rights are of value only for the living... Moreover, without adequate nutrition, the value of rights is greatly diminished... (M)alnutrition curtails growth, constrains mental and physical development, and limits the possibilities of action".[29]

However, in human rights terms, a compartmentalised approach to the right to food is both empirically unworkable and theoretically unacceptable. Its artificiality is best demonstrated by scrutinising one such proposal. In 1978 Ernst Haas argued that the positive focus of United States human rights foreign policy should be confined to:
"certain rights which **are** consistent with the American tradition and **are** compatible with all the major foreign policy objectives. They do not raise any of the nagging moral and practical issues. No problem of priorities arises. Moreover, these rights have already been legitimated by a number of recent international meetings. Prominent among them is the right to adequate food and nutrition. The right is personal, capable of being defined in scientific terms, universal, and subject to efficient implementation through international programs and national contributions... They can be embraced by communists, fascists, liberals, and ordinary authoritarians. They are of equal appeal to Muslims, Hindus, Christians, and atheists. They threaten no government and they do not pit legal and philosophical traditions against each other".[30]

19

But Haas' analysis is invalid on almost every score. Implementation of the right to food internationally would clash with a great number of existing US foreign policy objectives. Contrary to his assertion, the question of priorities and the range of issues which must be addressed are both extraordinarily complex (commodities agreements, terms of trade, land reforms, the equitable domestic and international distribution of available resources, rural versus urban development etc.). Moreover, it is debateable whether the right to food is capable of being defined in scientific terms; and the construction of effective implementation mechanisms is possible but immensely challenging. And finally, few issues have proven as politically threatening to governments as hunger (see Spitz's chapter, *infra.*).

Empirically, it is clear that in the vast majority of cases progress towards the realization of the right to food has gone hand in hand with the enjoyment of other rights such as those concerning popular participation in decision-making, the rights to freedom of association, expression and information, and the rights to education, health care, etc.[31] Those groups which are completely excluded from the decision-making processes affecting them are unlikely to maintain access to adequate food for very long. Similarly, for urban dwellers in particular, realization of their right to work will generally be a condition precedent to enabling them to command access to the food they require. In most instances, the false dichotomy which is embodied in the slogan "bread or freedom" has been invoked historically in order to justify repressive policies which have not in fact led to greater availability of bread for the masses.[32]

Acceptance of the view that any given human rights has precedence over all others also opens up an ideological minefield which can only result in the destruction of the existing consensus as to what values constitute human rights. Thus while recognizing the interdependence of the entire range of rights, the objective must be to maximize the enjoyment by each individual of his or her rights in so far as they are compatible with the rights of all other individuals. Under the International Covenant on Economic, Social and Cultural Rights, limitations on the right to food can only be imposed: (1) in conformity with the law; (2) in so far as is compatible with the nature of the rights; and (3) for the purpose of promoting the general welfare in a democratic society (Covenant, article 4). What exactly is meant by the term "the nature of the rights" is unclear, although given the "fundamental" nature of the right to food (article 11(2)), relatively few limitations upon its enjoyment would seem to be compatible except in so far as limitations upon the rights of some are necessary to ensure the enjoyment of minimum standards by others (for example, measuring to discourage wastefulness or gross over-consumption).

On the other hand, limitations upon other rights such as the right to private property, would seem to be required in a number of situations in order to enable land reform or other radical but essential measures through which the right to food may be realized, to be undertaken.[33] Thus, for example, article 21(1) of the American Convention on Human Rights provides that "the law may subordinate... use and enjoyment (of property) to the interest

20

of society".

While the "general welfare" may in times of crisis be more effectively promoted by non-food rather than food-related expenditures (e.g. defence spending in the face of an invasion) such situation would be relatively rare. Moreover, the qualification "in a democratic society" also imposes a significant limitation on the discretion of the government in so far as "the general welfare" must be defined in accordance with the conditions prevailing in a democratic society rather than, for example, those prevailing under a military regime which has unilaterally decreed "national security" or "modernization" to be priority goals.

Finally, any proposed limitations on the right to food which could result in death by starvation are clearly unacceptable. Apart from violating the right to food provisions, such limitations would also violate the right to life which, according to the Human Rights Committee is "the supreme right from which no derogation is permitted even in times of public emergency which threatens the life of the nation".[34]

5. The Right to Food in Existing International and Regional Human Rights Instruments

As noted earlier, the right to food has, despite its neglect in practice, been formally recognized in a wide range of human rights instruments. The most important such provision, article 11 of the Covenant on Economic, Social and Cultural Rights, is dealt with in the next section. In both this and the following sections it is proposed to review only a limited range of relevant provisions. In particular, reference is made only to recognized human rights which are **directly** applicable to the right to food, as opposed to other, indirectly related, rights such as freedom of association (e.g. for rural workers), freedom from torture (e.g. through food deprivation) or the right to health care.

5.1. The Charter of the United Nations and the Universal Declaration of Human Rights[35]

Under Articles 55 and 56 of the UN Charter all States Members accept the international legal obligation "to take joint and separate action" in co-operation with the UN to achieve *inter alia* higher standards of living, conditions of economic and social progress and development, solutions of international economic, social, health and related problems, and respect for human rights. The main purpose of the Universal Declaration of Human Rights, adopted by the General Assembly without dissent in 1948, was to spell out the human rights content of this Charter obligation.

The only direct reference to food is contained in Article 25, paragraph 1, which refers equally to a range of other economic and social rights. It states: "Everyone has the right to a standard of living adequate for the health and

21

well-being of himself and of his family, including food, clothing, housing and medical care and necessary social services...".

During the drafting of the article by the Commission on Human Rights several more specific proposals were made for articles dealing with the right to food, including drafts by Cuba and Panama. One such formulation, which was in comparatively strong terms, provided that "everyone without distinction as to economic and social conditions, has the right to the preservation of his health through the highest standard of food... which the resources of the State or community can provide...".[36] In the course of debate, however, a clear preference emerged for a single integrated provision dealing equally with the various component parts of an adequate standard of living.[37] The right to food is thus broadly stated, without any degree of specificity, but in such a way that it clearly goes beyond a right only to be free from hunger. Thus the amount of food to which every human being has a right is that which is adequate for his health and well-being and not merely for his bare survival.

The issue of the status of the Universal Declaration in international law is an old and vexed one but it retains a degree of relevance in relation to those States which have not yet ratified the Human Rights Covenants. At the time of its adoption the Universal Declaration was conceived by most States not as international law *per se* but as "a common standard of achievement" to which all aspired. However, it has since been argued that it now forms part of binding international law by virtue firstly of the fact that it is an authoritative interpretation of the Charter provisions, and secondly of the extent to which it has been reaffirmed and cited by the international community and individual States.[38] But whatever position is taken, it would appear to be difficult for any State to argue that it has not, by one means or another, accepted that there exists a human right to food, as stated in the Universal Declaration.

Reference may also be made to four other provisions of the Universal Declaration, to the substance of each of which we shall return later. They are:

(1) article 3 which provides that "everyone has the right to life";
(2) article 22 relating to the realization, through national efforts and international co-operation of economic, social and cultural rights;
(3) article 28 which provides that "everyone is entitled to a social and international order in which the rights and freedoms set forth in this Declaration can be fully realized"; and
(4) article 29 (1) which states that "everyone has duties to the community...".

5.2. The International Covenant on Civil and Political Rights

The drafting of the Covenants began in 1947 and culminated in the adoption by the General Assembly in December 1966 of the International Covenant on Economic, Social and Cultural Rights and the International Covenant on Civil and Political Rights.[39] Both Covenants had received sufficient ratifications to enter into force by early 1976. The right to food is mentioned

22

only in the former instrument but at least two articles of the latter Covenant warrant particular mention in the present context.

5.2.1. Article 1 - The Right to Self-Determination

Article 1 is the only provision common to both Covenants:
"1. All peoples have the right to self-determination. By virtue of that right they freely determine their political status and freely purpose their economic, social and cultural development.
2. All peoples may, for their own ends, freely dispose of their natural wealth and resources without prejudice to any obligations arising out of international economic co-operation, based upon the principle of mutual benefit, and international law. In no case may a people be deprived of its own means of subsistence".

The right to self-determination, as proclaimed in this article, has been the subject of endless debate and many, often conflicting, interpretations. Nevertheless, it is generally agreed that the enjoyment of the right to self-determination by peoples is basic to their enjoyment of all other human rights. It is also clear that enjoyment of the right to food must be one of the essential elements enabling people to freely pursue their economic, social and cultural development. However, due on the one hand to the essential political significance of the right and the controversial context in which it has most often been invoked, and on the other hand to its complexity and vagueness, relatively little effort has been made by States, the UN or academic commentators to develop its content from this perspective. It is arguable, however, that a government would be in violation of article 1 if it permitted the exploitation of the country's food-producing capacity (natural resources) in the exclusive interests of a small part of the population or of foreign (public or private) corporate interests while a large number of the State's inhabitants are starving or malnourished. Regardless of the issue of violations, however, there remains a strong incentive for States which are genuinely committed to achieving and maintaining their right to self-determination to ensure food self-reliance which, in the view of one commentator, is "the cornerstone of genuine self-determination".[40]

Moreover, very little attention has been given to the meaning and implications of the final sentence of the second paragraph. The outright prohibition against depriving peoples of their own means of subsistence relates directly to their control of their natural wealth and resources. Yet neither the *travaux préparatoires* nor subsequent academic analyses shed great light on the precise meaning of this sub-norm. Nor is it referred to at all in either the 1962 General Assembly resolution on Permanent Sovereignty over Natural Resources[41] or in the 1970 Declaration of Principles of International Law concerning Friendly Relations and Cooperation among States.[42]

Yet at least *prima facie*, this sub-norm would seem to be of major significance for the right to food in an era when the proliferation of cash crops for export appears to be a major threat to the adequate production of subsis-

23

tence foods for the masses in a growing number of countries. According to Cassese, the sentence introduces an exception to the earlier part of the paragraph. It may, in his view, "be read to nullify even arrangements 'freely made' by the people 'for their own ends' if these arrangements deprive the people of its means of subsistence. It presumably nullifies the obligation to pay any compensation required under international law where such compensation would deprive the people of its means of subsistence".[43] But while Cassese's interpretation clearly explains the significance of the subsistence provision *vis-à-vis* the rest of the paragraph and in the context of the controversial and central legal issue of compensation for nationalization, it sheds little light on the potential importance of the provision in terms of the right to food. An indication of this potential was provided during the drafting stage when, in response to objections that the provision was vague and ambiguous, one delegate offered the following examples of cases where, in his view, large groups of people had been deprived of their means of subsistence and in which the subsistence provision could have been invoked to obtain relief:

"A tribe in Tanganyika had been deprived of its ancestral land and had been resettled elsewhere against its will; and in Nauru the only source of national wealth, phosphates, was being unwisely overexploited by a British company, with the result that in about 50 years", time the population of the island would have to be resettled elsewhere because no resources would remain".[44]

In so far as these examples give a valid indication of the purport of the provision it would be appropriate for the Human Rights Committee, which is charged with supervising States' compliance with their Covenant obligations, to concern itself in the future with cases where this provision is alleged to have been violated by virtue of the deprivation of a people of its subsistence food production. However, in view of the complexity of the issue, its essentially economic and social nature, the difficulty of demonstrating causality, and the Committee's generally cautious approach, it is unlikely that the Committee[45] will tackle such issues in the foreseeable future.

5.2.2. Article 6 - The Right to Life

The second civil and political right which is sometimes cited as being relevant to the right to food is the provision in article 6 of the International Civil and Political Rights Covenant that "every human being has the inherent right to life... No one shall be arbitrarily deprived of his life." However, while philosophically and physiologically the right to food must be considered to be an important component of the right to life, there are arguments against applying a broad conceptualization to its legal interpretation. To date the weight of academic opinion has favoured the conclusion that the right to life is a civil right and that it amounts essentially to a right to be safeguarded against (arbitrary) killing.[46] Thus has been argued that it cannot reasonably be interpreted as freedom to live as one wishes[47] or as a right to an appropriate standard of living[48] and nor can it be invoked to "guarantee any person against death from famine or cold or lack of medical attention."[49] This interpretation is reinforced by the fact that the Commission on Human Rights, when drafting the Universal Declaration, rejected a proposal according to which the right to life would have encompassed the right to subsistence and to support for those not able to satisfy their own needs.[50]

More recently, however, the Human Rights Committee, in its General Comments on article 6, has criticized what it terms unduly narrow interpretations of the right to life and has urged States parties to the Covenant to take positive measures to protect the right, including *inter alia*, "measures to eliminate malnutrition and epidemics".[51] The implication of this approach is that a State party's failure to take appropriate measures to deal with serious hunger and malnutrition would constitute a violation of its obligations under article 6 of the Covenant. It is to be hoped that, in the future, information made available informally by NGO's to members of the Committee will enable it to apply this reasoning in appropriate cases.

5.3. The Geneva Conventions of August 12, 1949 and the Protocols

In any comprehensive survey of international legal provisions concerning the right to food it is essential that reference be made to the four Geneva Conventions and their two Protocols.[52] The Geneva Conventions constitute the essence of modern international humanitarian law and are designed to protect war victims.[53] These include first and foremost combatants who are unable to continue fighting (the sick, wounded, shipwrecked and prisoners of war) and also the civilian population which is not involved in military actions. Thus, for example, Convention III relating to "the Treatment of Prisoners of War" provides in article 26 that:

"The basic daily food rations shall be sufficient in quantity, quality and variety to keep prisoners of war in good health and to prevent loss of weight or the development of nutritional deficiencies. Account shall also be taken of the habitual diet of the prisoners. The Detaining Power shall supply prisoners of war who work with such additional rations as are necessary for the labour on which they are employed... Collective disciplinary measures affecting food are prohibited".

A number of other provisions in the same Convention also relate to the right to food.[54] In Convention IV which concerns "the Protection of Civilian Persons in Time of War" article 55 is of particular significance and states *inter alia* that:

"To the fullest extent of the means available to it, the Occupying Power has the duty of ensuring the food and medical supplies of the population; it should, in particular, bring in the necessary foodstuffs, medical stores and other articles if the resources of the occupied territory are inadequate".

In 1977 the Diplomatic Conference on the Reaffirmation and Development of International Humanitarian Law Applicable in Armed Conflicts adopted two Additional Protocols to the Geneva Conventions. Protocol I

25

relates to the protection of victims of international armed conflicts and Protocol II concerns the protection of victims of non-international armed conflicts. Several provisions of these Protocols are of relevance to the right to food. In particular note should be taken of article 14 of the Second Protocol which provides that:

"Starvation of civilians as a method of combat is prohibited. It is therefore prohibited to attack, destroy, remove or render useless, for that purpose, objects indispensable to the survival of the civilian population, such as foodstuffs, agricultural areas for the production of foodstuffs, crops, livestock, drinking water installations and supplies and irrigation works."

The positive side of this obligation is also dealt with in Protocol II, article 18(2) of which states that:

"If the civilian population is suffering undue hardship owing to a lack of the supplies essential for its survival, such as foodstuffs and medical supplies, relief actions for the civilian population which are of an exclusively humanitarian and impartial nature and which are conducted without any adverse distinction shall be undertaken subject to the consent of the High Contracting Party concerned".[55]

The Geneva Convention and the Protocols thus contain a significant number of provisions designed to ensure enjoyment of the right to food both by civilians and by former combatants in time of war. In some respects the relevant provisions are more detailed and comprehensive than those provisions of international law which govern realization of the right to food in peace-time.

Because of this complexity it is not possible to analyse them within the confines of the present chapter but we should at least be mindful of the type of issues which they address. In particular, in considering the need for a Convention on the Right to Food, it must be asked why the people of the world are not entitled to equally strong protection against hunger in times of peace as in time of war.

5.4. Other International Human Rights Instruments

It would be of very limited value for present purposes to seek to draw up an exhaustive inventory of specific provisions in international human rights instruments which constitute recognition of, or have some direct bearing on, the right to food. Nevertheless, it is appropriate to note that there is a large number of such provisions.[56] They range from, on the one hand, comprehensive provisions such as paragraph 20(1) of the Standard Minimum Rules for the Treatment of Prisoners ("Every prisoner shall be provided by the administration at the usual hours with food of nutritional value adequate for health and strength, of wholesome quality and well prepared and served") and Principle 4 of the Declaration of the Rights of the Child ("The child shall have the right to adequate nutrition...") to, on the other hand, such more limited provisions such as Article 5 of the Convention on the Elimination of All Forms of Racial Discrimination which seeks to ensure non-discriminary "access to any place or service intended for use by the general public such as ... hotels, restaurants, cafés ...". The latter provision thus deals with discrimination as a political act but not as an economic one.

5.5. Regional Instruments

None of the three main regional human rights instruments contains any specific reference to the right to food. In the case of the European Convention on Human Rights[57] this is not surprising, since economic, social and cultural rights are excluded from the Convention and are dealt with instead in the European Social Charter of 1961.[58] Nevertheless, that Charter also omits reference to the right to food. The most relevant undertaking by Contracting Parties is to take appropriate measures to "remove as far as possible the causes of ill-health" (article 11). Such a link between food and health is explicitly made in the American Declaration of the Rights and Duties of Man, of 1948, article XI of which provides that "every person has the right to the preservation of his health through sanitary and social measures relating to food, clothing, housing, and medical care, to the extent permitted by public and community resources".[59]

The American Convention on Human Rights, of 1969,[60] contains only one reference to economic, social and cultural rights (article 26), by which "States Parties undertake to adopt measures, both internally and through international co-operation, especially those of an economic and technical nature, with a view to achieving progressively, by legislation or other appropriate means, the full realization of the rights implicit in the economic, social, educational, scientific, and cultural standards set forth by the Charter of the Organization of American States as amended by the Protocol of Buenos Aires". In recent years, the Inter-American Commission on Human Rights has, perhaps somewhat belatedly, turned its attention to the existence of this provision. In its 1980 report it stated that "the essence of the legal obligation incurred by any government in this area is to strive to attain the economic and social aspirations of its people, by following an order that assigns priority to the basic needs of health, nutrition and education".[61] The Commission also called upon Member States to provide it with information on nutrition levels and the measures which they have adopted in order to improve these levels.[62]

In another, now forgotten, instrument, adopted in the same year - the Inter-American Charter of Social Guarantees - the American States (with the US dissenting) proclaimed *inter alia* that "workers have the right to share in the equitable distribution of the national well-being, by obtaining the necessary food, clothing and housing at reasonable prices". However, the very next sentence of the Charter provides one indication of the reasons why the Charter has subsequently been completely ignored: "To achieve these purposes the state must sponsor the establishment and operation of popular farms and restaurants and of consumer and credit cooperatives...".[63]

The most tangible outcome of these initiatives has been the preparation of

27

a "draft additional protocol to the Convention" which deals with economic, social and cultural rights.[64] Under article 11 of the 1983 draft the States parties "would recognize and, as far as they are able, undertake to adopt the most suitable measures so that the inhabitants of their respective territories have adequate food, clothing and housing". The degree of obligation flowing from such a provision would seem to be unnecessarily weak and it is to be hoped that an effort will be made to strengthen and elaborate upon the proposed formulation of the right to food. Under article 12(2) of the draft, States would pledge themselves to adopt suitable programs designed *inter alia* to achieve "reforms leading to equitable and efficient land tenure systems, increased agricultural productivity, expanded use of the land, diversification of production and marketing of agricultural products."

The third, and most recent, regional initiative, the Banjul (African) Charter of Human and Peoples' Rights, was adopted by the Organization of African Unity's Assembly of Heads of State and Government in June 1981.[65] While the Charter has not yet received the number of ratifications required for its entry into force (being a majority of Member States of the OAU) its provisions are still of considerable interest. In a number of respects it is a progressive and innovative statement of rights since it proclaims, for the first time in a potentially binding international legal instrument, rights such as the right of peoples

(1) to economic, social and cultural development (article 22);

(2) to national and international peace and security (article 23); and

(3) to a general satisfactory environment favourable to their development (article 24).

At the same time, however, the formulation of specific economic, social and cultural rights as contained in the Charter is brief and relatively vague. Thus while the Charter proclaims "the right to enjoy the best attainable state of mental and physical health" and "the right to education" there is no reference to the right to food or to the right to be free from hunger or any comparable formulation. Nor does the Charter proclaim the right to an adequate standard of living. The report of the Rapporteur on the drafting of the Charter does not indicate that any proposals were made for the inclusion of such rights.[66] Formulations which could perhaps be interpreted to cover the right to food, such as the rights to existence and to development are proclaimed as the rights of peoples and not of individuals. Thus neither the right to food as an individual nor as a collective human right is contained in the African Charter of Human and Peoples' Rights. Given the paucity of information available by way of *travaux préparatoires* it is only possible, at this stage, to speculate that the drafters were wary of the practical implications of including such a right, given the recurring food shortages which have plagued different parts of the African continent in recent years. It may be reasonable to presume that, at least in this respect, they followed the example of the other two major regional human rights instruments.

Perhaps the most plausible explanation for the omission of the right to food from the regional instruments is that the right to work is viewed as a more fundamental right, the realization of which should permit the satisfaction of nutritional needs. In the event of its non-realization the focus presumably is on the right to social security. The other reason for omission, especially in the case of the European instruments, is the real or supposed difficulty to which consideration is given in section 12 *infra* of ensuring implementation of rights such as the right to food through the means traditionally employed in human rights instruments. Nevertheless, at a time when unconscionably high levels of unemployment have become commonplace, when anti-inflationary policies are pursued at the direct expense of employment, and when more and more governments are embracing austere social and economic policies, it may be necessary to revise earlier assumptions, which in effect take realization of the right to work for granted, and to formulate specific commitments to promotion of the right to food within the framework of regional human rights instruments.

6. The International Covenant on Economic, Social and Cultural Rights

The primary focus in the present analysis is on article 11 of the International Covenant on Economic, Social and Cultural Rights which proclaims the right to adequate food as well as the right to be free from hunger. Its pre-eminence among international right to food norms is due to the following factors:

(1) it represents a codification of the earlier norm contained in the Universal Declaration of Human Rights;
(2) its content was significantly shaped by the most important of the international food agencies at that time - FAO;
(3) it is more detailed and specific than most other relevant international legal norms;
(4) 81 States (as at 1 July 1984) have formally accepted the obligation in international law to take steps to achieve progressively the full realization of the right; and
(5) a mechanism has been established under the Covenant to monitor States Parties" compliance with their obligations, including those relating to the right to food.

The detailed (and perhaps sometimes tedious) scrutiny to which article 11 is subjected below is justified not only by its importance for the reasons given above but also because a detailed understanding of the existing norm is an essential starting point for future efforts to give greater practical meaning to the right to food within the framework of international law.

The starting point for the analysis is the legislative history of article 11. The circumstances in which the provision was drafted explain a great deal about both its characteristics and shortcomings. In addition consideration of the *travaux préparatoires* enables us to verify the validity or otherwise of an interpretation based upon the plain meaning of the text and to clarify the meaning of provisions which are otherwise ambiguous or obscure.

29

6.1. The Drafting of Article 11

Between 1947 and 1954 the Commission on Human Rights worked on the drafting of the International Human Rights Covenants.[67] During this period most of the main specialized agencies, including ILO, UNESCO and WHO, played an active, and in some respects decisive, role in formulating those economic, social and cultural rights which were relevant to their respective mandates.[68] Notably absent, however, was FAO which apparently ignored the various invitations issued by the Commission to the specialized agencies to take part in the drafting process.

By 1951 the Commission had prepared a single covenant embracing both sets of rights. In an introductory paragraph to the part dealing with economic, social and cultural rights, note was taken of the resolve of States Parties "to combat the scourges, such as famine..." and "to strive to ensure that every human being shall obtain the food, clothing and shelter essential for his livelihood and well-being".[69] But while the covenant contained separate articles dealing with social security, housing, standards of living, and health there was no reference to the right to food *per se* in the substantive articles. However, by 1954 when the Covenants were sent to the General Assembly the Commission's final draft remedied this omission by including two separate draft articles by which States Parties to the Covenant recognized:
(1) "the right of everyone to adequate food, clothing and housing" (article 11); and
(2) "the right of everyone to an adequate standard of living and the continuous improvement of living conditions".[70] Several Governments argued that article 12 rendered article 11 redundant.[71]

It was not until 1963 that the Third Committee was urged to attach greater importance to the right to food and to spell out its implications in more detail. The Director-General of FAO, Dr. B.R. Sen, in addressing the Committee, regretted the absence in the Universal Declaration of Human Rights of "an urgent call to mankind... to regard freedom from hunger as one of mankind's first freedoms".[72] In his view, article 25 of the Universal Declaration, which mentioned the right to food only as one of a number of components of an adequate standard of living, "had been couched in somewhat too general terms". Having warned of the possibility that there would be 3 billion persons underfed or malnourished by the end of the century, Sen urged that the Covenant should enumerate specific measures to be taken to implement the right to food. Accordingly he provided the Committee with the text of a draft article dealing with the right to freedom from hunger and the measures required for the realization of the right.[73] The statement of States' obligations in the first paragraph of the FAO text is significantly stronger and more urgent than the formulation finally adopted in the Covenant. It required States Parties to the Covenant to "undertake, individually and through international co-operation, to develop programmes aimed at achieving freedom from hunger within the shortest possible time". Given the absence of specific time-frames for the realization of other rights the latter phase could have been interpreted as calling for priority to be given to freedom from hunger over other rights. The FAO proposal was subsequently reflected both in a Saudi Arabian draft of a separate article[74] and a proposal by Chile, Columbia, Ecuador, and Uganda for an additional paragraph on the right to freedom from hunger.[75] These two proposals were referred by the Third Committee to a working group of interested delegations which produced an integrated text [76] sponsored by 11 States. While the general principle of the right to freedom from hunger was unanimously endorsed, most of the debate centred around the question of whether it was necessary to elaborate upon the principle in any detail. Although not among the sponsors of the draft, the Romanian delegate strongly supported it on the grounds that "hunger could not be combated effectively by paternalistic measures designed solely to mitigate the problem and to avert a revolt of the starving".[77] Thus, in his view, it was necessary to promote increased production, agrarian reform, the training of relevant personnel and the teaching of sound nutritional principles. Other representatives attached importance to the fact that, although the food problem was essentially a matter for economic and technical organs, "governments should be reminded of the human rights aspect of the question".[78]

Several delegations expressed strong opposition to the FAO proposal to include specific implementation measures in the Covenant. In their view it was sufficient to state succinctly that everyone is entitled to freedom from hunger and to leave questions of implementation to the relevant UN agencies and to the General Assembly's Second Committee which dealt with economic questions. According to the representative of Pakistan, measures to implement the right "would have to form part of general plans for rural economic development, which would naturally differ from country to country, and it would therefore be wrong to attempt to include in the draft Covenant...uniform directives which States would be bound to follow".[79] In the same vein, the Netherlands representative argued initially that the proposed draft was:
(1) too detailed; (2) covered matters which went beyond the competence of the Third Committee; (3) was not consistent with the bald statements relating to the rights to housing and clothing; and (4) was more appropriate to a declaration than to a legally-binding instrument.[80] In the event, when the vote was taken in the Third Committee on article 11, paragraph 2, as finally included in the Covenant, Pakistan was the only State to abstain in a vote of 88 in favour, none against and one abstention.[81]

While the objections noted above did not deter the Third Committee from adopting a detailed text, including measures of implementation, they did nevertheless raise a number of issues which still require to be considered today if the normative content of the right to food is to be further developed in an acceptable and useful way.

6.2. A Legal Analysis of Article 11

In order to make effective use of any norm of international human rights

31

law it is necessary to establish:
(1) its content;
(2) the subjects or beneficiaries;
(3) the object or duty-holders; and
(4) mechanisms to promote compliance.

6.2.1. General Characteristics of Article 11

Before examining these four aspects, note should be taken of the general characteristics of the formulation contained in article 11 *vis-à-vis* other human rights formulations. In a number of respects article 11 follows a format which is common to most of the substantive articles in the Covenant, in that: (1) it commits States Parties to recognition of the right and to the adoption of certain general measures for its realization; (2) the right is to be enjoyed by "everyone"; and (3) the formulation is neither significantly more nor less detailed than that of other rights. In other respects, however, article 11 is different. First, the right to be free from hunger is the only right in either Covenant which is stated to be "fundamental". Secondly, the essential role of "international co-operation" in achieving realization of the right, which is mentioned twice in article 11, is not emphasized with respect to any other specific right in the Covenant. Finally, paragraph 2 (a) is unique among UN human rights instruments in that it incorporates the concept of "equitable distribution... in relation to need", the potentially significant implications of which are considered below.

6.2.2. The Content of the Norm

The Correct Terminology

The "right to food" is in fact a shorthand expression encompassing two separate norms contained in article 11. The first, stated in paragraph 1, derives from the "right of everyone to an adequate standard of living for himself and his family, including adequate food" and can be termed the right to adequate food. The second, proclaimed in paragraph 2, is the "right of everyone to be free from hunger". In most analyses which have been undertaken to date the two have been treated as being synonymous with a preference nevertheless being shown for the latter.

It is submitted that, while on the one hand there is a substantial difference between the two norms, with the first being much broader than the second, on the other hand the term "right to adequate food" is the appropriate overall one since there is no indication that paragraph 2 was intended by the drafters or by States which have ratified the Covenant to restrict or narrow the scope of the right proclaimed in paragraph one. Moreover, if the paragraph 2 formulation was taken in isolation as the definitive statement of the right, the Covenant would constitute not an elaboration and codification of the

Universal Declaration as intended, but a considerable reduction in the scope of the right proclaimed in 1948. The reason for the discrepancy between the two paragraphs in the Covenant is a simple historical one and is explained by the fact that the formulation in paragraph 2 was proposed by the FAO in 1963 in order to provide added legal force to support the worldwide Freedom from Hunger Campaign which the organization had launched in 1960.[82]

Minimalist or Maximalist Approach?

The practical implications of taking, as the primary norm, the right to adequate food rather than the right to be free from hunger are substantial. Whereas the former facilitates the adoption of a maximalist approach, the latter, which is in fact a sub-norm, is able to be fully satisfied by the adoption of policies designed to provide a minimum daily nutritional intake. Yet both the principles of human dignity on which the International Bill of Human Rights is founded, and various provisions of the Covenants make it clear that the normative thrust is towards progressive improvement rather than a static concern with the satisfaction of bare minimum needs. While it may be appropriate to focus on freedom from hunger as a means by which to mobilize public support and as a starting point for national and international efforts, such an approach should be seen only as the first step towards realization of the primary norm which is the right to adequate food.

In terms of quantity the notion of adequacy implies enough food to facilitate a normal, active existence rather than a minimum calorific package which does no more than prevent death by starvation. The adequacy approach is also favoured by the significant practical difficulties in devising an effective minimalist approach. As Sen notes: "There are significant variations related to physical features, climatic conditions and work habits. In fact, even for a specific group in a specific region, nutritional requirements are difficult to define precisely. People have been known to survive with incredibly little nutrition, and there seems to be a cumulative improvement of life expectation as the dietary limits are raised. In fact physical opulence seems to go on increasing with nutrition over a very wide range... There is difficulty in drawing a line somewhere, and the so-called 'minimum nutritional requirements' have an inherent arbitrariness..."[83]

In terms of quality the adequacy standard goes further than the freedom from hunger sub-norm in focusing on the cultural appropriateness of the food. As Margaret Mead emphasized in the early 1950s, "to introduce adequate nutrition, it is important to bring about changes that are in keeping with the established food habits of the people, and are acceptable within the framework of their value system".[84] Moreover, there is a strong case in policy terms for emphasizing the norm itself rather than the sub-norm. The OECD Development Assistance Committee has explained it thus: "Experience with the African Club du Sahel indicates that no nation this century would be likely to accept a minimal standard of life as an objective of policy

33

for more than a temporary emergency period. More serious is that attempts to reach agreement on minimal poverty lines are certain to be deeply resented by developing country leaders and people as overly technocratic and paternalistic on the part of the affluent North".[85]

Specific objectives and means

In general terms article 11 (1), in conjunction with article 2 of the Covenant, makes it clear that States Parties are required to take all appropriate steps to ensure realization of the right to food. Without in any way limiting this overall requirement article 11(2) proceeds to spell out certain objectives as well as particular means by which they might be achieved. Before analysing these specific provisions it is useful to recall that strong doubts were expressed by a number of speakers in the course of the *travaux préparatoires* as to the general advisability of trying to spell out particular measures by which the right should be implemented. Thus it was argued that "any hastily drafted elaboration of article 11 (1), or a new provision, might detract from the clarity which should characterize a statement of principle in an international convention".[86] Even those who argued in favour of elaboration conceded that it was possible only to give a "broad indication of the measures required" and that " a clear distinction should be maintained between the principle and the modalities".

Such caution was certainly justified. Probably no other detailed provision in the Covenant was drafted in such unusual haste (only five partial meetings, spread over five days including a weekend, were devoted to the entire exercise). The result, perhaps not surprisingly, is a relatively confused and by no means all-embracing mixture of means and ends. In interpreting the provision of article 11 (2) it is essential to keep constantly in mind three principles of interpretation: (i) article 11 (2) does not purport to be exhaustive and does not exclude the need for States to pursue other means and ends which may be required for realization of the right to food; (ii) the basic objective is realization of everyone's right to adequate food and progress in achieving the subsidiary ends listed in article 11 (2) must always be judged against that objective; and (iii) where difficulties of interpretation arise, the requirements of article 11 should be "interpreted and applied within the framework of the entire legal system prevailing at the time of the interpretation" [87] rather than at the time of the drafting or adoption of the provision.

In essence article 11 (2) is divided into sub-paragraphs dealing respectively with the national (article 11 (2) (a)) and the international (article 11 (2) (b)) dimensions of the right to food. The text of the latter, which requires that measures be taken to ensure an equitable distribution of world food supplies, is relatively straightforward although its precise implications are debateable. By contrast the former sub-paragraph is poorly drafted and confused despite the fact that it incorporates most of the key words which should be in such a provision. As Dobbert notes,[88] the original text proposed by the Director-General of FAO in 1963 was shorter, more concise and more readily able to be interpreted and applied. The principal objectives specified in article 11 (2) (a) are:

(1) to improve methods of food production with a view to promoting realization of the right to food;

(2) to improve methods of food conservation with a view to promoting realization of the right to food; and

(3) to improve methods of food distribution with a view to promoting realization of the right to food.

In addition, the article lists other matters which, although presented as though they were only means for the achievement of the three main objectives, can be more accurately characterized as secondary or complementary objectives. They are:

(4) making full use of technical and scientific knowledge;

(5) disseminating knowledge of the principles of nutrition; and

(6) developing or reforming agrarian systems.

Despite the absence of an appropriate comma, it seems safe to assume that the final phrase, "in such a way as to achieve the most efficient development and utilization of natural resources", applies to the paragraph in its entirety rather than only to objective (6).

6.2.3. The Subjects and Beneficairies of the Norm

The distinction between the subjects and beneficiaries of international law reflects a longstanding ideological controversy which need not concern us in detail here. Briefly, it is argued on the one hand that the Covenants create duties and confer rights only upon States Parties and that beneficiaries other than States derive their entitlements only through the latter. On the other hand, a strong case has been made that the duties assumed by States Parties to grant rights to individuals involves recognition of the individual as a subject of international law in his own right.

The principal holders of the right to food under the terms of article 11 are individuals. The right is formulated in terms of "the right of everyone". Whereas sub-paragraph 2 uses only this phrase, the terminology used in sub-paragraph 1 is "the right of everyone...for himself and his family". This phrase is taken directly from article 25 of the Universal Declaration and is not used elsewhere in the Covenant. It was included at a stage in the drafting process when article 25 was conceived of primarily as a right to social security.[89] Since that right was usually associated with breadwinners and extended through them to their families, and since the vast majority of the world's formal labour force at that time was male, such terminology is readily understood. Nevertheless changed perceptions and circumstances would seem to demand that no particular significance be attached to this phrase today.

Given that the individual is the principal subject of the right to food, the question which then arises is: to what exactly is he or she entitled? In practical terms, the answer will depend on the circumstances of the individual and of his or her geographical location at a given time. From the present perspective the most important point is to recognize the need to develop, at the national level, a set of relevant legal norms which reflects and seeks to satisfy the State's international legal obligation to promote the realization of the right of everyone to adequate food.

There is also another level at which one can identify a holder of the right to food: the State. Whether this is a collective right attaching directly to peoples or to States or whether it is rather an aggregation of the human rights of individuals which is articulated through the medium of the State is an important theoretical question, but it is of limited practical relevance in the present context. Article 11 does not specifically identify States as holders of the right to food. Nevertheless by imposing duties upon States to act, "through international co-operation", the article implicitly vests rights in certain States as a corollary of the duty of all States to act. Moreover, in practical terms, the obligation of States Parties "to ensure an equitable distribution of world food supplies in relation to need" can only be operationalized on an inter-State basis. The shield (or the sword) of State sovereignty severely restricts the possibility of implementing such an obligation at any other level. [90]

The question of which States might be entitled to make claims on the grounds that they are subjects of the right to food can only be answered on the basis of an assessment of the overall availability of food at the national level by comparison with the aggregated needs of the State's inhabitants for adequate food. The closest the international community has come to making such a global assessment is the category of "most seriously affected countries" which were those which, in the wake of the 1973 oil price rises, were deemed to be in need of emergency assistance to pay for minimum import requirements of food, fertilizer and industrial inputs.[91] This categorization is effectively obsolete today. Many other criteria could however be taken into account in assessing whether or not a particular country enjoys an equitable share of world food supplies in relation to need. While it is beyond the scope of this paper, consideration could be given for example to: (1) the official UN classification of least developed countries[92] (which, while taking account of food needs, does not specifically involve the application of a food-related criterion); (2) the guidelines and criteria for food aid, approved by the World Food Programme's Committee on Food Aid Policies and Programmes;[93] and (3) the concept of food priority countries used by the World Food Council.[94]

6.2.4. The Objects or Duty-Holders of the Norm

It is generally accepted that most, if not all, human rights have a corresponding duty which attaches to a particular entity or entities. The United Nations has not, however, adopted a "duties" counterpart to the Universal Declaration of Human Rights or to the Covenants and those instruments contain only relatively brief provisions relating to duties, other than the specific obligations assumed by States Parties.

Article 29 (1) of the Universal Declaration provides that "everyone has

36

duties to the community in which alone the free and full development of his personality is possible". That provision is also reflected in the preamble of the Covenant which states that "the individual, having duties to other individuals and to the community to which he belongs, is under a responsibility to strive for the promotion and observance of the rights recognized in the present Covenant". Article 29 is significantly less specific than a number of alternative formulations which were considered at the drafting stage but it has nevertheless been interpreted by some commentators as involving a substantial range of duties for the individual.

The only detailed study on the subject of duties which has been undertaken within the UN framework is one presented to the Sub-Commission in 1980 by Mrs. Erica-Irene Daes.[95] The study is, however, so broad-ranging and, in places, confused that it does not enable any specific conclusions to be drawn as to the duties which may attach to the right to food.

A more rewarding approach would seem to be the application of Henry Shue's typology of three duties which correlate to every basic right.

As applied to what he terms a "subsistence right" such as the right to food these are:

a. Duties not to eliminate a person's only available means of subsistence - duties to avoid depriving.

b. Duties to protect people against deprivation of the only available means of subsistence by other people - duties to protect from deprivation.

c. Duties to provide for the subsistence of those unable to provide for their own - duties to aid the deprived."[96]

It is beyond the scope of this chapter to analyse in any detail the implications for various entities of approaching the right to food primarily in terms of duties. Nevertheless such an analysis will have to be undertaken sooner or later if the relevant duties are to be spelt out and an appropriate system of accountability established. Such a system is an indispensable component of a comprehensive, balanced, practical and effective approach to the right to food.

In analyzing the duties relating to the right to food which derive from the relevant provisions of the Covenant four main categories of duty-holders can be distinguished. They are: (1) States in respect of their domestic duties; (2) States in respect of their external duties; (3) Individuals; and (4) The international community.

6.2.4.1. State's Domestic Duties

In broad outline the nature of States Parties' duties to promote the realization of the right to food within the territory under their jurisdiction can be ascertained from reading article 11 in conjunction with other relevant provisions of the Covenant. The fundamental obligation of each State Party is to take steps, to the maximum of its available resources, with a view to achieving progressively the full realization of the right of everyone, without discrimination, to adequate food (article 2 (1) and (2) and article 11). Before considering the substance of this obligation as it relates specifically to the right to food, two general aspects of the obligation itself warrant examination. The first concerns the obligation "to take steps" and the second relates to the obligation to devote all "available resources". While these two aspects are closely related, they are not identical.

The obligation to devote all available resources has been seen by some commentators to be so vague as to amount to a non-duty. However construction of the language of the Covenant in this way would largely undermine its *raison d'être* as well as being contrary to the intentions of the framers of the Covenant. The latter point is illustrated by the rejection in 1952 of a United States-sponsored amendment which would have further restricted the obligation so as to require that steps be taken only "to the maximum of the resources which may be used for the purpose". As one State representative observed, the wording contained in the final version of the Covenant was preferable to the diluted US version "because it meant that without exceeding the possibilities open to them, States must do their utmost to implement economic, social and cultural rights".

Clearly the obligation does not require that a State should expend resources which it does not have or that it is bound to spend all its resources on satisfying these rights. Nevertheless it does comport some freely accepted limitations on the State Party's freedom to allocate its resources, and also accords a degree of priority, over and above other goals, to promotion of the rights specifically proclaimed in the Covenant. This does not necessarily mean that an authoritative statement can be made as to a State Party's duties in a particular situation. For example, if a State's total resources are sufficient to ensure full domestic realization of the right to food, is it entitled under the terms of the Covenant to opt instead to devote its resources to other objectives such as building nuclear power facilities or luxury hotels, or reinforcing its military strength at the expense of causing hunger? Or can a government say: yes, there are people starving who could be fed but the country's need for foreign exchange earnings compels us to export food crops? Obviously there are no easy answers in practice to such questions although there may be situations which cannot under any reasonable interpretation be justified, when judged against the obligations assumed under the Covenant. In this respect, the government is accountable to its people for the manner in which it allocates its resources and for the consequences of such allocations in terms of food availability. Moreover, these allocations may justifiably be taken into account by other States and by the international community in assessing what is required in the circumstances to satisfy their obligation to provide assistance to the State concerned to ensure realization of the right to food.

The obligation of States Parties under article 2 and 11 is not, however, only a question of appropriate budgetary allocations. Although the Covenant does not contain any provision which is equivalent to article 2 of the International Covenant on Civil and Political Rights which specifically requires States to take "necessary" legislative and other measures, it is reasonable to assume on the basis of the *travaux préparatoires* and of the practice of States

38

in their reports under the Covenant that the "steps" required to be taken include the adoption of some type of legislative, executive and/or administrative measures oriented specifically towards the realization of the right in question. The validity of such an emphasis on the role of law is also confirmed by the provisions of: article 2 (2) whereby States Parties "undertake to guarantee" the exercise of the relevant rights without discrimination on certain grounds; article 3 by which States Parties "undertake to ensure the equal right of men and women to the enjoyment" of the relevant rights; and article 4 whereby limitations on the enjoyment of rights are restricted to those "determined by law". In addition, article 11 (1) commits States Parties to "take appropriate steps to ensure the realization of this right".

In so far as a requirement to take legal or administrative measures can be deduced from the Covenant it does not amount to an obligation to ensure immediate realization. This is made abundantly clear by the use of the phrase "achieving progressively". Nor does it enable us to assume that any particular policy approach (e.g. food stamps or soup kitchens) must necessarily be adopted. In practice, the policies and methods chosen will differ according to the needs and circumstances of each country. Nevertheless the leeway provided by this provision does not obviate the need to adopt at least rudimentary laws, regulations and/or programmes designed to establish appropriate policies and to form the basis on which progressive realization can be built. As an indication of good faith this could be expected to include the drawing up of a coherent, and as far as possible, comprehensive plan setting out the steps to be followed in seeking to realize progressively the right to food. Article 11 (2) gives an indication of some of the matters which should be addressed in the context of specific legislative or administrative measures. But by no means does it constitute a definitive list. Thus, for instance, with respect to the undertaking to develop or reform agrarian systems (article 11 (2) (a)) it is clear from the *travaux préparatoires* that where the existing situation is considered to be satisfactory there is no obligation to undertake reforms.[97] In such circumstances measures should, however, be taken to promote the continuing development and improvement of the system of agrarian land tenure. In this regard the World Food Council has emphasized the conviction that political priority and integrated national action - within the framework of integrated national plans through some form of food system, strategy or plan - are essential to effectively address food problems and to encourage increasing external support".[98]

In summary, it is submitted that the following obligations are incumbent upon States Parties to the Covenant with respect to domestic promotion of the right to adequate food:
(i) to accord, in the context of budgetary allocations, a degree of priority to satisfaction of the right to food over other objectives not covered by the Covenant;
(ii) to consider where appropriate, the creation of some administrative and/or judicial procedure for reviewing situations where violation of the right to food is alleged;
(iii) to take steps to uarantee enjoyment of the right to food without discrimi-

nation (article 2 (2) and article 3 of the Covenant);
(iv) to adopt a national food strategy covering both long-term production and distribution goals and necessary short-term or medium-term interventionary measures designed to alleviate existing hunger as rapidly as possible;
(v) to monitor, on a regular basis, the extent of hunger and malnutrition within the State and to take appropriate remedial action where necessary; and
(vi) to take measures to ensure that its own people are not in any case deprived of its own means of subsistence, including food (article 1 (2) of the Covenant) and to investigate any situation where such deprivation is alleged to be occurring.

6.2.4.2. States' External Duties

The General Assembly has, on several occasions, recognized that "in order fully to guarantee human rights and complete personal dignity, it is necessary to guarantee the right to (*inter alia*) ...proper nourishment, through the adoption of measures at the national and international levels, including the establishment of the new international economic order".[99] Similarly food has figured prominently in various NIEO-related instruments such as the Programme of Action on the Establishment of a New International Economic Order. [100] This emphasis on the international dimensions of the right to food accurately reflects the approach adopted in the Covenant.

The duty of international co-operation (Article 11(1))

With respect to external duties States Parties to the Covenant are obliged to take steps through international assistance and co-operation, especially economic and technical, to the maximum of their available resources with a view to achieving progressively the full realization of the right to food (article 2 (1) and article 11). Although the potential beneficiaries of this provision are not specifically limited to States Parties, the Covenant cannot readily be interpreted as vesting legal rights in non-State Parties. States are also required to avoid depriving any people of its own means of subsistence (article 1 (2)). The "essential importance of international co-operation" is further recognized in article 11 (1) but it is stated to be "based on free consent". The significance of this qualification is open to debate. The *travaux préparatoires* do not enlighten us but the qualification was presumably inserted as a safety clause against any assumption that food-surplus States have an automatic responsibility to make transfers to food-deficit States. Nevertheless, "free consent" cannot reasonably be interpreted as rendering the commitment to international co-operation (either in paragraph 1 or 2 of article 11) **entirely** optional and thus meaningless. Nor can it defeat the overall responsibility provided for in article 2. It should thus be taken as meaning that while an obligation to international co-operation exists, the form which such co-operation will take is to be determined in accordance with the free consent of the State concerned. If such an interpretation is accepted the relevant reservation proposed by the Carter Administration to be attached to US ratification of the Covenant would be inadmissible. The proposed reservation, which has no equivalent among the reservations lodged to date by States Parties, states: "It is also understood that paragraph 1 of Article 2, as well as Article 11,...import no legally binding obligation to provide aid to foreign countries".[101]

It is submitted that in fact the Covenant does import a legally binding obligation to co-operate internationally (which may sometimes involve the provision of aid) with other States, in certain circumstances, to ensure the realization of, *inter alia* the right to food. Such an obligation falls very short (fortunately) of suggestions such as one that the United States' "amber waves of grain" may one day be designated as part of the "common heritage of mankind" with access to it being shared globally.[102] Nor by any stretch of the imagination does it mean, as suggested in 1976 by a US State Department official, "guaranteed food aid for those countries with insufficient foreign exchange ... (as well as) worldwide rights to agricultural inputs, to investment capital, to technology, and to markets and commercial supplies".[103]

The duty to co-operate internationally to ensure the realization of the right to food is not limited to the need under appropriate circumstances to provide assistance. Indeed, given the extent to which food selfreliance is now recognized as a fundamental goal of most countries, the duties to avoid depriving and to protect from deprivation are almost certainly of greater importance. Without trying to draw up an inventory of the policy requirements which could derive directly from these duties, reference can be made to two of the most controversial issues in this area: food aid and transnational agribusiness.

In the case of food aid there is substantial evidence that large-scale, long-term, institutionalized aid programmes are frequently geared to increasing subsequent cash sales and to developing a local preference for imported foods (e.g. imported wheat rather than available home-grown rice) - thus creating continuing dependence and a drain on foreign exchange reserves. Moreover a large proportion of food aid is given either in order to dispose of unwanted surpluses or for narrow security and political reasons[104] and often has the effect of depressing local food prices and discouraging production, at the expense mainly of the poor. In recipient countries food aid is often used to reinforce existing inequalities. In one study of food aid to Bangladesh, 27 per cent went to the army, police and civil bureaucracy, another 30 per cent to predominantly middle-class ration card-holders and much of the remainder was used to keep prices low for the volatile urban population.[105] Thus there is now widespread support for the view that "policies stressing short-term, disaster-related food aid and direct relief for the poorest would be much more beneficial than the present long-term institutionalized programmes. Low cost food imports should never be allowed to compete with local food production and thus to destroy local initiative."[106]

For countries which have accepted the Covenant obligation to co-operate internationally in promoting the realization of the right to food, the duty to protect from deprivation requires that careful consideration be given to the impact of their food aid policies.

The second controversial area relates to the impact of the activities, particularly in developing countries, of transnational agribusiness corporations. An enormous literature has developed in recent years arguing that these activities have been singularly detrimental in terms of their impact on the right to food of the masses.[107] According to Susan George, unless TNC's control of food production and distribution processes is significantly weakened, "continued malnutrition and starvation will be the only prospect for those hundreds of millions who will never become 'consumers': the invisible poor".[108] Another commentator, recalling Bertold Brecht's statement that "famines do not occur. They are organized by the grain trade" claims that the grain "companies thrive upon and in fact encourage a system that excludes the hungry".[109] Despite the fact that the secrecy so staunchly maintained by the leading grain companies makes "it next to impossible to tell who is selling what to whom'[110] the duties of States Parties to the Covenant can arguably be interpreted as including a duty to take reasonable steps to mitigate the adverse consequences in terms of hunger of the activities of domestically based corporations. Realistically however, such standards of accountability will only be acceptable, if at all, to the relevant States when they are strictly defined and carefully negotiated. Nevertheless, the requirements of the Covenant constitute a useful starting point for the negotiation of instruments such as the WHO code of conduct for the marketing of breastmilk substitutes as well as constituting an important basis on which to mobilize public opinion. With respect to such issues, it is appropriate to recall the conclusion of the US Commission on World Hunger that "while it would be unrealistic to assume that economic conflicts of interest can be eliminated entirely from international economic relations, the United States can take steps to reduce existing conflicts between its national goals and the needs of hungry people".[111]

A duty of a different type which flows directly from the obligation of States Parties to co-operate internationally, is the duty of governments to seek international assistance in situations where widespread starvation would otherwise occur. The relevance of this duty was most dramatically illustrated in Ethiopia in early 1973 when the government of Emperor Haile Selassie sought to avoid adverse publicity by refusing to acknowledge the existence of a serious famine. As a result hundreds of thousands of people are estimated to have died. In analysing how such a tragedy could have been permitted to happen Green has written:

"Perhaps the most serious crime that a government can commit, short of a campaign of genocide against its own people, is consciously to ignore the existence of a major disaster, or knowingly to deny the needed relief... And yet, for this most serious of crimes, there is no international remedy, nor even any means of calling attention to it."[112]

Although he was writing before the entry into force of the Covenant his analysis would probably be the same today. However, at least in theory, the

Covenant does provide a mechanism by which attention could be called to such a serious violation of a State Party's duties under the Covenant. Only time will tell whether the Covenant will be used in this way, although the experience to date is not encouraging.

The duty to ensure an equitable global distribution (Article 11(2)(b))

States Parties to the Covenant also undertake to take measures "to ensure an equitable distribution of world food supplies in relation to need" and in so doing to take "into account the problems of both food-importing and food-exporting countries" (article 11(2)(b)). The latter requirement, introduced by its sponsor without significant explanation,[113] is, however, able to be understood by reference to the setting in which it was adopted. It reflects the fear of grain-exporting (developed) countries that the FAO Freedom From Hunger Campaign, which was launched in 1960 - three years prior to the drafting of article 11 - might interfere with the effective (i.e. profitable) operation of international grain markets.[114] Although the merits of such a provision were extremely dubious even at that time, it would clearly seem to be an anachronism today, in an age when the practice of "the global farm producing for the global supermarket" meant for example that in 1973, 36 of 40 of the world's poorest countries exported agricultural commodities to the United States and that agricultural exports from the Sahelian countries actually increased during the early 1970's, despite the drought and widespread hunger.[115]

However, of more relevance than the distinction between food-exporting and food-importing States is the use of the word "problems". In rejecting a proposal that the word "interests" be used in its stead the sponsors of the relevant draft stated that it was intended to indicate that "the distribution of food supplies should be based not solely on the interests of the countries involved or on purely economic grounds, but also on social and humanitarian considerations".[116] Such an interpretation is of very considerable significance since it precludes the adoption of either a narrow economistic approach to the duty stated in article 11(2)(b) or of an exclusively trade-oriented approach.[117]

What, then, is involved in ensuring "an equitable distribution of world food supplies in relation to need"? The provision derives from the original draft proposed by FAO in 1936, although the original terminology was much more flexible and the implied obligation was considerably weaker ("...national and international action should be geared to the realization of this right by paying particular attention to: (a) policies to ensure that world food supplies are shared on a rational and equitable basis".).[118] In its broad legal sense the term "equity" requires that account be taken of considerations of reasonableness and good faith. Its use in this context however serves only to convey a broad sense of fairness or reasonableness and it confers a wide discretion on those charged with interpreting and applying the provision. In Brownlie's view, "as a general reservoir of ideas and solutions

43

for sophisticated problems" the concept of equitable principles in international law "offers little but disappointment". [119] Nevertheless, in terms of article 11, the concept of equity is capable of offering some practical guidance since it has a basic point of reference which is the right of everyone to adequate food and to be free from hunger. Further light is shed on its meaning by its juxtaposition with the concept of "need". As noted above in connection with the subjects and beneficiaries of the right, the term "in relation to need" can be accorded a reasonably specific meaning by the application in a given situation of indicators of nutrition. Thus a country with a sizeable population of malnourishred would be "in need" provided that the problem was not simply a function of a highly inequitable internal distribution of food supplies. The qualification "in relation to need" is also important in that it permits discontinuation of the quest for equity once needs (assessed in terms not of bare essentials but of adequacy as required by article 11 (1)) are satisfied. Beyond that point, surplus food supplies are not subject to equitable distribution.

The reference to world food supplies is also significant since the term "supplies" goes beyond the idea of surpluses. The provision could thus involve a duty to consume less in times of general shortages so that even if no surpluses were produced, available supplies could be distributed more equitably on a global basis.

Having considered the different elements involved in interpreting article 11 (2)(b) the next question is: what specific duties does it involve in practice? In view of the generality of the stated duty the response can only be tentative, not authoritative. While the compilation of an inventory of specific duties may be intellectually satisfying it will be of limited practical value until such time as it is incorporated into a legally binding instrument designed to elaborate upon the existing broad obligations contained in article 11. The following duties *inter alia* could be included.

Duties to avoid depriving

1. The duty to avoid international policies and practices which deprive other States of their means of subsistence or which promote an inequitable distribution of world food supplies.
2. The duty to mitigate national policies which have the effect of promoting an inequitable distribution of world food supplies.
3. The duty not to use food as an international sanction.

Duties to protect from deprivation

4. The duty to ensure that international trade and aid policies and practices contribute as far as possible to the equitable distribution of world food supplies.
5. The duty to regulate the activities of domestically-based entities (includ-

44

ing transnational corporations and state trading enterprises) whose activities do, or might, have a significant impact on the distribution or world food supplies.

Duties to aid the deprived

6. The duty of food-surplus States to contribute to emergency buffer shemes and to assist in cases of internationally declared emergencies.

7. The duty to co-operate as far as possible with multilateral programmes which are aimed at ensuring an equitable distribution of world food supplies.

Before turning to the question of the duties of individuals passing reference should be made to two important, related issues: (i) the use of food as an international sanction and (ii) the relationship of the right to permanent sovereignty over natural wealth and resources with other relevant principles.

(i) Use of food as an international sanction

The proliferating use in recent years of both unilaterally and multilaterally imposed restrictions on the sale or transfer of food to countries such as Iran, Poland, the USSR and Afghanistan raises the question of the compatibility of such sanctions with existing international instruments. Morally, the use of food sanctions has long been frowned upon.[120] Legally, the position is less clear, except with respect to the provisions of the Geneva Convention which are applicable in times of war and with respect to economic warfare in general. In regard to the latter Whiteman has argued that economic warfare undertaken "with the purpose of upsetting... the world's food supply" is either an emerging or already existing peremptory norm of international law (*jus cogens*).[121] However, the position with respect to limited sanctions against a particular government is more complex. In 1981 the General Assembly adopted the Declaration on the Inadmissibility of Intervention and Interference in the Internal Affairs of States which "solemnly declares" *inter alia*: "...the duty of a State not to use its external economic assistance programme or adopt any multilateral or unilateral economic reprisal or blockade and to prevent the use of transnational and multinational corporations under its jurisdiction and control as instruments of political pressure or coercion against another State..."[122]

But since that controversial Declaration, the soundness of which is highly questionable in terms of international law, was adopted with 6 recorded abstentions and 22 "no" votes (mainly OECD member States) it is far from being determinative of the issue. However in another resolution, adopted later in the same session by consensus, the Assembly reaffirmed "that food is a universal human right... and, in that context stresses its belief in the general principle that food should not be used as an instrument of political pressure".[123] By contrast, although the General Agreement on Tariffs and Trade is generally designed to outlaw discriminatory trade measures, Article XXI nevertheless preserves the right of a contracting party to take "any action which it considers necessary for the protection of its essential security interests... taken in time of war or other emergency in international relations".[124]

45

The position under the Covenant is similar although slightly more restrictive. The duties under article 11, which include the duty to co-operate internationally to promote realization of the right to food, may be derogated from only in accordance with article 4. That article is however not formulated in such a way as to provide an indication of the legitimacy or otherwise of sanctions unless the sanctioning state could claim that its actions are for the purpose of promoting the general welfare in a democratic state (e.g. upholding national security?). In reality, international law as reflected in the Covenant and elsewhere is unlikely to be the deciding factor in a situation involving sanctions. Nevertheless the duty to co-operate and the specific provisions of article 11, both support the view that there is a general duty not to use food as an international sanction and never to do so in cases where starvation and death are the inevitable consequences.[125]

(ii) The right to permanent sovereignty over natural wealth and resources

A second issue, which is too complex to be dealt with satisfactorily here, concerns the relationship between the right to permanent sovereignty over natural wealth and resources, the principle of non-intervention and non-interference in the internal and external affairs of States, and the duty to make resources, including food, available to States in need.[126] A number of questions arise in this regard. For example, how is the duty to co-operate internationally and to ensure an equitable distribution of world food supplies in relation to need (article 11 of the Covenant) to be reconciled with article 25 which states that: "Nothing in the present Covenant shall be interpreted as impairing the inherent right of all peoples to enjoy and utilize fully and freely their natural wealth and resources".

Similarly some western scholars have posited the existence of an emerging right of access to resources which is seen to be of particular relevance to the industrialized world's needs for oil and other natural resources.[127] In contrast the Group of 77 (the developing countries) while calling for greater equity in international relations has at the same time vigorously rejected concepts, such as access to supplies, as being "incompatible with the aspirations, unity and solidarity of the developing countries". [128] Can a valid distinction, based perhaps on human rights instruments, be made between the right of developing countries to access to food supplies as opposed to the right of industrialized countries to access to oil supplies? There is a clear need to attempt to reconcile these potentially conflicting developments in modern international law.

6.2.4.3. The Duties of Individuals

The debate over whether individuals have a personal duty to contribute towards the realization of the world hunger problem has long occupied philosophers and others[129] but has rarely been addressed from an international

46

legal perspective. Such commentators have implicitly, if not also explicitly, minimized the responsibility of individuals by arguing that "the free competitive market is the only device that will provide the discipline and the incentives necessary to cause undernourished people to solve their own problems".[130] Others have focused very strongly on the duties of individuals. In one view "any discussion of world poverty that does not come round to demanding a radical change in our habits of consumption and waste, our tastes, our profligate standard of living, our values generally, is a hypocrisy".[131] Similarly, Singer has argued at some length that "everyone earning an average or above average income in an affluent society, unless he has an unusually large number of dependents or other special needs, ought to give a tenth of his income to groups working to end starvation".[132]

In terms of international human rights laws the individual does, according to the Covenant, have a duty to strive for the promotion and observance of the right to food, which is owed both to other individuals and to the community to which he belongs. At a minimum this would seem to involve duties not to over-consume and not to waste food. The range of duties could of course be considerably expanded in line with Shue's categories discussed above. In practice, the important point is that States Parties to the Covenant are not only entitled, but are required to give careful consideration to measures designed to promote the observance, on the part of individuals, of their relevant duties with respect to the right to food.

6.2.4.4. The Duties of the International Community

It may in some respects seem futile to seek to ascribe specific duties to an entity as vague and amorphous as "the international community". Nevertheless, in practice, the term can readily be interpreted as referring to the various international organizations which have been established by states to deal with the problems and challenges of the global food system. A study prepared in 1976 listed 89 multilateral intergovernmental bodies with food-related missions.[133] Since then the number has surely increased, if only because international proliferation is a time-honoured response (particularly at the international level) in situations where the political commitment required of the most powerful actors in order to implement readily apparent reforms, is absent.

Various commentators have suggested that this large network of international food agencies is fragmented, competitive and averse to co-ordination and that they are in so far as real power has been tested in them, beholden to the dominant interests of the wealthy producer states.[134] The dominant agency, FAO, has been accused of lying "becalmed and inactive"[135] and, more generally, it has been persuasively argued that since the principal interests of the international food bureaucracies are closely tied to the preservation of the *status quo*, no redefinition of selfish and short-sighted national interests can be expected to emerge from them.[136]

It is, however, far beyond the scope of this chapter to examine the validity of these assessments. For present purposes it is sufficient to note the important roles of the international agencies as information gatherers and as the principal forums within which the most pressing issues will continue to be discussed. It is thus pertinent to make some critical observations as to the shortcomings of their role, to date, with respect to the right to food.

(1) International agencies are committed, in theory, to promotion of the right of everyone to adequate food.

(2) In a variety of areas, the norms governing the international food system are the outcome of practices and patterns of behaviour which have been legitimated by international organizations.

(3) In reality "most practices legitimated by international organizations are simply multilateralized versions of the policies and preferences of powerful member-states".[137]

(4) The people most severely affected by world hunger have had little, if any, direct influence on international policy-making.

(5) Many international agencies have in the past been primarily concerned with production increases which, *per se*, are not necessarily going to promote the realization of the right to food.

(6) The policies promoted by international agencies have often had the effect, intentionally or otherwise, of increasing dependency on agricultural exports and on export markets.[138] Such a situation has often been detrimental to domestic enjoyment of the right to food.

(7) None of the agencies has made a concerted effort to explore the precise content of the right to food as an international legal norm.[139]

(8) Relatively few agencies see themselves as advocates of the right to food except in the broadest possible sense. They tend rather to fall back on what one critic has termed the standard FAO reply: "We only do what the government wants".[140]

(9) No legally binding instruments dealing directly and specifically with the right to food have ever been promulgated by international agencies.[141]

Any inquiry as to whether a particular agency is fulfilling its duty to promote the realization of the right to food must be based on a clear statement of the specific implications of the right for the agency concerned and must involve a critical appraisal of the agencies' activities in all relevant spheres. It is thus wholly inadequate to assert, as FAO first did in 1950[142] and has continued to do since,[143] that everything done by the Organization contributes, almost by definition, in one way or another to promotion of the right to food. The question to be asked is not whether a particular agency's activities are ultimately contributing to the promotion of the right to food but whether they are doing so in the most direct, effective and appropriate manner. Consider, by way of illustration, the example of a charitable organization which serves meals of caviar and champagne to a few poor people. The organization is promoting the human right to food of that group but it is unlikely to be doing so in the most nutritious way or to the benefit of the largest number.

On the basis of available evidence few, if any, of the major international agencies would pass such a test. Despite increasing emphasis in recent years

48

on questions of nutrition, agrarian reform and rural development and greater attention to the impact of different policies in terms of equity and the "food entitlements" of specific population groups, including the euphemistically so-called "most disadvantaged", none of the agencies has yet undertaken a serious overall review of its policies and practices to assess their impact on the realization of the right to food. It is to be hoped that if the urgent review of the policies and performance of the UN system food agencies, which the Brandt Commission called for in 1983,[144] is undertaken, the right to food will be the starting point.

7. The Present State of the Law

The foregoing survey leads to a somewhat ambivalent conclusion as to the present status of the right to food norm in international law. On the one hand, it is clear that attempts to distil from article 11 (in conjunction with other relevant articles) any grand design for a **comprehensive, ordered, operational** approach to implementation of the right to food, either at the national or international level, is misplaced. Thus the provisions of article 11 are in some respects both insufficiently detailed and sufficiently confused as to ensure that any such exercise would be largely speculative and ultimately frustrating.

On the other hand, despite the relative generality and temporal indeterminacy of the duties of States to implement the Covenant's provisions on the right to food, their importance should not be under-estimated. In addition to representing an international obligation on the basis of which they can be accountable, politically as well as legally, States Parties have also made a formal commitment against which their own peoples may assess their domestic policies. Moreover, since the board thrust of the norm is clear, article 11 provides a sufficient basis to enable a determination in some cases that particular acts, or omissions to act, are either in conformity with, or in conflict with the norm.[145]

In addition the position relating to the right to food of detained persons, prisoners of war, children and handicapped people is relatively straight-forward.

The next step then is to determine what lines of enquiry need to be pursued in order to move towards a clearer understanding of the means by which the right to food norm may be made operationally significant across a broader policy spectrum. Before doing so, it is necessary to consider the extent to which existing approaches to implementation have succeeded in shedding light upon the normative content of the right. For this purpose it is proposed to examine: (1) the approach which human rights bodies have adopted to the right to food; (2) the effectiveness or otherwise of the Covenant's implementation procedures as applied to the right to food; and (3) the existing international food regime.

Part III Implementation

8. The Right to Food in Human Rights Forums

Until very recently the theoretical aspects of the right to food have been ignored by the various inter-governmental human rights forums. In the UN context, the only general study ever undertaken on economic, social and cultural rights (which was completed in 1973, after a preliminary Secretariat study) failed to address the issue in any useful way. Thus, for example, after providing detailed statistics on matters of only secondary relevance such as "estimated per capita calorie and protein content of national average food supply" the study concluded that "as a first step to a more serious attack on the problem of hunger and malnutrition, there is need for a comprehensive and more regular survey of food consumption. Special attention should be given to national health programmes. The network of mother and child care centres, for example, should be used for the implementation of such programmes".[146] In other words, hunger *per se* was addressed rather than the right to food, and the relevant proposals were of breathtaking vagueness.

In 1977 the Commission on Human Rights rejected an NGO proposal to undertake a study on the right to food[147] - a proposal which however was subsequently accepted when it emanated from the Sub-Commission in 1982.[148]

Attention to the practical aspects of the right to food has also been slow to develop. In 1977 the Commission decided that in its study of human rights violations it had previously concerned itself mainly with political rights and that in future it should correct the imbalance by also studying violations of economic, social and cultural rights. [149] To date, however, the Commission's general debate on violations has rarely heard allegations of violations of the right to food - a shortcoming for which NGOs and individual governmental representatives, rather than the Commission itself, are to be blamed.

A notable breakthrough has occurred in the context of reports prepared by Special Rapporteurs on the human rights situation in particular countries. In this regard the precedents set by detailed reports in South Africa and Chile have in recent years been followed in a range of other cases with the result that previously ignored economic rights issues are now usually taken into account. (Not always, however, as in the report on Poland in 1984 which essentially dealt only with civil and political rights.) Nevertheless, the manner in which the right to food has been addressed leaves much to be desired. For example, a 1984 report on the situation in El Salvador devoted only 3 of its 47 pages to economic, social and cultural rights, and most of those dealt almost exclusively with the issue of agrarian reform. The actual impact of the failure to achieve such reform was not analysed, however.[150]

Probably the main failing of most such reports has been the absence of any conceptual framework within which to analyse issues such as the right to food. For example, a 1984 report on the situation in Guatemala includes a section on "social and economic reforms" (not "rights") in which the Special Rapporteur begins by saying that "it would be incorrect to stray too far into the purely economic field". But he then proposes an increased emphasis on the production of food export crops and observes that "many Guatemalans are prepared to give up their traditional subsistence way of life... to add a cash crop to their basic family food production". In his view "this type of development demonstrably conduces to the standards set by Article 11 of the Covenant...".[151] Although such an assertion is directly at odds with experience elsewhere, the report does not analyse the matter further.

By contrast, some of the country reports prepared by the Inter-American Commission on Human Rights have been considerably more detailed and structured in their treatment of the right to food. Thus, for example, a 1979 report on Haiti provides statistical data on matters such as per capita nutritional intake, the ability of the population in terms of average income to afford basic minimum consumption standards, infant malnutrition, and rural/urban differentials.[152]

In general, most UN human rights reports which have dealt with the right to food situation in particular countries have failed to establish any conceptual framework for analysis; have not made use of available statistical and other data; have not examined the various component parts of the right to food; have not considered the extent to which the right is enjoyed by different sectors of the population; have not sought to determine the nature of the links between hunger and government policies; have not concluded that violations of the right to food have occurred; and have not made any specific recommendations relating to the right to food.

9. The Implementation Procedures of the Covenant in Operation

Articles 16 to 23 of the International Covenant on Economic, Social and Cultural Rights provide for the creation of an elaborate set of procedures for the supervision of States' compliance with their obligations under the Covenant, including those relating to the right to food. The focal point for the procedure is a sessional working group of experts established for the purpose by the Economic and Social Council. It has met annually since 1979 and has examined detailed reports submitted by the States Parties to the Covenant containing information on the measures adopted and the progress made in achieving the observance of the various rights. Reports are also submitted by the relevant UN Specialized Agencies including the FAO. The experience to date under this procedure is reviewed below in the Chapter by Gert Westerveen.

For present purposes it is sufficient to note that, despite frequent re-evaluations of the Working Group's approach and methods, its performance has been singularly disappointing. For the most part, the following assessment, made in 1981, remains valid:

"The examination of reports has been cursory, superficial and politicized. It (the Working Group) has neither established standards for evaluating reports nor reached any conclusions regarding its examination of reports... (Its reports give) no indication as to how States Parties are complying with the provisions of the Covenant".[153]

The result is that, in contrast to the achievements of its counterpart established under the Covenant on Civil and Political Rights (the Human Rights Committee), the Working Group has not succeeded in developing even an embryonic jurisprudence by reference to which some of the specific normative implications of right to food could be ascertained. A vicious circle is thereby created in which neither the States Parties nor the Working Group is clear as to the core issues which should be addressed with respect to the right to food. The only way out of this impasse is through the development of a more detailed and precise framework (ideally in the form of a binding instrument) on the basis of which States Parties reports could be prepared and against which their compliance could be evaluated. Regrettably, however, no such effort has yet been undertaken despite the highly pertinent provisions of Article 23 of the Covenant (to which we will return in section 13 below).

10. The International Food Regime

The notion that a "regime" exists in every substantive issue area in international relations in which patterns of behaviour can be discerned, has recently gained prominence in the literature.[154] In this sense, an international regime has been defined as a set of "implicit or explicit principles, norms, rules and decision-making procedures" around which the expectations of relevant actors converge.[155] Although objections to the concept have been raised by some commentators,[156] it is nevertheless a very useful analytical tool with which to identify the major norms and principles which influence, if not quite govern, the behaviour of state elites (the principal actors) as well as other relevant entities (including multinational corporations and even non-profit non-governmental organizations) in a field such as food.

Particular variations of the regime concept have been termed "Grotian" and, in a number of respects, these are highly compatible with interpretations of international law according to which patterns of state behaviour, in a diversity of contexts, can generate expectations about future conduct which in turn can be transformed over time into specific prescriptive or proscriptive rules of law.

In the food field, recent analyses by Hopkins and Puchala[157] are of particular interest in that they provide an overview of the norms which have characterized the post-1945 international food regime.

In their view the following eight norms "tend either to be embodied in the charters of food institutions, or to be recognized as 'standard operating procedures' by food managers":

1) Respect for a free international market;
2) National absorption of adjustments imposed by international markets;
3) Qualified acceptance of extramarket channels of food distribution;

4) Avoidance of starvation (in the context of famines);
5) The free flow of scientific and crop information;
6) Low priority for national self-reliance;
7) National sovereignty and the illegitimacy of external penetration; and
8) Low concern about chronic hunger.[158]

In general terms, their conclusion is that the norms of the post-war era have been unsupportive of behaviour directed towards alleviating malnutrition and chronic hunger.

In order to move towards a new global food regime which would support goals such as food security, nutritional well-being, enhanced human welfare, economic stability and global interest, Hopkins and Puchala propose the following guiding principles: (1) universal rural modernization is imperative; (2) adequate nutrition is a central human right; (3) internal equity in food distribution is an international concern; (4) investment is a global responsibility; (5) food aid should be used as insurance, not surplus disposal; (6) famine relief is an international responsibility; (7) comprehensive information should be widely published; (8) food markets should be stable; and (9) multilateral capacities must be enhanced.[159]

It would be particularly instructive to compare both the present and the proposed regimes with the right to food norms identified earlier in this chapter as forming part of the existing international human rights law. For present purposes, however, it must suffice to note the striking extent to which the two sets of norms diverge and the extent to which each has been developed with almost total disregard for the other. In particular such a comparison underlines the virtual irrelevance in terms of international practice of many of the norms embodied in the Covenant, including those relevant to the right to food.

Either one of two conclusions could be drawn from such a comparison. The first is that the relevant human rights norms are so "soft" as to be non-law and that it is mistaken or naive to treat them as being other than symbolic. The overall thrust of the present analysis is that such a conclusion is both unwarranted and unacceptable. The alternative conclusion is that steps should immediately be taken to diminish, and ultimately eliminate, the gaps which exist between the norms governing the global food regime on the one hand and food-related international human rights norms on the other.

The most compelling criticism of that conclusion is that it is incompatible with the existing distribution of political and economic power, in the interests of which the present regime has been shaped. Thus, in a strong critique of Hopkins' and Puchalas' proposals, Bergesen has argued that while their vision is highly desirable it is entirely unrealistic. In his view the global food regime is, and will continue to be, dominated by a "combination of international economic laisse-faire and political unilateralism" which will ensure the continuation of the *status quo*.[160] He questions where any new norms could be derived from and concludes that the issue of hunger could only be transferred from the academic to the political agenda if there were "a fundamental change of grassroots perceptions and an equally far-reaching change of elite priorities in the Western countries".[161] The remaining parts of this chapter are devoted to arguing that human rights law provides the source of the necessary norms as well as a potential means by which to stimulate grass-roots consciousness.

Part IV: Future Development

The analysis in the previous part of this chapter has shown that none of the existing international approaches to implementation has succeeded either in shedding light upon the precise normative content of the right to food or in developing a conceptual framework within which future efforts might be pursued. In the remaining sections of the chapter consideration is given to the usefulness of adopting a human rights approach to the problem of hunger and an effort is made to identify a range of measures which could contribute to the long-term realization of the right to food.

11. Towards Development of the Covenant's Obligations: The International Level

The fundamental problem confronting scholarly efforts to give substance to the right to food is the prevailing hostility to the very concept of economic and social human rights. D'Amato, for example, considers them to be "incoherent...so-called rights" which are inconsistent with real (i.e., political) rights, "since they may involve redistribution of privately held resources".[162] In a later chapter in this book, van Hoof rebuts a number of comparable arguments which have been put forward by other commentators. Nevertheless, Western governments in particular remain reluctant to take seriously the notion of economic human rights. The most prominent example is that of the Reagan Administration, which has opposed United States' ratification of the Covenant on the singularly unconvincing grounds first that it sets unrealistic goals for poor countries and secondly that the idea of economic and social rights is easily abused by repressive governments.[163]

The persistence and acceptance of such attitudes serves to reinforce the vicious circle which presently exists whereby the failure to take economic rights seriously has discouraged efforts to develop their content and explore their implications, which in turn has facilitated their continuing neglect. It is submitted that the most effective way of breaking this circle is to tackle one of the key obstacles to the overall acceptability of the notion of economic rights: the vagueness and imprecision of the obligation incurred by States Parties to the Covenant to take steps to achieve progressive realization of the relevant rights. Since the obligation assumed by States under the International Civil and Political Rights Covenant is in a sense more immediate (each State "undertakes to respect and to ensure to all individuals within its territory and subject to its jurisdiction the rights recognized in the present Covenant...") than that assumed under the other Covenant, some commentators

54

have argued that economic, social and cultural rights are merely hortatory, aspirational or programmatic rights.[164] But while it is true that the requirement of progressive realization is less absolute than the requirement to ensure respect, this difference does not in any way diminish, or derogate from, the legal character of the obligations assumed under the Economic, Social and Cultural Rights Covenant. As Henkin has stated, "the rights it recognizes are as 'human', universal and fundamental as are those of the Civil and Political Rights Covenant".[165]

But while the legal character of economic rights may not be in doubt, the nature and scope of the relevant obligations remain extremely vague. In section 6 above an effort was made to explore the nature of States' obligations in the specific context of the right to food. In addition, however, further consideration needs to be given to the broader issue. Such work should be predicated upon two basic assumptions. First, the Covenant was drafted with the intention of imposing obligations upon the States ratifying it. Secondly, the legal obligations contained in the Covenant have been accepted in good faith by the States Parties.[166]

On the basis of these assumptions one of the most promising starting points would seem to be the notion that economic rights entail programmatic obligations. The meaning of the term "programmatic" is seldom considered since it is used primarily in order to relegate economic rights into the limbo of utopian reform programmes. One definition, suggested by a delegate during the *travaux préparatoires* referred to those rights, "recognized in principle, which could in fact be legally enforced only after economic or social programmes of greater or less duration had been carried out".[167] However, such an approach does not take us very far, either in theory or in practice. It would seem to be both more productive and more in line with the intent of the Covenant's framers to treat programmatic rights as those rights, the realization of which must be the specific objective of a clearly defined programme. Such a programme should be directed first of all to defining (in the specific context of the State concerned, but also taking account of relevant international standards) the scope and content of the right in question and, secondly, to specifying the means which are to be used to promote realization of the right as so defined. It is assumed that the international community has a potentially important role to play in drawing up general guidelines which might be used in such national undertakings.

With respect to the right to food it is particularly appropriate to note that the World Food Council has in recent years promoted the concept of national food sector strategies as "a means by which a country can achieve greater food self-sufficiency through an integrated effort to increase food production, improve food consumption and eliminate hunger. It consists of a review of a country's food situation and, based on this review, a coherent framework of policies, programmes and projects to realize the government's food objectives".[168]

Without attempting to assess the adequacy or otherwise of the World Food Council's approach, a commitment on the part of all countries to the adoption of some kind of national food strategy is clearly one of the essential "steps" required to promote implementation of the right to food in accordance with article 2 and 11 of the Covenant. Such strategies should embrace both long-term production and distribution goals as well as necessary short- or medium-term interventionary measures designed to alleviate existing hunger as rapidly as possible. The most important function of such strategies is to inform the residents of each State of the problems which their government has identified and of the measures which are being taken in response. Maximum public participation should be encouraged in the preparation of such strategies.

Having adopted an appropriate programme or strategy the next step must be to monitor the results on a regular basis and to respond appropriately to any reports of continuing hunger or malnutrition. In cases where the resources required either for monitoring or for responding to identified "violations" of the right to food are beyond the means of the government in question, the responsibility of other States and of the international community as a whole could come into play.

In addition to developing the concept of programmatic obligations other measures which could be taken at the international level include:

(a) the establishment of effective nutrition monitoring systems;[169]

(b) endorsement of the concept of "human rights impact statements", first proposed in 1979,[170] so that the impact of major proposed development projects or programmes on for example, enjoyment of the right to food, would be assessed before their implementation is begun; and

(c) the appointment of a group of experts to make recommendations as to the most effective means of supervising States' compliance with their right to food obligations.

12. Towards Effective Implementation at the National Level

In an address to Congress in 1944 President Roosevelt urged the adoption of a second bill of rights dealing with economic issues. Among the rights to which he referred were "...the right to earn enough to provide adequate food..., the right of every farmer to raise and sell his products at a return which will give him and his family a decent living... (and) the right to adequate protection from the economic fears of old age, sickness, accident and unemployment". [171] Forty years later, the world at large has made relatively little progress towards the implementation of these rights, as legal rights.

The Covenant envisages implementation of the various rights "by all appropriate means, including particularly the adoption of legislative measures". Such an open-ended formulation is clearly not intended to limit the range of measures which could potentially be used to give effect to economic rights to the essentially curative (*post-hoc*) and individualistic techniques traditionally employed by civil rights lawyers in Western countries. While legislative measures are seen to be important components of the overall approach, they are, by implication, not sufficient. Other appropriate means could, according to the needs, circumstances and traditions of a given society, embrace a wide range of measures covering the entire spectrum of social, economic and political structures.

Although the present paper is concerned primarily with the creative use of **law** in promoting realization of the right to food, it is essential to bear in mind the inherent limitations of such an approach and the equally important need for measures to resist or counter the potential "bureaucratization" of the issue. Some of these measures are dealt with below in the chapter by Dias and Paul.

Constitutional and (other) legislative measures have in fact not been extensively used to give recognition to the right to food as a human right. There are relatively few exceptions in this regard. Apart from States in which the provisions of the Covenant have been incorporated directly into municipial law, or in which constitutional guarantees of an adequate standard of living have been included, reference may be made to the Indian Constitution (article 47) in which "the raising of the level of nutrition" is declared to be a primary duty of the State and the 1979 Statute on the right of Nicaraguans in which (article 38) "the State recognizes the fundamental right of Nicaraguans to be protected against hunger".

Some of the reasons for the reluctance of States to give legislative recognition to the right to food were noted above (section 3.3). In addition, it is sometimes argued that the right to food is not able to be defined with the degree of precision required for legislative purposes. But this argument is belied by experience with other, no less vague, formulations. Municipal courts have been able to give effect in a wide range of situations to concepts such as "due process" or "equal protection". In many such cases the courts have adopted the attitude that while they may be unable to define the term precisely, "they know an abuse when they see it". Thus for example, as Schachter has recently pointed out, the concept of "human dignity" has been given effect in decisions by the European Court of Human Rights and the Western German Constitutional Court.[172] Vagueness is thus a poor justification for refusing legislative recognition to the right to food.

Above and beyond any value such recognition may have in terms of offering a potential remedy to an aggrieved individual, a formal commitment to the concept of the right to food can also have important hortatory value. In legal systems in which provision exists for public action forms of adjudication (e.g. through liberal provisions governing standing to litigate) recognition of the right to food could provide the basis for a wide range of claims on behalf of vulnerable groups as well as helping to legitimize various extra-legal activities. In addition, in certain types of cases, the burden of proof could be schifted from the hungry complainants to the State or other responsible actors.

The provision of an "effective remedy" to those whose rights have been violated is required under the political rights Covenant (article 2(3)) but not under its economic rights counterpart. This however does not preclude the adoption of a private remedies approach in municipal law or even in the context of a regional human rights arrangement. The fallacy of the oft-stated view that economic rights such as the right to food are completely non-justifiable, and are therefore unable to be protected by any judicially administered remedy, is clearly demonstrated by the diversity of forms of action which has been developed, mainly in the West, to enable private action to be taken to remedy deficient administrative performance. In the United States, for example, such remedies include: rights to contest regulatory impositions, hearing rights concerning government benefits, implied rights of action, and rights to require an administrative agency to take enforcement action.[173] While such remedies certainly have significant limitations, and may or may not constitute the optimal means by which to achieve their overall purpose, the mere fact of their existence nevertheless attests to the possibility of devising appropriate forms of action through which at least some dimensions of the right to food could be made enforceable. This is not to suggest that such an approach, which may work in the context of Western legal and administrative systems, is necessarily either feasible or at all appropriate in other contexts, particularly in the Third World.

Nevertheless, in both Western and Third World contexts the right to food could provide an ideal focus through which to pursue efforts to move away from an unduly individualistic bias in legal reasoning and forms of action.

13. Towards a Right to Food Convention

In 1975 the US Congress adopted a joint "resolution declaring as national policy the right to food", in which it resolved, *inter alia*, that "(1) every person in this country and throughout the world has the right to food - the right to a nutritionally adequate diet - and that this right is henceforth to be recognized as a cornerstone of US policy; and (2) this right become a fundamental point of reference in the formation of legislation and administrative decision in areas such as trade, assistance, monetary reform, military spending and all other matters that bear on hunger..."[174]

Despite the importance attached to it at the time of its adoption this symbolic commitment has failed to have an tangible impact whatsoever on US food policy. Experience at the international level with respect to rhetorical statements on the right to food has been equally disappointing.

As long ago as 1963, a Special Assembly of eminent personalities of world stature met in Rome and issued a Manifesto on Man's Right to Freedom from Hunger, in the course of which they stated "with all the emphasis at our command that freedom from hunger is man's first fundamental right".[175] Later in the same year the First World Food Congress, involving more than 1300 participants from more than 100 countries, adopted a Declaration in which they asserted "that the persistence of hunger and malnutrition is unacceptable morally and socially, is incompatible with the dignity of human beings and the equality of opportunity to which they are entitled, and is a threat to social and international peace."[176] In 1966, the FAO Conference acknowledged the designation of 1968 as International Year for Human Rights by declaring "that the future of mankind and the peace of the world cannot be secure unless man's fundamental right to be free from hunger is universally realized". The Conference also requested all FAO Member States to study the possibility of ratifying the International Covenant on Economic, Social and Cultural Rights, "and to undertake all necessary measures to achieve man's right to freedom from hunger and want".[177]

Innumerable other examples could also be cited to demonstrate that the international community has frequently purported to approach the problem of hunger and malnutrition from the perspective of human rights and that the right to food has been singled out for priority action time and again. There can be no doubt that if good intentions and carefully drafted declarations, communiques and programmes of action adopted by international gatherings could, without further ado, feed the starving and satisfy the malnourished, all would be well. However, it is not. The ineffectiveness and practical irrelevance of most of the targets which the international community has set for itself over the years with respect to realization of the right to food can be gauged from a review of some of the time horizons which have been established in this regard. Thus, for example, a comparison of the target adopted in December 1980 in the International Development Strategy for the Third United Nations Development Decade with that endorsed only nine months later, in September 1981, by the UN Conference on the Least Developed Countries clearly demonstrates the casualness and lack of specific commitment with which such targets are set. While the former instrument declares that "hunger and malnutrition must be eliminated as soon as possible and certainly by the end of this century", [178] the latter calls upon the least developed countries to "prepare strategies, plans and policies...which will...(eliminate) hunger and malnutrition as rapidly as possible and at the latest by 1990".[179] The ten year discrepancy in otherwise identical targets can only be explained by the lack of practical, if not symbolic, importance attached to the goal in question. An even stronger indication of the ineffectiveness of such non-binding targets is provided by the resolution by which the World Food Conference in 1974 resolved dramatically:

"that all Governments should accept the removal of the scourge of hunger and malnutrition, which at present afflicts many millions of human beings, as the objective of the international community as a whole, and should accept that within a decade no child will go to bed hungry, that no family will fear for its next day's bread, and that no human being's future and capacities will be stunted by malnutrition".[180]

Five years later, the FAO stated in an official report to its biennial Conference that "the World Food Conference target of mid-1985 was not only ambitious; in practice it has been ignored."[181]

The plethora of non-binding instruments relating to the right to food, with their chameleon-like provisions, attests to the ineffectiveness of elaborating instruments which do not contain appropriate follow-up mechanisms to ensure that States comply with the obligations they have freely entered into.

The voluntary character of declarations and suchlike has time and again been proven to be unsatisfactory in the field of food. The World Food Council's conclusion in 1980 that "the challenge posed by the Universal Declaration on the Eradication of Hunger and Malnutrition (of 1974)...is yet to be adequately addressed"[182] is equally applicable to the ambitious goals established in other comparable non-binding instruments.

There is thus a particularly strong case in favour of moving towards the elaboration and adoption of binding, or at least potentially binding, international legal instruments dealing with the right to food in general as well as particular technical aspects thereof. In recent years there has been a growing, albeit reluctant, recognition of this fact.

In 1979 the World Food Council acknowledged that progress towards the eradication of hunger would be "helped by the establishment of benchmarks by which such progress could be projected and assessed". [183] In 1981 Prime Minister Gandhi of India, addressing the FAO Conference, specifically endorsed an earlier proposal made by President Kaunda of Zambia for the drawing up of a "Hunger Elimination Treaty".[184] Most recently, in 1984, FAO has proposed the preparation of a "World Food Compact" which would be a codification of already agreed food security objectives. However, since the proposed Compact would not impose any "financial or binding obligations on its signatories" but "would represent a moral commitment",[185] it is difficult to escape the conclusion that the outcome will be yet another frustrating exercise in tokenism.

The analysis above (section 6) of article 11 of Covenant demonstrates that while the basic norm is clearly enunciated, no amount of strict legal construction or interpretation of the subsidiary norms will suffice to produce a clear and widely acceptable framework within which the right to food could be effectively operationalized. As foreseen in article 23 of the Covenant, the adoption of a convention or a series of protocols spelling out the normative implications of the right is an indispensable element for such operationalization. While the proposal for a right to food convention will assuredly not win overnight acceptance, efforts should begin immediately to identify the various options which might be pursued and to urge concerned governments to place the proposal squarely on the international agenda.

Conclusion: The Usefulness of a Right to Food Approach

No amount of legal analysis of the relevant international human rights provisions, no amount of posturing by statesmen and bureaucrats and no amount of academic debate and dissection of the "technical" issues can conceal the fact that the eradication of hunger and malnutrition has **not**, in practice, been a priority concern of the vast majority of governments. The political will has clearly been absent. The constituency of the starving and malnourished has usually only been able to exert sufficient political pressure in times of the direst emergency. In ordinary times the voices which are muted by hunger are simply not heard in the corridors of power.

Against this background, the key question is whether approaching the problem of hunger from a human rights perspective is anything more than an exercise in academic futility. The thrust of the response in this chapter is that it is not. In addition to the reasons given below it must be admitted that this response is also predicated on the belief that **excessive** realism (defeatism) is more destructive in the long term than what may presently be dismissed as naive idealism. Whereas the former ensure the maintenance of the *status quo*, the latter at least points the way to a better future. In brief the advantages offered by a right to food approach include the following:

(1) It serves to underline the ethical/moral dimensions of issues which are too often portrayed as exclusively technical matters.

(2) By approaching the problem from the perspective of a human rights framework, as defined by international legal obligations which governments have already accepted, it may be easier to rebut the unjustified but widespread assumption that there exists at present no accepted normative framework relevant to national and international food policy-making.

(3) spurious rights which are often claimed to have priority - such as: the absolute right to private property; the right to unfettered freedom of choice; the right to contract freely; and the right to open competition - are exposed for what they are worth in the overall human rights framework.

Macro-economic considerations such as balance of payments problems, export-led growth strategies, economic stabilization programmes or laissez-faire world trade policies are also put into an appropriate perspective.

(4) In matters of food policy the burden of proof is shifted from those claiming assistance to those in a position to provide it and from those calling for fundamental structural changes to those who benefit from the status quo and thus reject the need for change.

(5) The barriers of state sovereignty and domestic jurisdiction are significantly lowered (although by no means demolished) and some aspects of issues such as internal equality or the obligation of States to provide aid or support necessary reforms, become legitimate issues on the international agenda.

(6) The accountability of governments and of international organizations, in terms of the impact of their policies and programmes on enjoyment of the right to food, is emphasized.

In brief the adoption of a human rights framework facilitates the transfer of food issues from the purely technical and academic arenas to the serious political agenda, from which they have long been absent (notwithstanding a brief springtime of rhetoric around 1974). The myth of the political neutrality of any given food policy strategy is thereby exposed. Finally, and most importantly, focusing on the right to food provides a rallying point around

61

which to mobilize the starving masses. In reality, the major contribution which well-fed academics, technicians and bureaucrats can make is simply to emphasize the legitimacy of the right to food as a fundamental human right.

For, in the final analysis, appropriate policies will be adopted not as a result of technocratic altruism but only in response to widespread and insistent popular outrage. For that reason, an emphasis on the role of law must not be permitted to obscure the importance of viewing the concept of the right to food essentially as a mobilizing force, as a rallying point, through which people themselves are encouraged to assert their rights by making use of all appropriate legal and extra-legal means. The concept of human rights is too often assumed to be of only systemic relevance and viewed only in macroterms. In fact its primary role is both more modest and more fundamental - it is to imbue and develop in all people the belief that they possess certain inalienable rights and that they are entitled, perhaps even obliged, to do all in their power to realize those rights for themselves.

Notes

(1) Among the literature on the right to food see Christensen, The Right to Food: How to Guarantee (1978); Dobbert, "Right to food", in Dupuy (ed.), The Right to Health as a Human Right (1978) at 184; Nielsen, Wangel and Blyberg, The Right to be Free from Hunger: A Struggle for Self-Reliance (1978); Collins, "The right to food and the New International Economic Order" Unesco doc. SS-78/CONF.630/6 (1978); Caldwell, "The legal factor in the food-population equation" in MacDonald et.al. (eds.), The International Law and Policy of Human Welfare (1978) at 601-14; "International law and the food crisis" in Proceedings of the American Society of International Law (1975) at 39-63; Nanda, "The world food crisis and the role of law in combating hunger and malnutrition", 10 The Journal of International Law and Economics (1975); Eide, et.al. (eds.), Food as a Human Right (1984); Gustafson (ed.), Right to Food: Humanist Perspectives (1979); and The First Human Right (1968).
(2) UNICEF, The State of the World's Children 1984 (1984).
(3) UN doc. E/CONF.65/3 (1974) para. 176.
(4) Reutlinger and Selowsky, Malnutrition and Poverty: Magnitude and Policy Options, World Bank Staff Occasional Paper No. 23 (1976) at 2-3.
(5) Poleman, "World food: a perspective", 188 Science (1975) at 510-18.
(6) Eberstadt, "Has China failed?", 26 The New York Review of Books, April 5, 1979, at 36.
(7) See Crittenden, "World agencies statistics on world hunger often greatly exaggerated, experts contend", International Herald Tribune, October 8, 1981, at 7.
(8) Sixth Report of the Global Health Situation 1973-1977 Part I: Global Analysis (1980) at 142.
(9) Berg, Malnourished People: A Policy View (1981) at 1.
(10) Brown and Shue (eds.), Food Policy: The Responsibility of the United States in the Life and Death Choices (1977) at 3.
(11) Berg, n. 9, at 2.
(12) Sen, Poverty and Famines: An Essay on Entitlement and Deprivation (1981).
(13) Berg, n.9, at 3.
(14) See Isenman and Singer, "Food aid: disincentive effects and their policy implications", 25 Economic Development and Cultural Change (1977) at 205-37; and Maxwell and Singer, "Food aid to developing countries", 7 World Development (1979) at 225-47.
(15) Gwatkin, et. al. Can Health and Nutrition Interventions Make a Difference? (1980) at 34.
(16) See generally, Brown and Shue (eds.), op.cit. n. 10; Aiken and La Follette (eds.), World Hunger and Moral Obligation (1977); Gewirth, "Starvation and human rights" in Human Rights: Essays on Justification and Applications (1982); and Fishkin, The Limits of Obligation (1982).

62

(17) See the articles by Hardin and Fletcher in Aiken and La Follette (eds.), *op.cit.* n. 16; and Nozick, Anarchy, State and Utopia (1974), chap. 3.
(18) Haverberg, "Individual needs: nutritional guidelines for policy?", in Brown and Shue (eds.), *op.cit.* n. 10, at 229-30.
(19) See section 10 below.
(20) International Court of Justice, Reports (1962) at 547.
(21) Kullmann, "Fair labour standards" in international commodity agreements", 14 Journal of World Trade Law (1980) at 535.
(22) Proceedings of the American Society of International Law (1975) at 39-63.
(23) UN doc. E/1980/6/Add. 16 (1980) para 21.
(24) Rowles, "Law and Agrarian Reform in Costa Rica' 14 Lawyer of the Americas (1983) 399 at 514-15.
(25) Spitz, "Livelihood and the food squeeze", Ceres, May-June 1981, at 30.
(26) FAO, Approaches to World Food Security (1983) at 92.
(27) UN doc. A/2910/Add. 2 (1955) Annex I.A.
(28) Sen, n. 12, at 49.
(29) Gorovitz, "Bigotry, loyalty and malnutrition", in Brown and Shue (eds.), *op.cit.* n. 10, at 131-32.
(30) Haas, Global Evangelism Rides Again: How to Protect Human Rights Without Really Trying (1978)at 45-46.
(31) See the discussion of the "myth" that "societies that have eliminated hunger have done so only by denying people's rights. There appears to be a trade-off between freedom and ending hunger", in Lappé and Collins, World Hunger: Ten Myths (1979) at 34-38.
(32) See UN doc. E/CN.4/1488 (1981) paras. 122-91.
(33) See United Nations, Progress in Land Reform - Sixth Report (1976) 161-65. In Utopia, Thomas More even considered war to be "perfectly justifiable" "when one country denies another its natural right to derive nourishment from any soil which the original owners are not using themselves". (Penguin Books ed., 1965) at 80.
(34) Report of the Human Rights Committee, UN doc A/37/40 (1982) Annex V, para. 1.
(35) G A Res 217 A (III) (1948).
(36) UN doc. E/600 (1947) Annex A, article 25.
(37) See Verdoodt, Naissance et signification de la Déclaration universelle des droits de l'homme, (1964) at 233-41.
(38) See generally Humphrey, "The universal declaration of human rights: its history, impact and juridical character", in Ramcharan (ed.), Human Rights: Thirty Years After the Universal Declaration, (1979) at 21-37.
(39) G A Res. 2200 A (XXI) (1966).
(40) Collins, *op.cit.*, n.1, at 33.
(41) G A Res. 1803 (XVII).
(42) G A Res. 2625 (XXV).
(43) Cassese, "The self-determination of peoples", in Henkin (ed.), The International Bill of Rights: The Covenant on Civil and Political Rights (1981) at 92-106.
(44) UN doc. A/C.3/SR.674 (1955) para. 8.
(45) Cassese, *op.cit.*, n. 43, at 111-13.
(46) Dinstein, "The right to life, physical integrity, and liberty", in Henkin (ed.) *op.cit.*, n. 43, at 114-115.
(47) Scheuner, "comparison of the jurisprudence of national courts with that of the organs of the convention as regards other rights", in Robertson (ed.) Human Rights in National and International Law (1968) at 214-239.
(48) Przetacznik, "The right to life as a basic human right", 9 Revue des droits de l'homme, (1976) at 585-603.
(49) Robinson, The Universal Declaration of Human Rights: Its Origins, Significance and Interpretation (2d ed., 1958) at 106.
(50) UN doc. E/CN.4/21 (1947) at 59.
(51) Report of the Human Rights Committee, UN doc. A/37/40 (1982) Annex V, para. 5.
(52) See The Geneva Conventions of August 12, 1949 and Protocols Additional to the Geneva Conventions of 12 August, 1949 (Geneva, International Committee of the Red Cross, 1970 and 1977 respectively).

(53) The predecessor to the Third Convention of 1949 was the Geneva Convention Relative to the Treatment of Prisoners of War of July 27, 1929. It provided in article 11 that "the food ration of prisoners of war shall be equivalent in quantity and quality to that of the depot troops".

(54) See e.g. article 15 concerning the maintenance of prisoners; article 51 concerning working conditions; and article 72 concerning entitlement to receive relief shipments of food and other necessities.

(55) It has been argued that this provision, by requiring the consent of the party concerned before action can be taken, amounts to a step backward in international law since the pre-existing law was vague and was capable of being interpreted so as to permit the provision of relief without such consent. See Eide, "The new humanitarian law in non-international armed conflict" in Cassese (ed.), The New Humanitarian Law of Armed Conflict (1979) at 277-294.

(56) See generally, Human Rights: A Compilation of International Instruments, UN doc. ST/HR/1/rev.2. (1983).

(57) European Treaty Series No. 5 (1951).

(58) Ibid., No. 35 (1961).

(59) Pan American Union, Final Act of the Ninth Conference of American States, (1948) at 38-45.

(60) Organization of American States Treaty Series No. 36 (1969).

(61) Annual Report of the Inter-American Commission on Human Rights, OAS doc. OEA/Ser.G, CP/doc. 1110/80 (1980) at 152.

(62) Ibid., at 153.

(63) Ninth International Conference of American States, Bogota, Colombia, March 30 - May 2, 1948, Report of the Delegation of the USA (1948) Appendix 2, at 251-59.

(64) OAS doc. OEA/Ser.P/AG/doc. 1656/83 (1983).

(65) OAU doc. CAB/LEG/67/3/Rev.5 (1981); 21 I.L.M. 58 (1982).

(66) OAU doc. CM/1149 (XXXVII), Annex I.

(67) "Annotations on the text of the draft International Covenants on Human Rights: prepared by the Secretary-General", UN doc. A/2929 (1955).

(68) Alston, "The United Nations specialized agencies and implementation of the International Covenant on Economic, Social and Cultural Rights", 18 Columbia Journal of Transnational Law, (1979) at 82-90.

(69) UN doc. E/1992 (1951) Annex I, article 19.

(70) UN doc. A/2929, chap. VIII.

(71) UN doc. A/2910/Add.1 (1955) Annex; and A/2910/Add.3 (1955).

(72) UN doc. A/C.3/SR.1232 (1963) para. 6.

(73) Ibid., The draft text read as follows:
"1. The States Parties to the present Covenant recognize the right of everyone to be free from hunger. They undertake, individually and through international co-operation, to develop programmes aimed at achieving freedom from hunger within the shortest possible time.
2. The States Parties to the present Covenant recognize that, with a view to achieving the full realization of this right, national and international action should be geared to the realization of this right by paying particular attention to:
(a) Policies to ensure that world food supplies are shared on a rational and equitable basis;
(b) Economic, technical and other measures to increase the production of food;
(c) The adaption of existing institutions, including systems of land tenure and land use, to the requirements of economic and social progress; and
(d) The promotion and full utilization of scientific and technical knowledge and a massive education of the population in order to improve methods of production, conservation and distribution of food."

(74) UN doc. A/C.3/L.1172.

(75) UN doc. A/C.3/L/1175 and Add.1.

(76) UN doc. A/C.3/L/1177 and Rev.1.

(77) UN doc. A/C.3/SR.1266 (1963) para. 55.

(78) "Report of the Third Committee" UN doc. A/5655 (1963), para. 95.

(79) UN doc. A/C.3/SR,1264 (1963), para. 4.

(80) UN doc. A/C.3/SR.1266 (1963), paras. 57-63.

(81) UN doc. A/C.3/SR.1269 (1963), para. 2.

(82) UN doc. A/C.3/SR.1266 (1963), para. 56.
(83) Sen, *op.cit.*, n. 12 at 12.
(84) Mead, Cultural Patterns and Technical Change (1953) at 213.
(85) OECD, Development Cooperation - Efforts and Policies of the Members of the Development Assistance Committee - 1977 Review (1977) at 21.
(86) UN doc. A/C.3/SR.
(87) "Legal consequences for States of the continued presence of South Africa in Namibia (South West Africa) notwithstanding Security Council Resolution 276 (1970)", I.C.J. Reports (1971) at 31.
(88) Dobbert, *op.cit.*, n.1, at 194.
(89) Verdoodt, *op.cit.*, n. 37, at 233-41.
(90) One problem which could arise if the concept of equitable distribution in relation to need is applied only at the level of the State rather than to smaller units is that regions which are suffering from famines, but where the national or even the local supply of food has either not declined or declined only slightly (Sen, *op.cit.*, has examined several such cases) would not necessarily qualify directly for assistance.
(91) G A Res. 3202 (S-VI) (1974) Section X.
(92) UNCTAD Res. 122 (V)(1979); G A Res. 34/203 (1979); and "Report of the United Nations Conference on the Least Developed Countries", UN doc. A/CONF.104/22 (1981).
(93) "Food aid for the least developed countries (A perspective for the eighties): contribution by the World Food Programme", A/CONF.104/7/Add.22 (1981) Annex 1.
(94) In the "Manila Communique of the World Food Council" food priority countries, which "should be accorded special treatment by Governments and agencies of the United Nations" are defined as "countries which require special attention because of the seriousness of their food problems, their economic or resource limitations, their being victims of frequent natural calamities and their potential for increasing food production". UN doc. A/32/19, Part One, para.1.A.1.
(95) UN doc. E/CN.4/Sub.2/432/Rev.1 (1980).
(96) Shue, Basic Rights: Subsistence, Affluence, and U.S. Foreign Policy, (1980) at 6.
(97) UN doc. A/C.3/SR.1267 (1963), para. 4.
(98) UN doc. A/36/19 (1981), para. 7.
(99) G A Res. 34/46 (1979) para. 7; cf. also Res. 35/174 (1980), preamble; and 36/133 (1981) para. 7.
(100) G A Res. 3202 (S-VI), section I.
(101) Message from the President of the United States, transmitting four treaties pertaining to human rights, Sen. Exec. C,D,E, and F, 95th Cong., 2d Sess. vii (1978).
(102) Cleveland, "Does everything belong to everybody?", The Christian Science Monitor, 19 December 1978, at 22.
(103) The Right to Food Resolution, 94th Cong., 2d Sess., 68 (1976).
(104) See Wallerstein, Food for War - Food for Peace: United States Food Aid in a Global Context (1980) at 15; and Lappé, Collins and Kinley, Aid as Obstacle (1980).
(105) Hartmann and Boyce, Needless Hunger: Voices from a Bangladesh Village (1979) at 46.
(106) George, "Impact of the food systems of industrialized countries on society and the environment in developing countries", UN doc. ENV/SEM.LL/R.18 (1979) para. 55.
(107) For an attempt to relate the two issues see Kowalewski, "Transnational corporations and the third world's right to eat: the Carribbean", 3 Human Rights Quarterly (1981) at 45-64.
(108) George, How the Other Half Dies: The Real Reasons for World Hunger (1977) at 191.
(109) Morgan, Merchants of Grain (1980) at 446.
(110) *Ibid.*, at 282.
(111) Overcoming World Hunger: The Challenge Ahead (1980) at 184.
(112) Green, "Afterword" in Shepherd, The Politics of Starvation (1975) at 87.
(113) UN doc. A/C.3/SR.1264 (1963) para. 6.
(114) Report of the Conference of FAO, 12th Session (1963) at 24-25.
(115) Collins, *op.cit.*, n.1, at 6.
(116) UN doc. A/C.3/SR.1268 (1963) para. 16.
(117) The interpretation proposed by Dobbert (*op.cit.*, n.1, 193) that article 11 (2)(b) "envi-

sages primarily international exchange of goods, normally through trade channels" would thus seem unduly restrictive.

(118) *op.cit.*, n.73.

(119) Brownlie, "Legal Status of Natural Resources in International Law (Some Aspects)", Académie de droit international, Recueil des cours, 1979, I, vol. 162 (1980), at 288.

(120) Doxey, "Oil and Food as International Sanctions", 36 International Journal (1981) at 311-34; and Wallensteen, "Scarce goods as political weapons: the case of food", 13 Journal of Peace Research, (1976) at 277-98.

(121) Whiteman, "Jus Cogens in international law, with a projected list", 7 Georgia Journal of International and Comparative Law (1977) 609, at 625-26.

(122) G A Res. 36/103 (1981) Annex, para. 2, part II, (k).

(123) G A Res. 36/185 (1981) para. 10, based on the 1981 report of the World Food Council, UN doc A/36/19, para. 20. Similarly, in 1980 the Council had, in response to the 1980 US embargo on grain exports to the Soviet Union, stated that: "Without getting itself involved in judging this action, the Council may say that unilateral use of food as a political instrument has been condemned in the past and this condemnation must be reaffirmed". UN doc. WFC/ 1980/7, para. 8.

(124) 55 UN Treaty Series 194.

(125) At the 1981 FAO Conference the French Minister for Agriculture quoted President Mitterand as saying that "it is no longer acceptable that the food power of the rich exporting countries be used as a means of speculation or of political pressure to the detriment of the poorest. It is unacceptable that food power be employed as a food weapon". FAO doc. C 81/ PV/5 (10 Nov. 1981), at 7 (in French).

(126) See generally, Brownlie, *op.cit.*, n.119.

(127) E.g. Perkins, The Prudent Peace: Law as Foreign Policy (1981) chap. 12.

(128) Declaration of the Ministers for Foreign Affairs of the Group of 77 in UN doc. A/34/ 533 (1979) Annex, para. 4.

(129) In practical terms such an approach is important since it serves to reassure those who argue against the provision of foreign aid on the grounds that it is a bottomless pit into which all of a country's resources could be poured with the main result being the impoverishment or ruin of the donor.

(130) Shuman, "Food Aid and the Free Market" in Brown and Shue (eds.), *op.cit.*, n.10, at 162.

(131) Rosjak, quoted in Caldwell, *op.cit.*, n.1, at 603.

(132) Singer "Reconsidering the famine relief argument", in Brown and Shue (eds.) *op.cit.*, n.10, at 49.

(133) Referred to by Hopkins and Puchala, "Perspectives on the International Relations of Food", 32 International Organization (1978) 607. See generally "Principal organizations and bodies of the United Nations system concerned with food and and food-related problems", UN doc. WFC/1981/7 and Add. 1.

(134) Thompson, "International organizations and the improbability of a global food regime" in Balaam and Carey (eds.), Food Politics: The Regional Conflict (1980) at 191-206; and Shefrin, "The agricultural agencies: objectives and performance", 35 International Journal (1980) at 263-91.

(135) Strange, "Cave! hic dragones: A critique of regime analysis", 36 International Organization (1982)at 483.

(136) Bergesen, "A new food regime: necessary but impossible", 34 International Organization (1980)at 298.

(137) Hopkins and Puchala, *op.cit.*, n. 133,at 612.

(138) For example the Council of Ministers of the Organization of African Unity adopted a resolution in February 1982 in which it noted " that the strategy to development and economic growth recommended in the World Bank Report (entitled Accelerated Development in Sub-Saharan Africa: An Agenda for Action (1981... would in fact perpetuate the present structure of African economies and make them more dependent on agricultural exports and on external markets", OAU resolution CM/Res. 921 (XXXVIII) reprinted in UN doc. A/37/161 (1982) Annex, at 28.

(139) Symptomatic of this is the book published in 1976 by FAO of speeches made by the agencies' Director-General from 1968-1975, Addeke H. Boerma. It is entitled *Right to Food*

but the issue of the human right to food is nowhere specifically addressed in its pages.

(140) George, *op.cit.*, n. 108, at 231.
(141) The food quality and related standards adopted by the joint FAO/WHO Codex Alimentarius Commission are too technical to qualify as an exception to this rule.
(142) UN doc. E/CN.4/364 (1950) para. 111.
(143) "The entire programme of the Organization is a contribution to the advancement of certain fundamental human rights and in particular of the right to food", FAO reply reproduced in UN doc. E/CN.4/1318 (1978) para. 19.
(144) Common Crisis (1983) at 132.
(145) See for example Falk's characterization of a government's deliberate refusal to satisfy basic human needs as a severe human rights violation, in Human Rights and State Sovereignty (1981) at 165-67.
(146) Ganji, The Realization of Economic, Social and Cultural Rights: Problems, Policies, Progress (1975) UN doc. E/CN.4/1108/Rev.1 and E/CN.4/1131/Rev.1, para. 81.
(147) See UN docs. E/CN.4/SR.1392, para. 2, and E/CN.4/NGO/222.
(148) Economic and Social Council Res. 1983/140.
(149) Res. 5 (XXXIII) para. 2.
(150) UN doc. E/CN.4/1984/25, paras. 30-40.
(151) UN doc. E/CN.4/1984/30, para. 5.12.3.
(152) OAS doc. OEA/Ser.L/V/II/46, doc. 46, Rev. 1 (1979) paras. 72-81.
(153) "Implementation of the International Covenant on Economic, Social and Cultural Rights: ECOSOC Working Group", 27 The Review of the International Commission of Jurists (1981) 26 at 28.
(154) Krasner (ed.) International Organization, Vol. 36/2 (1982).
(155) *Ibid.*, at 186.
(156) Strange, *op.cit.*, n. 135.
(157) *op.cit.*, n. 133; and Puchala and Hopkins, "International regimes: lessons from inductive analysis", 36 International Organization (1982) at 245-76.
(158) *Ibid.*, at 263-65.
(159) *Op.cit.*, n. 133, at 862-65.
(160) Bergesen, "A new food regime: necessary but impossible", 34 International Organization (1980) 285 at 301.
(161) *Ibid.*, at 302.
(162) D'Amato, "The concept of human rights in international law", 86 Columbia Law Review (1982) 1110 at 1129.
(163) International Herald Tribune (Paris), 11 February 1982 at 3.
(164) See the chapter by Van Hoof, infra.
(165) Henkin (ed.), *op.cit.*, n. 43, at 10.
(166) See Virally, "Review essay: good faith in public international law", 77 American Journal of International Law (1983) at 130.
(167) Un doc. A/C.3/SR.368 (1951), paras. 129-30.
(168) National Food Strategies to Eradicate Hunger (1982), at 7.
(169) World Health Organization, Food and Nutrition Strategies in National Development (1976) at 7.
(170) UN doc. E/CN.4/1334 (1979).
(171) 90 Congressional Record 57 (1944).
(172) Schachter, "Human dignity as a normative concept", 77 American Journal of International Law (1983) at 848-54.
(173) Stewart and Sunstein, "Public Programs and Private Rights", 95 Harvard Law Review (1982) at 1193-1322.
(174) The Right to Food Resolution, Hearings Before the Subcommittee on International Resources, House of Representatives, 94th Congress, 2nd Session (1976).
(175) FAO, 4 Freedom from Hunger Campaign News, September 1963.
(176) FAO Conference Res. 5/63 (1963).
(177) UN doc. A/CONF.32/16 (1968), para. 9.
(178) G A Res. 35/56 (1980) Annex, para. 28.
(179) UN doc. A/CONF.104/22 (1981), chap. I, para. 10.
(180) UN doc. E/CONF.65/20 (1975), chap. II, Res. I.

(181) FAO doc. C79/24 (1979), XV.
(182) UN doc. WFC/1980/7, para. 2.
(183) UN doc. WFC/1979/3, para. 163.
(184) FAO doc. C81/PV/4 (1981), 8.
(185) FAO doc. CFS:84/4 (1984) paras. 80-81.

Part II:
Philosophical perspectives

The right not to be hungry*

Amartya Sen
University of Oxford

1. RIGHTS AND METARIGHTS

Do people have a right to be free from hunger? This is asserted often enough, but what does it stand for? It is, of course, tempting to say: Nothing at all. But that piece of sophisticated cynicism provides not so much a penetrating insight into the practical affairs of the world, but merely a refusal to investigate what people mean when they assert the existence of rights that, for much of humanity, are plainly not guaranteed by the existing institutional arrangements.

It is useful to begin with Ronald Dworkin's distinction between "background rights" and "institutional rights":

Any adequate theory will distinguish, for example, between background rights, which are rights that provide a justification for political decisions by society in abstract, and institutional rights, that provide a justification for a decision by some particular and specified political institution. Suppose that my political theory provides that every man has a right to the property of another if he needs it more. I might yet concede that he does not have a legislative right to the same effect; I might concede, that is, that he has no institutional right that the present legislation enact legislation that would violate the Constitution, as such a statute presumably would. I might also concede that he has no institutional right to a judicial decision condoning theft. Even if I did make these concessions, I could preserve my initial background claim by arguing that the people as a whole would be justified in amending the Constitution to abolish property, or perhaps in rebelling and over-throwing the present form of government entirely. I would claim that each man has a residual background right that would justify or require these acts, even though I concede that he does not have the right to specific institutional decisions as these institutions are now constituted (Dworkin [1], p. 93).

A system of social security that guarantees to everyone a minimum income sufficient to buy enough food can be seen to make the right to be free from hunger an institutional right, provided it could be assumed that the decision-making within the family would lead to the income being expended for that purpose rather than some other. For a great many countries, however, such social security arrangements do not exist, and if the right in question is asserted in the context of such countries as well, they would clearly not be institutional rights, but merely background rights.

But sometimes the assertion would seem to be even weaker than what could be called background right in the sense of arguing that "the people as a

* This article has been reprinted from 'Contemporary Philosophy. A New Survey', vol. 2, pp. 343-360, with the permission of the author and the publisher.

whole would be justified in amending the Constitution" to make these claims institutional. Franklin Roosevelt's 1941 speech on "a world founded upon four *essential* freedoms", including "freedom from want ... everywhere in the world", was, in fact, quite unrevolutionary in its constitutional implications, despite the enormity of the "freedom" in question. Its importance rested primarily in acknowledging a shift in the political climate as a result of which the issues of hunger and want would enjoy an unprecedented standing in post-War discussion on public policy.

Dworkin's distinction between "concrete" and "abstract" rights must also be considered in this context. "An abstract right is a general political aim the statement of which does not indicate how the general aim is to be weighted or compromised in particular circumstances against the other political aims" (Dworkin (1), p. 93). The kinds of rights Dworkin mainly concentrates on in his examples are political in the narrower sense, but the distinction is quite general. The right to be free from hunger may be treated as an abstract right when the "trade-offs" with other objectives are not specified and other features of concrete application kept somewhat vague.

The right to be free from hunger has different status in different countries, varying from being concrete, institutional rights (in countries with elaborate social security systems with specified priorities) to abstract, background rights (in countries in which such rights are accepted without insitutional translation and without even concrete specification of priorities). I would now like to argue that the rights related to being free from hunger can take an even "remoter" form than an abstract, background right, *without* being empty of content, and in this context Dworkin's categorisation may require an extension.

A *metaright* to something x can be defined as the right to have *policies* $p(x)$ that genuinely pursue the objective of making the right to x realisable. As an example, consider the following "Directive Principle of State Policy" inserted in the Constitution of India when it was adopted in 1950:

"The state shall, in particular, direct its policy towards securing ... that the citizens, men and women equally, have the right to an adequate means of livelihood".

The wording was careful enough to avoid asserting that such a right already exists, but saying only that policy should be directed to making it possible to have that as a right. If *this* right were accepted, then the effect will not be to make the "right to an adequate means of livelihood" real - even as an abstract, background right - but to give a person the right to demand that policy be directed towards securing the objective of making the right to adequate means a realisable right, even if that objective cannot be immediately achieved. It is a right of a different kind: not to x but to $p(x)$. I propose to call a right to $p(x)$ a *metaright* to x.

Why do we need a different category of metarights given the very weak form of rights captured by Dworkin's concept of abstract, background rights? The reason is that the two general categories of rights and metarights deal with different subjects of entitlement. Corresponding to an institutional right to x (e.g., to a public arrangement for two meals a day for all), a back-

70

ground right permits one to claim that the state must see to it that x be achieved, and if it isn't, then to claim, as Dworkin puts it, "that the people as a whole would be justified to amending the Constitution ... or perhaps in rebelling or overthrowing the present form of government entirely". A metaright to x does not yield this claim. It concentrates not on the achievement of x, which might be currently unachievable, but on the pursuit of policies that would help to make x achievable in the future. Even an *abstract, background* right is concerned with x rather than with $p(x)$, which is the focus of attention of a metaright to x. The justification for amendment, rebellion, overthrowal, etc., would arise from the absence of such policy measures $p(x)$ rather than from the absence of achieved x.

It is not difficult to see why metarights of this kind have a particular relevance for economic aims such as the removal of poverty or hunger. For many countries where poverty or hunger is widespread, there might not exist *any* feasible way whatsoever by which freedom from them could be guaranteed for all in the very near future, but policies that would rapidly lead to such freedom do exist. The metaright for freedom from hunger is the right to such a policy, but what lies behind that right is ultimately the objective of achieving that freedom.

There are, of course, ambiguities as to ways of checking whether the measures taken by the government amount to a policy $p(x)$ aimed at securing a certain right x. There may be various ways of moving to x, at different speeds. Standards of acceptability are eminently arguable. But such ambiguities of specification are not unusual in dealing with rights in general. Debates on whether or not an abstract "right to free speech or dignity or equality" - to quote Dworkin's example - is being violated, need not be any less intricate than debates on whether or not a set of public measures amount to a policy directed towards securing the abolition of starvation. Indeed, sometimes it is patently clear that the policies pursued are *not* thus directed.

A metaright to x as a right to $p(x)$ can, of course, also be either institutional or background, and either concrete or abstract. The "Directive Principle" of the Indian Constitution that was quoted did not make this metaright an institutional one, nor concrete in terms of specified priorities. So it is best viewed as an abstract, background metaright. There is, however, no difficulty in conceiving of the same right being made institutional and concrete, permitting any individual to sue the government for not pursuing, with the required amount of urgency, a policy that is genuinely aimed at achieving the right to adequate means.

The rights related to adequate means could, thus, vary from being concrete, institutional rights to abstract, background metarights. Even the last is not vacuous since it can provide a ground for protest, or rebellion aimed at overthrowal of the government, if the metaright is systematically ignored by the government, but it is, of course, in some ways, a good deal weaker than rights of other specification. The point of this section has been to identify the variety of forms in which rights related to adequate means could arise. The content of these rights would vary tremendously depending on the particular form, and it is important to be clear about what is or is not asserted by a particular formulation of a right of this kind.

2. RIGHTS AND ENTITLEMENTS

I move now from the notion of rights to that of entitlements. It is usual to characterise rights as relationships that hold between distinct agents, e.g., between one person and another, or between one person and the state [1]. In contrast, a person's entitlements are the totality of things he can have by virtue of his rights. What bundle of goods he ends up with will, of course, depend on how he exercises his rights, and so the entitlements are best viewed as a *set* of bundles any one of which he can have by using his rights.

Being free from hunger is really a matter of entitlements rather than of rights only. Contrary to Alexander Selkirk's defiant claim in his island of solitude that:

"I am monarch of all I survey.
My right there is none to dispute,"

the usual two-agent rights are not relevant in this case since no one else was there, but he did have the use of "the fowl and the brute". In the social context a person's entitlements would depend, among other things, on all the rights he has vis-a-vis others and others have vis-a-vis him. If a right is best thought of as a relationship of one agent to another, entitlements represent a relationship between an agent and things - based on the set of *all* rights relevant to him.

Entitlements as a concept is quite a general one, and the "things" referred to need not be commodities but anything the person could conceivably wish to have including non-molestation in the streets, or the freedom to lecture on the immorality of the modern age to one's neighbour in the bus. But in this paper the focus is on economic entitlements only - in particular the entitlement to adequate means.

An illustration may clarify the notion of entitlements. Suppose the set of rights in question were those guaranteed by a typical private ownership market economy with the usual rights of ownership, inheritance, etc. Given a person's "endowments", including his own physical and mental abilities as well as his possessions guaranteed by the prevailing system of claims, immunities, etc.,[2] he has various opportunities of arriving at different bundles of goods and services to which he will be entitled depending on what acts of exchange, production, etc., he decides to undertake among the ones available. These acts involve creation of fresh rights and obligations vis-a-vis others by virtue of the contracts entered into, formally *or* informally. In selling a commodity and buying another, the rights of ownership of the goods in question change, and the same applies to the exchange of labour power with money or commodities involved in an act of wage employment. The output of the production process belongs, in this system, to the owner of the establishment, and he has also the obligation arising from the purchase (or renting) of inputs (including labour power) and possibly from the tax system prevailing in the country. Through these complex processes, a person's endowments are transformed into his entitlements, each process of the transformation being governed by the system of rights prevailing in the economy. A person is entitled to a good in this system if he acquires it through some ligitimised process, e.g., making it himself, obtaining it through voluntary donation from someone legitimately owning it.[3] Whether or not he is entitled to the good in question can be resolved only by referring to the system governing all these acts. And on that depends a person's entitlement to adequate means.

Most cases of starvation and famines across the world arise not from people being deprived of things to which they are entitled, but from people not being entitled, in the prevailing legal system of institutional rights, to adequate means for survival.[4]

3. LAW AND MORALITY

In legal theory following the tradition of Bentham [7] and Austin [8], a distinction is made between what law is and what law ought to be. The description of the prevailing system of rights does not, therefore, amount to its moral acceptability. This distinction between "legal validity and moral value" raises some conceptual problems, and it has been debated whether an iniquitous law should have the status of being taken at all as valid law. (See, for example, Kelsen [9].)

Herbert Hart has defended the distinction powerfully, especially in the light of the possible consequences of eschewing this distinction:

"What then of the practical merits of the narrower concept of law in moral deliberation? In what way is it better, when faced with morally iniquitous demands, to think "This is in no sense law" rather than "This is law but too iniquitous to obey or apply"? Would this make men more clear-headed or readier to disobey when morality demands it? Would it lead to better ways of disposing of the problem such as the Nazi regime left behind? No doubt ideas have their influence; but it scarcely seems that an effort to train and educate men in the use of a narrower concept of legal validity, in which there is no place for valid but morally iniquitous laws, is likely to lead to a stiffening of resistance to evil, in the face of threats of organized power, or a clearer realization of what is morally at stake when obedience is demanded. So long as human beings can gain sufficient cooperation from some to enable them to dominate others, they will use the forms of law as one of their instruments. Wicked men will enact wicked rules which others will enforce. What surely is most needed in order to make men clear sighted in confronting the official abuse of power, is that they should preserve the sense that the certification of something as legally valid is not conclusive of the question of obedience, and that, however great the aura of majesty or authority which the official system may have, its demands must in the end be submitted to a moral scrutiny. This sense, that there is something outside the official system, by reference to which in the last resort the individual must solve his problems of obedience,

73

is surely more likely to be kept alive among those who are accustomed to think that rules of law may be iniquitous, than among those who think that nothing iniquitous can anywhere have the status of law." (Hart [10], pp. 205-206).

Recently, these issues have been re-examined in the context of some general criticisms of the approach of legal positivism. In particular, strong arguments have been put forward disputing the claim that "the truth of legal propositions consists in facts about rules that have been adopted by specific social institutions, and in nothing else", making the counter-claim that "when lawyers reason or dispute about legal rights and obligations, particularly in those hard cases when our problems with these concepts seem most acute, they make use of standards that do not function as rules, but operate differently as principles, policies, and other sorts of standards" (Dworkin [1], pp. vii and 22). The inclusion of principles does, of course, make the distinction between legal validity and moral value that much less clear.

I have neither the competence nor the desire to enter into this debate on the content of law. But even if it is accepted that legal rights and obligations go beyond those established by institutional rules, this does not still eliminate the distinction between legal validity and moral value, despite the recognition that some moral principles can have legal force precisely by virtue of being principles. It is still possible to deny the moral acceptability of a given totality of rights as upheld by law including those arising from institutional rules *as well as* those related to moral principles and other standards. Disputing the *independence* of the two issues is not the same thing as rejecting the *distinction* between them. Indeed a non-vacuous assertion of interdependence must proceed from acknowledging that the two questions are not the same.

This distinction is of some importance to policy concerning poverty and starvation. The prevailing legal system of entitlements, based on a system of rights that may take quite a hard-nosed attitude towards poverty and starvation, will have to be contrasted with systems of entitlements that incorporate other moral principles in which freedom from hunger and basic wants has an important status. A nutritionally adequate diet may well be taken to be a part of a person's moral entitlements, even when it is not a part of his legal entitlements. If there is sufficient agreement on the principle behind these moral entitlements and the force of political organisation to back it up, the legal entitlements themselves may change eventually to incorporate the right to a nutritionally adequate diet. But no matter when this happens - even whether or not it *ever* does - statements on moral entitlements have interest of their own and have implications for the important problem of obedience and other questions of personal action and group activities.

The distinction between rights and metarights can be combined with the distinction between legal and moral claims, giving us four compound categories. Even if it is concluded that in a certain poor country the entitlement to a nutritionally adequate diet is neither a legal right, nor quite a moral right (the country may not even be able to provide it for everyone under current economic conditions), it could still be a moral metaright, and even conceivably - as discussed in Section 1 - a legal metaright (institutional or background, concrete or abstract). If it is accepted as a legal metaright, it immediately gives legal status to the demands for policies oriented to eliminating hunger and undernutrition. But even when such legality is not accepted (not even at the abstract, background level), there is the possibility of making a strong moral claim for such a metaright. Indeed, many political movements of far-reaching consequence begin with such a moral claim, e.g., a moral censure of a government's policies about hunger, leading later to stronger claims, and perhaps eventually to legal acceptance of the right to adequate food, brought about by evolutionary or revolutionary political changes.

4. MORAL RESPONSIBILITY AND CONSEQUENTIALISM

"When I hear anyone talk of culture I reach for my revolver", so runs an alleged witticism attributed to Hermann Wilhelm Goring. Talking of morality seems to provoke a similar reaction in many. Perhaps there is an aura of hallowed pomposity associated with the concept of morality, and the suggestion that freedom from hunger and basic wants is dictated by morality might be viewed in some quarters not so much as a proposition but as a lump in the throat. But moral this issue certainly is, both in the general definitional sense as well as in the more specialised sense of being closely related to "the critical principle, central to all morality, that human misery and the restriction of freedom are evils" (Hart [10], p. 82).

But if the hungry have the moral *right* to food, who has the moral *duty* to provide that food, or the means to it? So far, this right has been discussed mainly as a claim against the state. But depending on the nature of the morality chosen, other people could be thought to have that duty. It appears, however, to be the case that the common morality prevailing in Western society - indeed in most cultures - does not insist on this duty. Though regarding the activity of feeding the hungry to be praiseworthy, it is usual to maintain that the more affluent are not duty bound to sacrifice their own interests and those of their family members to reduce the suffering of others from starvation.

This position is at variance with a strong version of the consequentialist approach whereby anyone in a position to do something good (in *net* terms) is required to do so. Such an approach has been defended recently in a somewhat constrained form by Peter Singer [11] and in a more demanding form by John Harris [12].[6] It is, of course, widely conceded that if a person does harm to another by some positive action, he is morally responsible for the harm caused. What the general consequentialist argument does is to extend this responsibility to anyone who could have prevented the harm but willingly did not do so.

In whatever sense we are morally responsible for our positive actions, in the same sense we are morally responsible for our negative actions (Harris [12], p. 211).

If this is accepted, then the moral responsibility for preventing hunger falls on anyone who can prevent some hunger, and the only restraint comes from the possibility of competing claims of other morally good demands. Even conceding the force of many such claims, the moral duty to relieve starvation would frequently be the most compelling demand on a person's resources. (See Singer [11].)

Consequentialism as an approach has, however, been attacked from many different points of view, and some of these critiques would apply particularly to the demanding version of consequentialism under discussion, which morally attributes to the non-intervener the consequences of inaction and treats it in the same way as the consequences of positive action. This is not the occasion to go into an evaluation of consequentialism (some issues are discussed in my "Rights and Agency" [13]), but I should note that some commonly used moral arguments do employ consequentialist reasoning applied to inaction as well. Blaming a swimming-expert passerby for not saving a drowning child who cried for help is an obvious example. The real question is where the limits of one's responsibility are to be drawn and what types of causal dependence are to be regarded as morally relevant.

5. UTILITY AND WELFARISM

A consequentialist moral approach - indeed more generally a consequence-sensitive moral approach[7] - would have the need for a method of evaluating consequences, and here the scope of alternative approaches is considerable. A common complement of consequentialist (or consequence-sensitive) approaches is a general method of judging consequences that can be called "welfarism", of which utilitarianism is a special case.

Welfarism requires that states that are indistinguishable from the point of view of personal utility levels must not be treated differently from the point of view of moral desirability. No other characteristics of these alternative states should influence our moral judgement except insofar as they - directly or indirectly - affect individual utility levels.[8] If everyone would be exactly as well off in terms of his personal utility in state x as he would be in a, and also everyone would be just as well of in y as he would be in b, then x can be regarded as morally at least as good as y if and only if a is also regarded as morally at least as good as b.

The most well-known example of welfarism is classical utilitarianism, where states are judged in terms of the *sum of personal utilities* generated. Obviously, the operation of *summing* is not necessary so far as welfarism is concerned. If instead we identify the moral desirability of a state not with the personal utility aggregate in that state but with the personal utility level of the worst-off individual in that state (as with the so-called "maximin" criterion), this too will be a case of welfarism (as indeed "maximin" is).[9] Utilitarianism is, thus, only a distinguished member of a wider class of welfarist moral principles.

Welfarism is rampant in traditional welfare economics, even of the kind that takes utilitarianism as unacceptable or unusable. In fact, the so-called

"Bergson-Samuelson social welfare function", even when it eschews the use of cardinal utility and interpersonal comparisons of welfare (and is thus unable to accomodate utilitarianism altogether), is nevertheless typically given a thoroughly welfaristic formulation. Insofar as social welfare W is made a function of the level of personal utilities only, welfarism is implied. (See, for example, Samuelson [16] and Graaff [17].) It becomes possible to judge two states x and y without knowing anything about them except the personal utilities generated in each state.

Social welfare functions having the properties specified by Arrow [18] also implies something very close to welfarism. Three of Arrow's conditions for social choice, *viz*, independence of irrelevant alternatives, unrestricted domain and the Pareto principle together rule out the use of all information about the social states other than personal welfares, except in special cases of indifference. The Arrow impossibility result can be seen as a consequence of combining welfarism (ruling out the use of information other than personal welfares) with very poor personal welfare information (without interpersonal comparability and cardinality). (See Sen [14] and [19].) In fact, the main approaches of traditional welfare economics have all tended to be welfarist, and this particular feature of classical utilitarianism has been typically preserved in the later anti-utilitarian approaches.

Under welfarism a person's claim to an adequate diet and other means of living is based on the influence that these things have on his welfare level. In the special case of utilitarianism, the moral value of food going to a person depends on his marginal utility from it. This marginal utility has to be compared with the alternative marginal utilities that could be generated by denying him that food and using those resources in other ways. Under the maximin approach, the comparison has to be not between marginal utilities but between his general level of welfare compared with those of others, and his needs get priority over those of others if and only if he happens to be worse off in welfare terms vis-a-vis others who could gain from the denial of the fulfilment of his needs[10].

These welfaristic considerations may be thought to be in general rather favourable to giving a person a strong claim to having his basic needs fulfilled. When a person is so poor that these needs are unfulfilled, his marginal utility from these items can be taken to be very large, strengthening his utilitarian claim. Also his total welfare level can be taken to be very low, strengthening his maximin or leximin claim. Thus, it might be thought that a rejection of welfarism is likely to reduce rather than strengthen the moral claims to food and other basic means, which are favourably treated by welfarism.

This is indeed so in some important respects. For example, contrasted with theories of entitlement of the kind proposed by Nozick [21], utilitarianism or maximin would certainly be more favourably inclined to giving priority to the basic needs of a person. Indeed, both utilitarianism and maximin have been used very effectively to argue for social security arrangements of a type that would have little place Nozick's system of entitlements.

On the other hand, welfarism in general, and utilitarianism or maximin in particular, do make the claim to adequate means conditional on the appro-

77

priate personal utility values. They are thus context-dependent in a manner that someone asserting the *right* to be free from hunger could not really find acceptable. While it may not be very common to argue against social security provisions by asserting that a poor person's marginal utility from income (or basic means) is low, such arguments are not entirely unknown. Indeed, the "impossibility" of "really helping" the poor given their tendency to misuse charity has been a significant theme in social discussions as well as in literature.[11] Furthermore, the denial of interpersonal comparisons of utility has provided an easy means of shooting down welfarist defences of social transformation, and of debunking the welfaristic critique of economic inequality. (See, for example, Robbins [22] and [23].) The structure of welfarism makes it exposed to such counter-arguments since its context-dependent nature can be exploited to reverse a defence of these claims by changing the assumed context. (For example, see Robbins [23], pp. 656-637, who concentrated on utilitarian morality.)

Indeed, utilitarianism is particularly open to such manipulation. Since it bases a person's claims not on his being generally badly off but on the value of his *marginal* utility, there is scope for disputing this claim by questioning the assumed relationship between *overall* deprivation and marginal utility. Maximin is somewhat less open to this, since it concentrates on a person's overall utility level rather than on the magnitude of his marginal utility. But there have, in fact, been arguments that have treated deprived peasants as "innately happy", attributing a goodly bonus of utility to their traditional way of life. This is supposed to weaken the case for "intervening" in their lives, even though those lives may be hanging on a rather thin thread of material means of sustenance.

The assertion of a right to the basic means of living would demand something more than an acknowledgement of a claim that holds *if and only if* certain assumed utility conditions are fulfilled. Rights to basic means are widely accepted as defining things a person is entitled to (either in the immediate direct sense, or in the indirect sense of a metaright discussed in Section 1). The basis of this acceptance does not rest on welfaristic considerations only. In fact, the effect of asserting these claims as rights is to make them less context-dependent than all welfaristic claims must, of necessity, be. The main point is that the utility numbers do not summarise the relevant facts of a situation adequately, and it matters morally whether the low personal utility reflects the consequence of hunger or, say, being depressed by the success of one's neighbour. Misery arising from hunger may well be treated differently from the same amount of misery arising from other causes if the freedom from hunger is given a status of its own on top of what is implied by the case for freedom from misery as such. Human psychology is a complex thing, and misery can have many different causes. But the near universality of the suffering from hunger and its central role in a person's life give it a status of its own that is not adequately measured on the scale of utility.

I am not arguing here that the elimination of the misery of hunger must be given absolute priority over all other objectives including removal of other forms of misery, but that there is a case for distinguishing between misery from hunger and misery of other sorts. The special claim of the former, if acknowledged, will require different relative weights to be attached to different kinds of misery.[12] A welfarist system will not be able to discriminate in favour of freedom from hunger in this way.

6. CONCLUDING REMARKS

Without trying to summarise the arguments presented in this paper, I shall make a few general remarks to put the discussion in perspective.

First, rights can take many different forms varying in terms of concreteness, articulation, force and institutional reflection. Ronald Dworkin's categorisation (e.g., "abstract" or "concrete", "background" or "institutional"?) captures nicely many of the nuances involved, but would seem to require some supplementation in the form of a class of "metarights" (Section 1). A metaright to x is a right to some policy $p(x)$ that would help to make the right to x realisable. Metarights have the effect of broadening the right structure surrounding x. Whether such a metaright is unrealised would depend not on whether x fails to obtain, but on whether $p(x)$ fails to obtain. Metarights themselves can be categorised in the same way as rights can be, e.g. abstract or concrete, background or institutional, since metarights to x are nothing but rights to $p(x)$.

Second, rights related to not being hungry can, thus, take very many different forms in terms of concreteness, institutional reflection, etc., but it seems necessary also to consider in this context the class of metarights not to be hungry. This is particularly relevant to countries in which immediate abolition of hunger is impossible but policies that would rapidly achieve such a goal do exist (Section 1). The failure to fulfil metarights of this kind can provide legitimate reasons for revolt.

Third, the notion of "entitlements" relates to the system of rights (including metarights), and establishes a person's overall command over things taking note of all the rights involving interpersonal obligations (Section 2). Starvation relates directly to entitlements, and depends on endowments as well as opportunities of transforming endowments into entitlements.

Fourth, while the content of law may not be independent of moral principles and the boundaries are unclear, this does not disestablish the thesis that moral rights differ from legal rights (Section 3). The right not to be hungry and the corresponding metarights can strongly arise in such moral contexts, even when their legal status is weak or absent. The moral right not to be hungry has, thus, to be distinguished from the corresponding legal rights - in all its forms.

Finally, the field of application of moral rights depends crucially on two particular aspects - among others - of the moral framework, $viz.$, (i) whether the framework is consequentialist (Section 4), and (ii) whether it is welfarist (Section 5). Utilitarianism is both consequentialist and welfarist. While consequentialism tends to widen the scope of moral responsibility regarding hunger, welfarism need not have this effect. In a non-welfarist framework misery from hunger can be given a special status over and above claims arising from misery as such. This can also make the claim to food not conditional on the exact utility characteristics associated with various extents of hunger, focussing directly on the right not to be hungry. Thus the greatest scope for moral obligation to relieve hunger may arise in particular moral structures which are consequentialist but not welfarist.

Notes

(1) The merits of the two-agent characterisation of rights are disputed in Sen [13], and also in my "Equality of What?" in S. McMurrin, (Ed.), *Tanner Lectures on Human Values*, Volume 1, Cambridge: C.U. Press, 1980. The present paper, written primarily during 1977-78, retains the traditional two-agent format.

(2) For an elegant formal analysis of these different types of "simple rights" (e.g., claim, immunity, power and freedom) and more complex structures that incorporate these simple rights, see Stig Kanger [2] and [3]. See also the helpful textbook of Lars Lindahl [4].

(3) It also depends on whether or not others have legitimate claims on him that can be met by the disposal of the good in question. An indebted peasant's entitlements are severely curtailed by the rights of the moneylenders.

(4) I have tried to examine the role of entitlement systems in this context in Amartya Sen [5] and [6].

(5) In fact, the remark is found in Hanns Johst, *Schlageter*, 1932. Evidently, Goring found it profound enough to be repeated.

(6) For a critique of Singer's and Harris's position as well as some other reasons for greater acceptance of responsibility for relieving sufferings of others, see Susan James [13].

(7) A consequentialist approach judges the goodness of an action *entirely* by the goodness of its consequences. A non-consequentialist approach can, however, still be sensitive to the goodness of the consequences of an action while taking note of other features as well. Consequentialist approaches form a particular subcategory of consequence-sensitive approaches.

(8) For a formal characterisation of welfarism, see Sen [14] and [19].

(9) Maximin is associated with Rawls's Difference Principle, which is a part of the first principle of his two principles of justice (Rawls [15]). But they are not quite identical. The Difference Principle, while initially motivated in terms of interpersonal comparisons of welfare, is made to apply to the allocation of *primary goods* only (pp. 90-95). This makes it, in fact, essentially non-welfarist. Rawls's first principle dealing with liberty is, of course, heftily non-welfarist.

(10) This effect is not always guaranteed by maximin, but the lexicographic extension of it will have this effect; see Rawls [15], pp. 82-83) and Sen ([20], p. 138).

(11) Several nineteenth century novelists were much taken by the moral conflicts involved in this.

(12) This general question of differential weighting in a non-welfarist framework is considered in Sen [13]. See also Sen [19] an my "Utilitarianism and Welfarism", *Journal of Philosophy* 76 (1979).

BIBLIOGRAPHY

Arrow, K.J. [18] *Social Choice and Individual Values*. New York: Wiley, 1951. 2nd edition 1963.

Austin, J. [8] *Lectures on Jurisprudence*. 1863.

Bentham, J. [7] *Principles of Morals and Legislation*. 1789.

Dworkin, R. [1] *Taking Rights Seriously*. London: Duckworth, 1977.

Graaff, J. De V. [17] *Theoretical Welfare Economics*. Cambridge: Cambridge University Press, 1957.

Harris, J. [12] The Marxist Conception of Violence. *Philosophy and Public Affairs* 3 (1974).

Hart, H.L.A. [10] *The Concept of Law*. Oxford: Claredon Press, 1961.

James, S. [13] *The Duty of Relieve Suffering*. University of Connecticut and Newnham College, Cambridge, 1979.

Kanger, S. [2] *New Foundations for Ethical Theory*, Part 1. Stockholm 1957. - [3] Law and Logic. *Theoria 38 (1972)*.

Kelsen, H. [9] *General Theory of Law and State*. Cambridge, Mass., 1945.

Lindahl, L. [4] *Position and Change: A Study in Law and Logic*. Dordrecht: Reidel, 1977.

Nozick, R. [21] *Anarchy, State and Utopia*. Oxford: Blackwell, 1974.

Rawls, J. [15] *A Theory of Justice*. Cambridge, Mass.: Harvard University Press, 1971.

Robbins, L. [22] *An Essay on the Nature and Significance of Economic Science*. London: Macmillan, 1932. - [23] Interpersonal Comparisons of Utility. *Economic Journal* 48 (1938).

Samuelson, P.A. [16] *Foundations of Economic Analysis*. Cambridge, Mass.: Harvard University Press, 1947.

Sen, A. [5] Starvation and Exchange Entitlement: A General Approach and Its Application to the Great Bengal Famine. *Cambridge Journal of Economics* 1 (1977). - [6] *Poverty and Famines: An Essay on Entitlements and Deprivation*. Oxford: Clarendon Press, 1981. - [13] *Welfare and Rights*. (Text of Hogerstrom Lectures, given at Uppsala University Philosophy Department in May 1978.) Unpublished manuscript, but part of the text used in my "Rights and Agency", *Philiosophy and Public Affairs* 11 (1982). - [14] On Weights and Measures: Informational Constraints in Social Welfare Analysis. *Econometrica* 45 (1977). - [19] Personal Utilities and Public Judgements: Or What's Wrong with Welfare Economics. *Economic Journal* 89 (1979). - [20] *Collective Choice and Social Welfare*. San Francisco: Holden-Day, 1970 (distributions taken over by North-Holland, Amsterdam).

Singer, P. [11] Famines, Affluence and Morality. *Philosophy and Public Affairs* 1 (1972).

The Interdependence of Duties

by
Henry Shue

A complete account of a human right must specify the correlative duties and the relevant agents: what needs to be done in order to fulfill the right and who ought to do it. It soon becomes evident that besides the list of duties and the list of agents a third element is needed as well: a list of allocative principles to assign the duties among the agents. Granted even that a particular duty must be performed and that a particular agent must do something or other, why should specifically this agent perform precisely this duty? Is this burden not too much, or too little, to be borne by this party? Some basis is needed for answering such questions.

Except in a limiting case in which a right involved few duties which fell upon few bearers, the full specification of the correlative duties, the relevant agents, and the allocative principles for even a single right would be an enormous undertaking. Here I shall attempt through some illustrations merely to put a little more solid shading on this outline of the conceptual framework with an eye toward the case of the right to adequate food. I shall do nothing here to argue directly that there is a universal human right to adequate food, although I believe that strong indirect support could be provided by the demonstration that there is an assignment of the constitutive duties among governments, individuals, and other agents that not only is compatible with but draws upon widely accepted general principles of responsibility.

It is in part because there are multiple agents, or duty-bearers, with different kinds and degrees of responsibility toward various right-bearers, that we need to distinguish among duties. And we can see that different duty-bearers have different kinds and degrees of responsibility only by reflecting upon principles that allocate responsibilities among agents. So the questions of correlative duties, relevant agents, and allocative principles are deeply interdependent, as are the duties themselves.

Alternative Typologies

In 1980 I suggested that every basic right, and most other moral rights as well, could be analyzed using a very simple tripartite typology of interdependent duties of avoidance, protection, and aid. With some crude sub-divisions for the latter two general categories, the scheme of duties correlative to a right as I left it was:

Tripartite Typology of Interdependent Duties
I. To avoid depriving.

II. To protect from deprivation.
1. By enforcing duty(I) and
2. By designing institutions that avoid the creation of strong incentives to violate duty(I).

III. To aid the deprived
1. Who are one's special responsibility;
2. Who are victims of social failures in the performance of duties (I), (II-1), and (II-2); and
3. Who are victims of natural disasters.[1]

A number of people have agreed with the fundamental thesis that instead of engaging in the artificial, simplistic, and arid exercise of attempting to classify every right as flatly either negative or positive, it is more fruitful to examine the relatively negative (duties to avoid depriving), the relatively positive (duties to aid the deprived), and the intermediate (duties to protect from deprivation) elements that are mixed together in various proportions in the implementation of just about every right. A few people, especially Philip Alston and Asbjørn Eide, have constructively criticized and creatively revised my first stab at a framework for duties.[2] That discussion continues in the present volume.

There is, I take it, no great-typology-in-the-sky at which we are all guessing, and the question about which typology to employ is not one of the ultimate issues. Categories like avoidance, protection, and aid are general kinds of duties, not specific duties. At best such general categories help to organize the debate over precisely which duty falls to which agent. The bottom-line of the intellectual enterprise, however, must be the specific designation of what should be done by whom at a level of detail that will permit assessments of compliance by responsible agents themselves and, where appropriate, by others charged with supervision over their compliance. Typologies are of largely heuristic, mnemonic, pedagogical, and rhetorical value, and like many other ladders they can be left behind once we have reached the next level, which in this case consists of very specific duties. Still, since it is rarely easy to imagine, remember, teach, and explain previously unarticulated duties, any instruments that will really help us with these tasks are not to be ignored.

I am delighted to accept the re-naming of the first, most negative duty as the duty to respect. I chose the clumsy label of "the duty to avoid depriving" in order to emphasize the crucial point that even rights which had in the past been misleadingly classified as positive rights, including the right to adequate food, involved fundamental duties that are as purely negative as any duty can be - that are entirely a matter of refraining from interfering with the enjoyment of the substance of a right. On the other hand, the inclusion of "avoid", rather than saying simply "not depriving", was intended also to convey that even the duties that are as nearly negative as possible still demand some effort. One is not merely to hope one does not deprive others of their rights or merely "try" not to deprive them. One is to take (positive) steps not to deprive them: avoid depriving. To "respect" someone's rights is

84

precisely to take some trouble to see to it that one does not deprive the person of what he or she has a right to. Hence, the "duty to respect" rights is an accurate, and certainly more elegant, name for what I called the duty to avoid deprivation; I am quite content, then, with the trio of respect, protect, and aid.

Besides the great improvement of re-naming the first duty, people who have responded to the tripartite typology have tended to lengthen the list of duties but at the same time to lose the distinctive meaning of the third duty in my list, the duty to aid. I would like to comment first on the tendency to drop out the duty to aid; this will lead directly to a look at the tendency to add duties.

The important sub-committee of the International Lawyers Association, which is being chaired by Asbjørn Eide as it drafts a convention on the right to adequate food, and the chapter in this volume by G.J.H. van Hoof use the following four-part typology:

A. The duty to respect
B. The duty to protect
C. The duty to fulfill
D. The duty to promote.

All the discussions accompanying the alternative typologies are imaginative and insightful, and over the long run the rich commentaries may well prove much more valuable than any typology, including mine. For now, however, I want to concentrate rather narrowly on the typologies as such, especially the contrast between my three categories and the four categories in what I will for convenience call the Eide typology (Alston and van Hoof, who have other chapters here, are both also on Eide's committee of jurists).

Everyone involved agrees upon the duty to protect. As I have already indicated, I take "the duty to respect" to be the same as my "duty to avoid depriving" and am pleased to adopt the more elegant name. So, the Shue typology and the Eide typology both begin with the duty to respect and the duty to protect. Shue then concludes with **aid,** while Eide has **fulfill** and **promote.** I shall return shortly to the merits of the duties to fulfill and to promote as possible additions, but I want first to resist the omission of the duty to aid.

Two unrelated reasons of very different kinds support the retention on any list of a duty to aid. The second reason also raises doubts about the advisability of adding duties to fulfill and to promote. First, I think we all want to begin from where the world actually is now - both the typologies under discussion are intended to be thoroughly practical and not utopian. The current situation, unfortunately, is one in which hundreds of millions have already been deprived of food by the very political and economic institutions that ought to have been protecting their supplies of food. Our most urgent duty would be to assist these deprived, even if this were, strictly speaking, no longer a matter of protecting their rights, which have long been violated, but of assisting their recovery from past violations.

This leads, however, to the second reason for preserving the duties to aid, which is conceptual, not practical. What the Eide list contains besides duties to respect and protect (and instead of the duties to aid on the Shue list) are duties to fulfill and to promote. On the one hand, it might seem that the duties to fulfill and to promote simply represent a sub-division of the duty to aid and thus spell out more fully or explicitly what was already contained more summarily in the duty to aid. But this is not true. What is distinctive about the duty to aid is that it is what is owned to victims - to people whose rights have already been violated. The duty to aid is, if you like, largely a duty of recovery - recovery from failures in the performance of the duties to respect and protect. (This is not true of duty III-3 in the original typology - it is "pure" assistance, with no basis in fault or failure, since it is a response to purely natural disasters, of which there are relatively few).

On the other hand, it might seem that the Eide typology is concentrating directly upon what is involved in the realization of the right, while I have gone on to consider the response to failures in the realization of the right. In this sense I may seem to have crossed outside the boundaries of their effort and taken on an additional matter. What should be done now to assist those whose rights have already been violated may seem to be outside the scope of what should have been done earlier to guarantee the realization of the rights.

Think briefly of a different kind of right, say, the right to physical security. Suppose the current situation in a certain region is that landowners always send thugs to beat up sharecroppers who complain about the terms of their tenancy, and it has long been like this in the region. A plausible description, especially if some of the sharecroppers have never enjoyed physical security against beatings, is that their right to physical security needs to be fulfilled or promoted. But another perfectly reasonable description of the situation is that the sharecroppers have been deprived of their physical security and therefore need assistance. (Some people would counter that one can only be deprived of something if one had it to lose, although it seems natural to me to say, for example: throughout her life she was always deprived of the love she needed - she was utterly deprived of it, she never enjoyed it).

When people are deprived of things to which they have a right, it will usually be possible also to describe the situation alternatively as their needing to have their rights fulfilled or promoted. The situation does not wear either description on its sleeve. The description in terms of fulfillment and promotion seems, however, to be misleading in the following way. The description in terms of fulfillment and promotion suggests that the rest of us would be going beyond duties to respect and to protect if we acted upon duties to fulfill and promote. The rights of some people need to be "fulfilled" or "promoted," however, because other people have already failed to perform duties to respect and protect. Rather than going beyond respect and protection, we are having to go back and make up for failures in respect and protection. This is more clearly conveyed by saying that we are assisting the deprived. If our assistance enables them to enjoy adequate food, physical security, or whatever else they have been deprived of, their right will in fact have been fulfilled. This will be clearer if we return briefly to the more fundamental question of how to characterize a human right.

86

Rights as Social Guarantees Against Standards Threats

It can be useful to think of a human right as providing "(1) the rational basis for a justified demand (2) that the actual enjoyment of a substance be (3) socially guaranteed against standard threats".[3] "Substance" is merely a vague placeholder for whatever a right is a right to: freedom of the press, not being held in slavery, physical security, due process, adequate shelter, or whatever. Most relevant here is the dual third point that the general structure of a right includes two central elements: a threat and a guarantee, or protection, against that threat. The threats, human or natural, are there and real whether anyone recognizes them or not. The guarantee, or social protection, is there only if people decide to create it by constructing institutions and processes that will provide it.

The human rights we already enjoy are constituted by the rationally justified social guarantees we have already designed and constructed against the threats we have already recognized. The human rights we do not yet enjoy, but ought to enjoy, are the similar rationally justified guarantees against threats that already hang over us but are not yet clearly conceived or fully acknowledged. Human rights are enjoyed when social arrangements have been made on a rational basis so that we can work together to protect each other against recognized threats. New human rights evolve as we comprehend the seriousness and pervasiveness of previously ignored threats and come to realize that guarantees or social arrangements against those threats could be made effective without sacrificing anything of greater value. This is what has been happening in recent years with the right to adequate food.

Most controversies about which human rights should be acknowledged turn, then, around two points of debate: first, whether a particular threat is sufficiently serious, and is otherwise appropriate, to be the substance of a human right; and, second, whether the guarantees that would have to be built in order to protect people against that threat would not themselves create burdens or threats for those responsible for maintaining the guarantees that would be worse than the treat they protect against - in other words, whether the cure would be worse than the disease. It is the possibility that the cure might be worse than the disease - that the potential new right might conflict with a critical old right - which prevents us from immediately inferring a right wherever there is a serious threat. Not only must the threat itself pose a serious danger to a vital interest but the social arrangements that would be needed to guard against the threat must themselves not threaten other vital interests.

Including in the analysis of a human rights these elements of threat and guarantee makes it easier to explain how it is possible to make a mistake about a human right - to have the wrong right. Any actual social consensus may include superfluous "rights" that ought not to be recognized but are; or it may omit urgent rights that ought to be included but are not. A "right" is superfluous when either the threat is not as serious as alleged or the burdens and duties created by the social provisions necessary to deal with the threat are more of a problem themselves than the original threat would have been;

and, obviously, a critical right is missing when a threat is ignored or underestimated or when the burdens of cooperating to defend each other against that threat are exaggerated.

Noticing that rights are responses to threats also enables us to explain clearly how the list of human rights can legitimately, if only gradually, change over the centuries. The legitimacy of providing social guarantees against threats is always to be judged partly by assessing the seriousness of the threat against the availability of the human resources for dealing with the threat. The explanation of how the list of rights can change is simply that the kinds of threats against which the human society can feasibly protect its members changes, both because threats themselves advance and recede and, because the resources of society for dealing with threats, advance and recede.

The fact that the best protection against serious threats is often a social institution most not be allowed to obscure the other fact, with which it is perfectly compatible, that some of the worst threats to human rights are also social institutions, political and economic. As the partisans of civil and political rights never tire of repeating - correctly, as far as they are concerned - it was social institutions, specifically oppressive governments, against which the earliest rights were asserted. The *Magna Carta* demanded that the (royal) government get off the (noble) people's backs. And, never have rights been violated more seriously than by the regimes of Hitler and Stalin. All this is not merely true - it is extremely important.

What follows, however, is that what is needed is good government rather than bad government. What does not follow is that the best government is the least government. The best government is the government that most fully honors human rights. Sometimes this means simply not violating rights, which is in itself a major achievement, but sometimes too it means protecting rights whith institutions well-designed for the job. Which of these institutions should be governmental is an open question.[4]

Relevant Agents and Allocative Principles

It would be helpful to have before us a comprehensive list of categories of relevant agents, although naturally not every kind of agent will bear every kind of duty toward everyone. We can be quite sure that every agent has the duty to show respect toward everyone else, since any person or organization who was an exception to this duty would be at liberty to violate the right at will, leaving the "right" seriously compromised at best. Without some general principles of responsibility, however, we cannot firmly decide and clearly explain who owes what to whom. Philip Alston has moved the discussion significantly forward by focusing attention upon the four main categories of duty-holders for whom legal duties are already specific in the International Covenant on Economic, Social and Cultural Rights (ICESCR):

1. States in respect of their domestic duties;

2. States in respect of their external duties;
3. Individuals; and the
4. International Community.

I take the difference between (2) and (4) to be essentially the difference between unilateral action and multilateral action, especially broadly inter-governmental action through global agencies like (for the case of food) FAO, the World Food Council, and other elements of the "United Nations food network".

The full range of responsibility that includes even moral duties that ought not to be translated into legal duties involves additional categories of relevant agents. Just as the domestic and external duties of states can be distinguished, the duties of individuals can be divided along a somewhat analogous line, roughly the line between compatriots and strangers. The extent to which it is possible to justify the conventional wisdom that compatriots take priority, and how exactly one draws the compatriot/stranger distinction, are matters I have discussed other places and will not re-open here.[5] If citizenship or other forms of membership in societies or nations mean anything at all, members will presumably bear some duties toward each other that they do not bear toward outsiders. Some of these duties may be certain categories of duties correlative to human rights but not claimable initially, or even ultimately, against everyone else.

H.L.A. Hart's classic article, "Are There Any Natural Rights?" helped to make famous a distinction between special and general in application to rights and derivatively to their duties. I want to suggest that some duties are neither special nor general in Hart's sense. Hart said:

"When rights arise out of special transactions between individuals or out of some special relationship in which they stand to each other, both the persons who have the right and those who have the corresponding obligation are limited to the parties to the special transaction or relationship. I call such rights special rights to distinguish them from those moral rights which are thought of as rights against (i.e., imposing obligations upon) everyone . . ."[6]

Hart often proceeds as if his dichotomy of general rights and special rights were exhaustive. Many human rights, however, are neither general nor special, in Hart's sense. Human rights certainly do not arise out of special transactions or special relationships, and the rights cannot be fully claimed against everyone. The duty to respect falls upon, and can be claimed against, everyone, but many other duties fall upon only some people.

Hart's mistake is to attempt to discuss each right in an undifferentiated way, without distinguishing among its various different kinds of duties. Any given right partly can, and partly cannot, be claimed against everyone. A much clearer way to understand this is that the duty to respect falls upon everyone and some other kinds of duties do not. The fundamental problem with Hart's approach is the tendency to write as if each right were correlated with only one duty, which would, I suppose, be something like a duty to satisfy that right. If each right had only one duty, a general right might well have a general duty and a special right, a special duty.

Some of the duties correlated with some human rights fall upon some people, and not upon others, because of "special transactions" or "special relationships". It is not, however, that the right arises out of the relationship or transaction, but that the relationship or transaction provides the basis for the assignment of one or more kinds of duties. Thus, the typical human right will have a "general" duty to respect and some "special" duties to protect and assist. The rights itself is neither "general" nor "special".

I believe it is unpromising to hope that each right will somehow dictate the assignment of its constituent duties, as if each right could have an essence from which we would be able to deduce the specific assignments of responsibility for fulfilling it. Such a hope would exaggerate how much can be determined by purely theoretical considerations. It would also ignore the differences between the derivation of the list of correlative duties and the deprivation of the list of allocative principles. The categories of duties, as we have seen, can be established largely in the abstract, on the basis of general knowledge about human individuals and groups and the meanings of the concepts involved. If anyone is to be secure in the enjoyment of anything, no one else can be at liberty to interfere - hence, the duty to respect. Since some people can be expected to fail to fulfill their respective duties to respect, some protection of rights-holders against such rights-violators will need to be organized - hence, the duty to protect. Since even well-organized protection is bound to fail sometimes, some assistance will need to be organized for the victims of the rights-violations - hence, the duty to aid. Working out the categories of duties is not quite so simple as this suggests, since some difficult choices among alternative formulations must be made, but the point is that the reasoning is largely instrumental in a broad sense. Given what people are generally like and given what enjoying a right generally means, which specific tasks must be performed in order for people to enjoy rights? Which division of labour will do the job?

Thinking of the issue as a matter of a division of (moral) labour is helpful, because it clarifies the difference between deciding which tasks need to be done and deciding who should perform each task. Which division of labour will do the job of maintaining a household? Someone must earn the money to buy the food, someone must go and purchase the food with the money, someone must prepare and serve the food, and so forth. It is fairly obvious which tasks need to be done but not at all obvious who should perform which task. Should the husband earn the money to buy the food and the wife prepare and serve the food? Why not *vice versa?* Why shouldn't both tasks be shared? In order to decide these questions some principles for allocating responsibilities are needed: the assignment of the tasks among agents is not somehow obvious simply from the nature of the tasks.

The situation with most kinds of rights-based duties and their allocations is similar in the relevant respect: the nature of the task to be done will not dictate who should do the task. In addition to the list of categories of duties and the list of relevant agents, we need principles for allocating responsibility and - this is what is most important - those principles may be based on theories other than the theory of rights itself. To take an intrinsically very signifi-

90

cant example, consider the State. The State is generally considered to have among its central responsibilities the protection of the rights of everyone within the territory over which it is sovereign. These responsibilities could be exercised by some other kind of agent, including one created for this purpose. The fact that they are exercised by States has more to do with the reigning theory of sovereignty than is does with any particular theory of rights. The grounds for allocating duties of protection to States is not as much the nature of the rights in question or the nature of duties to protect as it is the nature of sovereignty as now conceived.

Another organization with enough power to protect rights, especially against the State itself, would be a rival sovereign.

Similarly, which individuals bear which duties to aid toward which victims of rights-deprivations depends upon much other than the nature of the rights in question and the duties to aid. It will be largely determined by theories of moral responsibility which set the proper bounds of self-interest, by theories of citizenship which draw the appropriate line between compatriots and strangers, by theories of the state which draw the appropriate line between individual responsibility and government responsibility, and so forth.

The point is that it would be asking too much of any theory about rights and their correlative duties to expect it to settle by itself all issues about how the duties are to be allocated among relevant agents. One reason why a theory of rights cannot be fully determinative of the allocation of rights-based duties is that there are many duties that are not rights-based. Establishing priorities among genuine duties is itself a major undertaking.

The Responsibility to Take Due Care

I would like now to provide an example of what I have been calling allocative principles. This principle is especially noteworthy because it shows how closely interdependent the duties to respect and to protect are. Specification of sensible, well-informed principles for the allocation of responsibility is, I think, one of the central tasks of contemporary political philosophy. I have elsewhere suggested - somewhat misleadingly - that we sometimes bear "responsibility through complicity - complicity by continuing acceptance of benefits."[7] The qualification "continuing" is a reference to information: continuing to accept the benefits of an institution after learning about the severe harms caused by that institution.

One may not have intended to cause anyone any harm at all, but once one knows that serious harm is resulting from the ongoing operation of some institution, the benefits of which one continues to accept, one can no longer claim to be ignorant of the harm to be done: "In such situations, knowledge is not only power but also responsibility, because it places us in a position to act".[8] We may initially have intended no harm, but we cannot maintain that we are ignorant of the harm to continue once we know that an institution upon which we have some influence is causing the harm and we do nothing to eliminate the harmful effects.

What me be misleading about the preceding is any suggestion that responsibility falls upon someone only if the person happens to blunder upon what amounts to some incriminating evidence about one of the social institutions that the person benefits from or supports. This would make degrees of responsibility contingent upon happenstance affecting which information one chanced upon. Thus, if my government were engaged in all sorts of mischief in Honduras but I did not know (or care to know) about it, I would have no responsibility for it. If my callous treatment is pushing my secretary toward a nervous breakdown but I have not noticed, then it would be her problem, not mine.

This is not what we think. On the contrary, we hold people responsible - to some degree, in some cases - for the harms to which they contribute not only unintentionally but even unknowingly. This is what "callous" means: you didn't need to will the harm because you were too insensitive to the needs of others to notice that you are harming them. We do sometimes condemn individuals and institutions for having failed to foresee and prevent serious harms. We hold them responsible for having failed, in short, to take due care. We have **responsibility to take due care.**

No one thinks that the manufacturers of Thalidomide intended to cause infants to be limbless, or even, as far as I know, that they willingly acquiesced after they had the information incriminating their drug. But people generally still held them responsible, because it is the business of drug firms to find out (all the effects) of new compounds. We held them responsible for not taking due care. If an obstetrician drops a baby and fractures its skull, we do not assume the act was intentional and charge him or her with murder. But we still hold the obstetrician responsible for not having taken due care - it is the business of obstetricians to handle babies without causing them harm.

Not everyone is as vulnerable as an infant, although it is well worth remembering that most of the people in the world's population now - not to mention most of the malnourished - are children. And most causal relationships are far less linear and simple than the mother's taking Thalidomide and the offspring's lacking arms or legs. But we do still believe that large and complex institutions and organizations like governments, corporations, armies, and unions ought to include in their plans mechanisms for taking due care.

One of the functions that some part of the organization should perform is to expect what would otherwise be unexpected harms and head them off. Not to do so is a failure in intelligence, in both senses of "intelligence."

Indeed, the failure to take due care is as much what the Greek would have called an intellectual vice as it is a moral vice in the narrower modern sense. If a post-Kantian moral vice consists of intending or willing evil, and an intellectual vice is a failure to see or to understand which actions are good and which are evil, then the failure to take due care may at least as often be a failure to foresee a harm as a willful failure to prevent it once foreseen. It is easier to think in terms of the moral failings of individuals than in terms of the intellectual failings of institutions. It is also anachronistic in this age of bureaucratic planning, both public and private.

92

Most of the people in circumstances in which they must (and may) invoke their rights to adequate food - circumstances in which they cannot provide for their own subsistence - are children. Many of the duties correlative to their rights fall upon their own better-off compatriots, but some of these duties fall upon affluent foreigners. Some of the duties are, then, what would traditionally have been called universal duties and what we might now more naturally call transnational duties. This is clear from the responsibility to take due care toward vulnerable whom one may affect.

The Transnational Duty to Build Adequate Institutions

We obviously lack at present adequate institutions for the performance of the more positive of these transnational responsibilities. The inadequacies of traditional government-to-government foreign aid, as well as the failings of intergovernmental organizations like the World Bank, are well-known and much-analyzed. Insofar as non-governmental transfers are taken to be "humanitarian" (in the sense of discretionary), we fail to signify that what are being fulfilled are indeed people's rights. Indisputably we are on an institutional frontier, and most of our efforts are fairly primitive.

Soon the argument is liable, however, to take the following general form, which is perverse: of course the prompt fulfillment of the rights to adequate food would be a fine thing, but the available institutions, national or international, are simply not now adequate for the task, so we won't be able to do very much better for a while, although we will certainly try our best, given the institutions that we have to work with. This is analogous to the residents on a rough and lawless frontier saying: "Gee, wouldn't it be nice if we had a sheriff with the authority to form a posse ad round up outlaws, but since we don't have any institutions of law and order here, I guess the best we can do is to let everyone fight for himself".

Building an adequate institution where is none is a difficult undertaking, even when the institution in question is as rudimentary as some minimal law enforcement. The transition from no institution to institution is made especially difficult because of the obvious challenge of motivating people to make the transition. Even if having the institution would be in everyone's interest, it is usually not in anyone's interest to act as if the institution is already in place before it actually is. It may be in my own interest that laws should be enforced, even against me as well as against other people, but is is not in my interest simply to obey model laws while others can get away with ignoring them. It only becomes in my interest to obey the law at the time when the law becomes enforceable. The challenge is making any law enforceable when it is not yet in people's interest to obey it. If the building of rudimentary institutions of law and order on the frontier is this complex, it is easy to imagine the difficulty with instituting new economic and social institutions of the kind that would function more effectively to enable people to enjoy their subsistence rights. The problem is, however, no different in principle.

If you think that people have a right not to be shot down in the street, you do not say fatalistically that if we had a sheriff, we could deal with this problem, but since we lack the relevant institution we will just have to keep struggling along. "To will the end is to will the means." In other words, if we really ought to accomplish some goals, then we really ought to take the necessary steps to get there. And if taking the necessary step means building some institution that may be long and hard in coming, then we ought to get started. What we ought not to do is to use the absence of the institutions as an excuse for failing to accomplish the purpose.

This is why I have called the excuse of inadequate institutions, not simply misguided, but perverse. The absence of the means for fulfilling a goal is being used as the excuse for not fulfilling it, when, if we seriously had the goal, we would be working on the creation of the necessary bridges from here to there.

When people do actually have a right to something like adequate food this does not mean merely that we should assist them in obtaining adequate food if it is easy and convenient to do so. It means that we have a duty, correlative to their right, to do what must be done in order for them to enjoy their right. In terms of my original typology, this is most nearly a duty of type II-2, a duty to protect by designing institutions. These institutions would, however, not only reduce the incentives to deprive people of their rights, but positively inhibit such deprivation, even unintended deprivation. Taking dure care is itself, I suppose, respecting rights. Building institutions that enable us more effectively to take due care is protecting rights. It is perfectly possible, as in the case of the frontier town without a sheriff, that before we can fulfill a right we must change existing institutions or build new ones. If so, then the energetic and imaginative building of the institutions that will fulfill the right is an urgent duty in response to that right.[9]

Conclusion

I have tried to indicate, then, that even without the addition of duties to fulfill and to promote rights, the original three categories of duties - respect, protect, and aid - and the complex ways in which they are interdependent already require substantial and imaginative institutional innovation. A concrete illustration is the allocative principle of the responsibility to take due care and the duty to protect by building adequate institutions.

Notes

(1) Henry Shue, Basic Rights: Subsistence, Affluence, and U.S. Foreign Policy (Princeton, N.J.: Princeton University Press, 1980), p. 60. Chapter 2, "Correlative Duties", is entirely devoted to the explanation of this typology.
(2) See the chapters individually and jointly by Alston and A. Eide in Asbjørn Eide, Wenche Barth Eide, Susantha Goonatilake, Joan Gussow, and Omawale, editors, Food as a Human Right (Tokyo: United Nations University, forthcoming).
(3) Shue, Basic Rights, p. 13.

(4) The preceding section will appear in Henry Shue, "Subsistence Rights: Shall We Secure These Rights?" in How Does The Constitution Secure Rights?, edited by Robert A. Goldwin and William A. Schambra (Washington: American Enterprise Institute for Public Policy Research, forthcoming).

(5) Chapter 6, "Nationality and Responsibility," of Basic Rights is devoted to this cluster of issues, as is the more recent essay, "The Burdens of Justice," Journal of Philosophy, vol. 80, no.1 (October 1983), pp. 600-608. Also see, in the same number of Journal of Philosophy, Charles R. Beitz, "Cosmopolitan Ideals and National Sentiment," pp. 591-600. For a very different view, see Michael Walzer, Spheres of Justice: A Defense of Pluralism and Equality (New York: Basic Books, 1983).

(6) Hart, "Are There Any Natural Rights?" in Rights, ed. by David Lyons (Belmont, Calif.: Wadsworth Publishing Co., 1979), p. 20. Hart's classic essay is found in many collections. It originally appeared in The Philosophical Review, 64 (April 1955), 175-191.

(7) Henry Shue, "Exporting Hazards," in Boundaries: National Authonomy and Its Limits, edited by Peter G. Brown and Henry Shue, Maryland Studies in Public Philosophy (Totowa, N.J.: Rowman and Allanheld, 1981), p. 136.

(8) Ibid.

(9) The preceding two sections will, for the most part, also appear in Henry Shue, "Subsistence Rights: Shall We Secure These Rights?" in How Does The Constitution Secure Rights?, edited by Robert A. Goldwin and William A. Schambra (Washington: American Enterprise Institute for Public Policy Research, forthcoming).

HONORE (Art. 22)

Reprinted with permission from 'Dessine-moi un droit de l'homme'
EIP-ISBN 2-88137-000-4

Part III:
The Role of International Law

The Legal Nature of Economic, Social and Cultural Rights: a Rebuttal of Some Traditional Views.

by
G.J.H. van Hoof

1. Introduction

A number of reasons are often adduced to explain the present failure of the international community to arrive at a more effective codification of international norms relating to the right to food. Alston has summarized the main arguments as follows. [1] First it is said that efforts to bring about more concrete norms in this field would be a waste of time since moral and humanitarian considerations alone will not move governments or other relevant actors to respect the right to food. Secondly, it is argued that the complexity of the issues involved in promoting realization of the right to food, and the absence of a universal consensus on either the causes of, or the solutions to, the problem, make it virtually impossible to establish effective machinery for the implementation of the right to food. Thirdly, it is not infrequently argued that civil and political rights are of prior importance and that the human rights belonging to the category of so-called economic, social and cultural rights, such as the right to food, can only be realized once freedom has been attained by the peoples of the world. [2]

This article highlights a number of aspects of the latter argument in some detail. Within the framework of this argument the issue of the legally binding or non-binding nature of the internationally proclaimed economic, social and cultural rights is raised very often , and, closely connected with it, the issue of the (alleged) fundamental differences between civil and political rights on the one hand, and economic, social and cultural rights on the other. A considerable number of people, particularly in the West, and including eminent and influential international lawyers, still hold views attributing a second-rate status to economic, social and cultural rights. In their extreme form such views may be summed up as follows: either the position is taken which expressly denies a legally binding character to economic, social and cultural rights, or those rights are alleged to differ from civil and political rights in such fundamental respects that it becomes impossible to escape the conclusion that the former are inferior from a legal point of view.

The present article aims at rebutting those views. In the first place, it will be argued that there is no reason to deny the economic, social and cultural rights (fully-fledged) legally binding status under international law. Secondly, it will be opined that a black-and-white distinction between civil and political rights on the one hand and economic, social and cultural rights on the other hand is mistaken, and that instead a more integrated approach encompassing both sets of rights is preferable.

Such an endeavour requires an examination in some detail of a number of theoretical aspects of international law in general and the international law of human rights in particular. At first sight such a theoretical approach hardly seems to fit in with the eminently practical objective of the realization of the right to food. However, on closer inspection these theoretical aspects turn out to have quite an impact in practice. For, views like the ones referred to above, which deny a legally binding status to economic, social and political rights hamper efforts aimed at a more meaningful codification of these rights in general and of the right to food in particular. To the extent that they are accepted, such views are likely to discourage scholars from further exploring the possibilities of devising more concrete norms designed to tackle the food problem. Similarly, they may constitute an incentive to decision-makers not to pursue policies designed to bring about a more effective implementation of everyone's right to adequate food.

In the following sections we will outline our own position on the basis of a discussion of the studies engaged in by two scholars, whose work is broadly representative of the prevailing school of thought concerning the legal nature of economic, social and cultural human rights. These authors are E. Vierdag [3] and M. Bossuyt. [4] We will confine our analysis to these two authors for reasons of manageability and because, albeit from somewhat different angles, they have dealt with the issues involved in an extensive and penetrating manner which covers most of the arguments advanced by others. Consequently, the reason for focusing on the studies of Vierdag and Bossuyt is not that these authors deserve to the singled out for criticism, but rather because they have very clearly outlined their respective positions.

In addition there are two other limitations on the analysis which follows. First, we will have to concentrate on the main themes of argumentation as put forward by Vierdag and Bossuyt. It would far exceed the scope of the present paper to deal with all the aspects of their detailed analyses. Secondly, it is necessary to start at the beginning and therefore to confine the analysis to the question of the legal nature of the economic, social and cultural rights laid down in the International Covenant and other relevant treaties and conventions. Consequently, without in any way underestimating its importance, particularly for practical purposes, we must leave out of consideration the question whether and, if so, how, States have incurred or can incur international legal obligations relating to economic, social and cultural rights, in particular the right to food, other than through entering into treaty-obligations.

2. The Thesis that Economic, Social and Cultural Rights are Not Really Law.

Vierdag is one of the staunchest protagonists of the thesis that economic, social and cultural rights are not really law. His study opens with the question: "What is the legal nature of the rights granted by the International

Covenant on Economic, Social and Cultural Rights (ICESCR)?". [5] In the final sentence of his study this question is quite unequivocally answered in the following way: "except in circumstances of minimal or minor economic, social or cultural relevance, and subject to the distinctions made above, the rights granted by the International Covenant on Economic, Social and Cultural Rights are of such a nature as to be legally negligible". [6]

This statement can hardly be misunderstood,nor does the remainder of Vierdag's study, leave doubt as to his position. In the same vein it is, for instance, observed with respect to Articles 6, 11 and 13 of the International Covenant that "the implementation of these provisions is a political matter, not a matter of law, and hence not a matter of rights". [7] More generally, Vierdag concludes that "In the ICESCR the word "right" appears to be used as it often is in political programmes, viz., in a moral and hortatory sense". [8]

It should be observed from the outset that it is quite remarkable to conclude with respect to provisions contained in a treaty such as the International Covenant, that their implementation constitutes a political, and not a legal matter, [9] and that its provisions are used in a moral and hortatory sense, and consequently are not legally binding. While it cannot be denied that the international law-making process is extremely cumbersome and that its outcome is often characterized by uncertainties, it is at the same time generally accepted that treaties, because of their highly formalized nature, constitute the most unambiguous and reliable source of international law. [10] One would therefore expect the legally binding character of norms contained in a treaty to be taken for granted.

The reasoning which leads Vierdag to the opposite conclusion with respect to (a number of) the provisions laid down in the International Covenant on Economic Social and Cultural Rights would in fact seem to consist of two closely intertwined elements. The core of his argument would seem to be on the one hand the proposition that the term "right" should be reserved "For those rights that are capable of being enforced by their bearers in courts of law, or in a comparable manner", [11] coupled on the other hand with the observation "that social rights are not directed at government action that can be described in terms of law. The creation of social and economic conditions under which social rights can be enjoyed is - as yet - not describable in terms of law. In order to be a legal right, a right must be legally definable; only then can it be legally enforced, only then can it be said to be justiciable". [12]

As far as the enforceability requirement is concerned, [13] it is allegedly derived from the practice of international law. To prove his point, Vierdag invokes "the international law standards on the treatment of aliens" and "the more recently developed field of the international protection of civil and political rights". With respect to the former he concludes that they "make legal remedies part and parcel of the rights of aliens". [14] Even assuming this point of view to be correct, it should be borne in mind that international law concerning the treatment of aliens differs in at least one vital respect from the international law of human rights in general. In the former case, private persons are protected vis-a-vis a foreign State in their capacity of nationals of another State, and therefore with the support of that latter State. In the case of the international law of human rights in general, private persons are protected first and foremost against their own State and in their capacity of human beings as such, with no particular State to add its weight to this protection. It hardly needs explaining that in the latter circumstances it becomes far more difficult to provide for a prototype of legal enforcement in the form of courts of law, or in a comparable manner. Consequently, the second field mentioned by Vierdag, viz., the more recently developed international protection of civil and political rights, constitutes a better standard for comparing the legal nature of economic, social, and cultural rights than international standards on the treatment of aliens.

As far as the political and civil rights are concerned, Vierdag adduces Article 8 of the Universal Declaration of Human Rights [15] and Article 13 of the European Convention for the Protection of Human Rights and Fundamental Freedoms [16] to substantiate his contention that international law has "recognized the availability of legal remedies as inherent in the granting of such rights". [17] Surprisingly enough, he subsequently concedes that these provisions are difficult to construe and that their texts raise a number of problems which are not easy to solve. [18] In fact Vierdag admits that, at least on the international plane, civil and political rights cannot very often be enforced through courts of law or in a comparable manner. Nevertheless, this does not prevent him from drawing the conclusion that the provisions mentioned are "a clear indication of the point under discussion: when there are rights of individuals in international law, there ought to be remedies". [19] However, it may at least be doubted whether this conclusion amounts to the same thing as the statement that international law has recognized the availability of legal remedies as inherent in the granting of rights, let alone whether it can be equated with the proposition that the availability of legal remedies constitutes a pre-condition for the legally binding character of norms under international law. In short, to my mind the arguments advanced by Vierdag are not very convincing.

Apart from that, it is submitted that the enforceability requirement is based upon an adverse comparison between national and international law, the result being a false concept of international law. To put it differently, one cannot simply "transplant" concepts and ideas derived from municipal legal systems into international law, because often these are not attuned to the realities of international relations. Every system of law, as a device for regulating and ordering relations in society, must at least to some extent reflect the basic features of the society it is to serve. It is almost a commonplace to acknowledge that there exist wide-ranging differences between most national communities on the one hand and the international community of States on the other. The most relevant differences for our purposes boil down to the fact that national communities are usually vertically structured or centrally organized, while international society is horizontally structured or characterized by a decentralized organization. [20] As a result, unlike international law, national systems of law are most of the time equipped with an institutionalized law-making process, an executive branch of government, and law-enforcing machinery. In international law these functions have

100

largely to be performed in a non-institutionalized way by the subjects of that law, viz. the States themselves. It is the exception rather than the rule that norms of international law can be enforced through courts of law, or in a comparable manner. However, this is generally considered an insufficient reason to deny to such norms the status of binding rules of international law. Similarly, it does not mean that there is no way to enforce, or rather to implement, such rules of international law. All that it implies is that rules of international law usually have to be enforced or implemented through methods different from those available in municipal legal systems. [21] So even if the availability of enforcement through courts of law constitutes a pre-condition for according a legally binding status to a norm in national legal systems, this does not justify the same conclusion with respect to international law.

Elsewhere I have argued that the constitutive element of rules of international law, viz., the criterion by which one can judge whether or not a rule is a rule of international law, is to be found in the consent to, or acceptance of, that rule on the part of the States concerned. [22] In other words, if a State has expressed its intention to be bound by a legal rule - in a more active way through consent, or in a more passive way through acceptance - the legally binding status of that rule has to be considered to be beyond doubt. In my view this conclusion flows cogently from the abovementioned horizontal structure or decentralized organization of the international community and the ensuing lack of an institutionalized law-making process, as a result of which States themselves have to act as the "law-givers" of international law. In this view, therefore, the availability of enforcement through courts of law or in a comparable manner cannot be considered a condition for the legally binding status of rules of international law. Obviously, it may be argued that such legal remedies are desirable because they may considerably enhance the effectiveness of the rules concerned, and that, consequently, an attempt should be made to provide for enforcement through courts of law also with respect to rules of international law. However, such considerations should not be used to deny legally binding status to rules of international law on the grounds that they cannot be enforced through methods similar to those prevailing in municipal legal systems.

What has been observed above with respect to the enforceability-requirement also applies to a large extent to the definability test proposed by Vierdag [23], since the question whether a rule is enforceable, in the sense of being justiciable, is dependent on whether it has been defined in a sufficiently concrete way. Because of his comparison between national and international law, Vierdag, in discussing the legal nature of economic, social and cultural rights, focuses almost entirely upon the "rights" (of individuals)-side. However important this aspect may be, if it is overemphasized, it tends to obscure the other side of the medal, which in my view is equally important, viz., the "obligations" (of States)-side. As a consequence the danger arises, for instance, of confusing the so-called direct effect of treaty provisions [24], for which the degree of concreteness of a rule is decisive, and the legally binding nature of a rule, for which it is not.

This is illustrated by Vierdag's discussion of number of landmark decisions of the Court of Justice of the European Communities. This discussion is designed to find out whether the EEC-Treaty could serve "as a model according to which the rights of the ICESCR might be enforced by e.g. municipal courts ...". [25] He concludes that it cannot because "in various cases the European Court of Justice has refused to accord direct effect to provisions that leave a certain discretion to Member States (or Community organs) in the performance of either negative or positive obligations", [26] while the obligations of States under the ICESCR are not defined in a sufficiently precise way to prevent a certain discretion in the performance of their obligations. [27] All this seems entirely correct. The point to make here, however, is that the Court in no way implied that the provisions in question were not legally binding for the State(s) concerned, despite their lack of direct effect; on the contrary, it expressly referred to them as "obligations".

In my view the "obligations"-side of the legal nature of economic, social and cultural rights should be explored further and might even prove more fruitful as a point of departure. [28] Vierdag devotes only a small section of his lengthy analysis to this aspect . [29] Moreover, for all practical purposes that section is confined to the conclusion that both the reporting system contained in the Covenant [30] and Article 2(1) laying down the obligation for States Parties to take steps with a view to achieving progressively the full realization of the rights recognized in the Covenant [31] will probably turn out to be ineffective, because the scope and content of these obligations cannot be sufficiently determined.

As I see it, this would seem to be putting the cart before the horse. Once it has been established that rules are legally binding, as are those contained in a treaty like the Covenant, they cannot readily be assumed to be empty shells. Rather, (international) lawyers should first try to deduce whatever obligations may be found from the rules concerned, even if these are vaguely formulated. To the extent that this is not possible, efforts should be made to elaborate more detailed rules and have them accepted by the States concerned. Finally, if the system of implementation pertaining to the rules concerned proves unsatisfactory, ways and means should be sought in order to enhance its effectiveness. If such a point of departure is not adopted, the allegedly negligible legal nature of rights such as those contained in the economic, social and cultural rights Covenant is likely to be made into a self-fulfilling prophecy.

3. The Thesis that there Exist Fundamental Differences between Civil and Political Rights on the One Hand, and Economic, Social and Cultural Rights on the Other

On this thesis we can be comparatively brief, partly because of what has been observed in the preceding section and partly because it is probably better known than the thesis that economic, social and cultural rights are not really law. Arguments that economic, social and cultural rights differ in fundamental respects from civil and political rights may vary in their implications. They may amount, or at least come close, to the proposition that economic, social and cultural rights are not really law. Alternatively, without denying the legally binding character of economic, social and cultural rights, it may be alleged that the differences between them and civil and political rights may be so great that the former are in fact considered to be second-rate human rights.

Bossuyt's approach would seem to be representative of the latter school of thought. [32] The differences he construes between civil and political rights on the one hand, and economic, social and cultural rights on the other are very far-reaching. The ultimate reason for these differences is, according to Bossuyt, to be found in the fact that the realization of the latter set of rights requires a financial effort on the part of the State, while in respect of the former this is not the case. [33] The fact that the implementation of at least a number of civil and political rights, such as the right to a fair trial and the right concerning periodic elections, may cost the State money, is dismissed by Bossuyt on the ground that the expenditure involved is very modest [34] and, at any rate, does not go beyond the minimum required to ensure the very existence of the State. [35] It is submitted, however, that in relation to the resources which at least some developing countries have available, the expenditure involved in, for instance, the holding of free and secret elections or the setting up of an adequate judiciary and legal aid system may be quite considerable.

Another, legally more tangible, argument used by Bossuyt is that civil and political rights require non-interference on the part of the State, whereas the implementation of economic, social and cultural rights requires active intervention by the State. The former are, therefore, said to create negative obligations, whereas the latter create positive obligations. [36] In this rigid form the distinction put forward by Bossuyt is, in my view, difficult to uphold. There are wellknown examples of civil and political rights which in fact demand active intervention on the part of the State, such as the right to a fair trial. Similarly, not all the rights categorized as economic, social and cultural, fit the mould of State-intervention. Freedom to form trade unions constitutes the classic example, although much depends on how exactly this freedom is defined. [37]

Despite these difficulties in the non-interference intervention dichotomy, Bossuyt deduces from it a difference in both the content and the character of the rights. As to the first aspect, Bossuyt argues that civil and political rights are of necessity invariable in their content, as minimum rights cannot vary from one country to another. Economic, social and cultural rights on the other hand are said to have a variable content depending upon the level of economic development of the State concerned. [38] But the case law concerning the European Convention for the Protection of Human Rights and Fundamental Freedoms sheds a very different light on the allegedly invariable content of civil and political rights. Although the Convention applies to a region consisting of a comparatively homogeneous group of States, it has nevertheless been interpreted by the European Commission and the European Court of Human Rights so as to deny the existence of a uniform European standard applicable in all cases. In other words, the fact that the content given to a particular right or freedom protected by the Convention may deviate markedly from one Contracting State to the other has not been judged to be incompatible with the Convention. [39]

As to the difference in character, Bossuyt asserts the existence of a fundamental distinction between the two categories of rights. To the civil and political rights he assigns an absolute character: "In recognizing civil rights, positive law can only protect those things that man already possesses". [40] Conversely, the economic, social and cultural rights can, according to Bossuyt, only be enjoyed "to the extent that these rights have become subjective rights". [41] It is difficult to rebut views ascribing an absolute character to one or another type of human rights, when they are, as seems to be the case here, based on some concept of Natural Law. For such concepts ultimately prove not to be scientifically verifiable to those who are not already convinced of their validity. [42] Nevertheless, I know of no convincing argument to support the contention that, for instance, the right to life is absolute because it emanates from human dignity, [43] while, for instance, the right to food does not have the same absolute character.

Finally, Bossuyt alleges that a number of consequences are to be drawn from the above-mentioned differences in nature and character. These consequences are said to be found in the different modalities in which the two sets of rights are applied *ratione temporis, ratione materiae*, and *ratione personae*. The following distinctions are alleged to exist: civil and political rights must be implemented immediately (immédiatement), while economic, social and cultural rights can only be realized progressively (progressivement); the former must be respected in their entirety (en totalité), whereas the latter may be accepted partially (une partie de ces droits); the first category has to be ensured to everybody (universellement), but, with respect to the second category, certain groups of the population may, or even must, be given priority (sélectivement). [44]

In my view these distinctions are far too rigid. This conclusion is confirmed by the practice of the international law of human rights. It suffices in this respect to recall briefly a few examples from the European Convention for the Protection of Human Rights and Fundamental Freedoms, which is generally considered one of the most developed instruments in the field of civil and political rights. With respect to the distinction *ratione temporis* it may be noted that the European Convention has derived a considerable part of its effectiveness from the dynamism with which it has been applied by its supervisory organs. [45] As a result the level of protection provided by the Convention has more or less continuously been raised, a situation to which the Contracting States have had to adapt. In some instances they have not been able immediately to meet the required standard. As far as the *ratione materiae* distinction is concerned, it is true that the Convention does not leave the Contracting States the choice of accepting only some of the right contained in it, as is the case in some instruments in the field of economic, social and cultural rights. Nevertheless, the Convention provides the possibility for States to make reservations and some States have indeed done so. [46] Furthermore, article 15 allows Contracting States, under certain circumstances, to derogate from their obligations under the Convention in time of war or other public emergency threatening the life of the Nation. [47] Finally, it should be borne in mind that the Convention is structured in such a way that the enjoyment of many of the rights and freedoms contained in it may be restricted to quite a considerable extent. [48]

Consequently, it cannot be said that the rights and freedoms laid down in the Convention must in all cases be respected in their entirety. The distinction *ratione personae* may be rebutted on the basis of article 16 of the Convention, containing the possibility for Contracting States to impose restrictions on the political activity of aliens, [49] and the so-called doctrine of "inherent limitations" developed by the Convention's supervisory organs. That doctrine allows for restrictions to be imposed on the rights and freedoms of persons with a special legal position, such as detained persons, psychiatric patients, soldiers, and civil servants. [50]

These brief examples are adduced to explain why the relevant distinctions are applied by Bossuyt in too black-and-white a fashion. This does not, however, detract from the fact that they may constitute useful tools for analysis, provided they are employed in a more flexible manner. In any event the distinctions should not be construed so as to result in the creation of an antithesis between civil and political rights versus economic, social and cultural rights. It is submitted that these distinctions cut across both categories of human rights, as has been illustrated by recent developments.

4. The Dynamic Nature of the International Law of Human Rights and the Ensuing Need for an Alternative Theoretical Framework.

One of the most important characteristics of the international law of human rights is its dynamic nature. This partly reflects the fact that this area of international law, or at least the considerably increased attention paid to it, is comparatively young. As a result, important parts of the field covered by it have not yet been sufficiently mapped out, which has been responsible for uncertainties and ambiguities. Secondly, and more importantly in this respect, the law of human rights is not only comprehensive, but also concerns the very foundations of society. Even more than other fields of law it is therefore influenced by developments in that society. Particularly in present times which witness far-reaching changes, the law of human rights finds itself in a state of more or less permanent development.

The societal changes which most affect the law of human rights may be summarized in the following two tendencies. On the one hand material changes have taken and are taking place, which can be described as a process of increased and increasing interdependence; on the other hand psychological processes have occurred which may be labeled by emancipation.

The increased interdependence is mainly caused by developments in science and technology which have been taking place since the Second World War. The effect of these developments is that relations in society have become more frequent, more intensive, and consequently more penetrating. In short, society has grown more complex. As a result people have become more dependent upon each other and upon the State in an increasing number of respects to an increasing extent. Moreover, the increased interdependence has not been confined to national societies. On the international plane, too, the interests of States and the populations of States have grown increasingly more intertwined. [51]

Parallel to and in interaction with these material changes, psychological processes have occurred which can be described as a general emancipatory movement. This movement is characterized in particular by the phenomenon that with respect to various aspects of life people have come to take on a less submissive, or rather more assertive attitude vis-à-vis the State. This has sometimes resulted in a more or less paradoxical situation. On the one hand more far-reaching demands are made upon the State in providing for the well-being and well-fare of its population; on the other hand such a deeper intervention on the part of the State is warded off on the basis of the argument that it encroaches upon traditional freedoms. This emancipatory movement, too, has an international dimension as is best exemplified by the rise of the Third World and the place it has subsequently come to claim within the international community.

As far as the international law of human rights is concerned, the upshot of the developments condensed in this brief survey is that traditional schemes for analysis have become obsolete in a number of respects.

In these circumstances the quest for innovative approaches to the promotion of human rights assumes particular importance. With respect to economic, social and cultural rights, it may be productive to approach the problem of implementation from the angle of obligations. In this regard four "layers" of State obligations may be discerned which, for lack of better terms, may be called: an obligation to respect, an obligation to protect, an obligation to ensure, and an obligation to promote. [52]

In general terms these different types of obligations can be defined in the following manner. The obligation to respect forbids the State itself to act in any way which would directly encroach upon recognized rights or freedoms. This aspect, therefore, closely resembles what in the traditional scheme was called an obligation of non-interference. The obligation to protect goes further, in the sense that it forces the State to take steps - through legislation or otherwise - which prevent or prohibit others (third persons) from violating recognized rights or freedoms. The obligation to ensure requires more far-reaching measures on the part of the government in that it has to actively create conditions aimed at the achievement of a certain result in the form of a (more) effective realization of recognized rights and freedoms. The obligation to promote is also designed to achieve a certain result, but in this case it concerns more or less vaguely formulated goals, which can only be achieved progressively or in the long term. The obligation to ensure and the obligation to promote together encompass, *inter alia,* what traditionally are called "programmatic" obligations within the framework of economic, social and cultural rights.

106

This model obviously needs to be elaborated and refined. Nevertheless, even in the form outlined above, it would seem to offer a number of possibilities to develop a more fruitful approach to the international law of human rights. First and foremost, it stresses the unity between civil and political rights, and economic, social and cultural rights, as long as it is recognized that the various "layers" of obligations can be found in each separate right or freedom. In other words, civil and political rights do not always consist only of obligations to respect and obligations to protect. Under the impact of the above-mentioned processes of increased interdependence and emancipation this type of right now sometimes involves obligations to ensure and even obligations to promote as well. An example is freedom of expression, which, at least in some countries, has come to include, apart from the prohibition of censorship, an obligation to create conditions favourable to the freedom to demonstrate (police-escort, police-protection, etc.) and to pluralism in the press and the media in general.

Conversely, economic, social and cultural rights are not always made up only of obligations to ensure and/or obligations to promote. They may also involve elements of obligations to respect and obligations to protect. For instance, the obligation to respect and protect the right to adequate housing, as laid down in Article 11 of the Covenant, would in my view be violated, if the government's policy, even in the least developed countries, allowed the hovels of poor people to be torn down and replaced by luxury housing which the original inhabitants could not afford and without providing them with access to alternative housing on reasonable terms. It bears reiterating therefore that obligations to fulfil and to promote cannot from a legal point of view too readily be assumed to be empty shells.

The foregoing may be illustrated a little further by briefly applying the model of the various "layers" of obligations to the right to food. The following examples of the different types of obligations can thus be discerned. The obligation to respect the right to food implies that a government may not expropriate land from people for whom access to control over that land constitutes the only or main asset by which they satisfy their food needs, unless appropriate alternative measures are taken.

Similarly, the obligation to protect the right to food includes the duty on the part of the State to prevent others from depriving people in one way or another, for instance by force or economic dominance, from their main resource base to satisfy their food needs, such as access to land, water, markets, or jobs.

The obligation to ensure the right to food requires a State to take steps in case members of its population prove incapable of providing themselves with food of a sufficient quantity and quality. In emergency situations a State must, to the maximum of its resources, make available the necessary food stuffs. Alternatively or in addition it must seek the assistance of other States to cope with the hunger problem. This raises the question as to the existence of an obligation on the part of other States to provide the required assistance to the best of their ability, as in my view can be deduced from article 11(2). In a more structural way the obligation to ensure the right to food may entail the duty of a State to initiate land reforms in order to improve the production and distribution of food. Although it is difficult *in abstracto* to indicate what measures a State has to take, in concrete situations particular measures can be said to be pertinent for the State concerned in order to meet its obligation to ensure the right to food. At any rate, a State violates this obligation when, in the face of food shortage, it does nothing.

The same holds, *mutatis mutandis*, for the obligation to promote the right to food. As was pointed out this type of obligation encompasses measures aimed at long term goals, and in the case of the right to food it may therefore consist of, for instance, the duty on the part of the government to set training programmes for farmers in an effort to improve methods of production and thus raise productivity in agriculture.

Apart from the fact that the model of various "layers" of obligations allows for a more integrated approach to the issue of human rights it would seem to offer an additional advantage in that it constitutes a more promising point of departure for dealing with the issue of enforcement or implementation of human rights. From the point of view of effectiveness it may be expected that different types of obligations require different forms of enforcement or implementation. The model of "layers" opens the possibility to tailor the system of enforcement or implementation to the various types of obligations.

Notes

(1). See Alston, in Eide et al.(Eds.), Food as a Human Right (1984), chap. 14.
(2). For our purposes it is not necessary to go into the details of the questions as to which rights belong to the category of civil and political rights, and which to the economic, social and cultural rights. The right to food is undoubtedly to be classified under the latter category. More generally, the distinction, as it is used in doctrine and in practice, is fairly clear since both categories are more or less "petrified" in on the one hand the International Covenant on Civil and Political Rights, and on the other hand the International Covenant on Economic, Social and Cultural Rights. See for more details on this question Bossuyt, "La distinction juridique entre les droits civils et politiques et les droits économiques, sociaux et culturels", 8 Human Rights Journal, (1975) 783-813; Bossuyt, "L'interdiction de la discrimination dans le droit international des droits de l'homme", (1976) 173-217; and Van Boven, "Distinguishing Criteria of Human Rights", in Vasak and Alston (Eds.), The International Dimensions of Human Rights (1982) 43 at 48-49.
(3). Vierdag, "The Legal Nature of the Rights Granted by the International Covenant on Economic, Social and Cultural Rights", 9 Netherlands Yearbook of International Law, (1978) 69-105.
(4). See the studies cited in note 2.
(5). Loc. cit. (note 3), 69.
(6). Ibid., 105.
(7). Ibid., 103.
(8). Idem.
(9). In this respect obviously much depends on how these concepts are defined; for more details on the relation between "law" and "politics" see Van Hoof, Rethinking the Sources of International Law, (1983) 24-28.
(10). Ibid., in particular 19-28 and 117-119.
(11). Loc. cit. (note 3), 73.
(12). Ibid., 93.

(13). According to Vierdag "saying that a right is "enforceable" is intended to mean that an authority of the state (or, for that matter, an international authority) is competent to receive complaints about violations of the right by anyone - executive state organ, official or private person - and to give redress by cancelling or rectifying the violating act or regulation, or by awarding compensation for damage, or both. If the authority in question is a court of law, the term "justiciable" may be preferred". Ibid., 73.

(14). Ibid., 72.

(15). "Everyone has the right to an effective remedy by the competent national tribunals for acts violating the fundamental rights granted him by the constitution or by law".

(16). "Everyone whose rights and freedoms as set forth in this Convention are violated shall have an effective remedy before a national authority notwithstanding that the violation has been committed by persons acting in an official capacity".

(17). Loc. cit. (note 3), 73.

(18). Idem.

(19). Ibid., 74.

(20). For more details see Van Hoof, op. cit. (note 9), 61-65.

(21). Very often such methods are based on the combined effect of considerations derived from the self-interest on the part of the States concerned and the element of reciprocity which is operative in international relations. Ibid., 258-261.

(22). Ibid., 57-60 and 76-81.

(23). Loc. cit. (note 3), 93.

(24). By direct effect is meant the possibility for private persons to derive from a State"s treaty obligations claims to individual rights which the courts must protect.

(25). Loc. cit. (note 3), 100.

(26). Idem.

(27). Ibid., 101.

(28). See also infra, section 4.

(29). See section 6.1.

(30). Loc. cit. (note 3), 94-95.

(31). Ibid., 95 and 101.

(32). See the studies cited in note 2.

(33). Op. cit. (note 2) 185; loc.cit. (note 2), 790

(34). Op. cit. (Note 2), 185; loc. cit. (Note 2), 790.

(35). Op. cit. (Note 2), 182; loc. cit. (Note 2), note 19.

(36). Op. cit. (Note 2), 185-186; loc. cit.(Note 2), 790

(37). See on this question Bossuyt, loc. cit. (note 2), 806-807.

(38). Op. cit. (note 2), 186; loc. cit. (Note 2), 790.

(39). The landmark decision in this respect is the Handyside-case; for more details see Van Dijk and Van Hoof, "Theory and Practice of the European Convention on Human Rights", (1984) 433-449.

(40). Op. cit. (note 2), 186; loc. cit. (Note 2), 790-791.

(41). Op. cit. (note 2), 187; loc. cit. (Note 2), 791.
In Bossuyt's scheme the absolute character of civil and political rights would seem to correspond with the institutional function of the international system of supervision by which they are protected: "La mise en vigueur d'une convention internationale de droits civils ne crée pas pour les personnes relevant de la jurisdiction des hautes parties contractantes des droits nouveaux, mais un nouveau mécanisme de côntrole de ces droits" (op. cit. (note 2), 190). This function is different with respect to economic, social and cultural rights: "En matière de droits sociaux, pour lesquels le mécanisme de contrôle reste généralement assez peu developpé, l'aspect normatif revêt une importance accrue". (Idem.)

(42). See also Van Hoof, op. cit. (note 2), 30-34.

(43). Bossuyt, op. cit. (note 2), 186; loc. cit. (Note 2), 790.

(44). Op. cit. (note 2), 187-188; loc. cit. (note 2), 791-792. A final distinction made by Bossuyt between the two sets of rights consists of differences in the mechanisms of protection which apply to both categories of rights. (Op. cit. (note 2), 185-188.) This issue has been discussed supra, section 2.

(45). See Van Dijk and Van Hoof, op. cit. (note 39), 460.

(46). Ibid., 449-454.

(47). Ibid., 398-408.

(48). Ibid., 420-422.
(49). Ibid., 408-410.
(50). Ibid., 422-424.
(51). For more details see Van Hoof, op. cit. (Note 2), 65-71.
(52). See Eide, "The Right to Adequate Food as a Human Right", UN doc E/CN 4/Sub.2/ 1983/25.

Obligations of Conduct and Result

by
Guy S. Goodwin-Gill[*]

By comparison with treaties dealing with civil and political rights there would appear to be fundamental differences in the nature of the rights and duties, including those relating to the right to food, which are formulated in the International Covenant on Economic, Social and Cultural Rights.[1] The briefest comparison of article 2 with its counterpart in the Civil and Political Rights Covenant is already revealing. In the latter, states undertake "to respect and to ensure", and to take the necessary steps "to give effect", to the rights recognized, while the rights themselves are clearly and specifically described. Article 2(1) of the former Covenant seems equivocal by contrast:

"Each State Party to the present Covenant undertakes to take steps, individually and through international assistance and co-operation, especially economic and technical, to the maximum of its available resources, with a view to achieving progressively the full realization of the rights recognized in the present Covenant by all appropriate means, including particularly the adoption of legislative measures."

This basic statement of obligation has encouraged many to describe the thrust of the Covenant as "programmatic and promotional",[2] rather than descriptive of individual rights.[3] The absence of any specific reference to remedies lends further support to the view that obligations of a somewhat different order are in contemplation. One recent commentator has made the point that the Economic and Social Rights Covenant "speaks in the language of rights, but refers to the realities of programs,"[4] which states are bound to undertake to guarantee minimum levels of well-being and progressively to increase such well-being.

The peculiar, in the sense of special, standing of "social welfare duties" is reinforced by regional comparisons. Thus the European Social Charter records parties' understanding that "legal obligations of an international character" are involved, but that their application "is submitted solely to the supervision provided for" elsewhere in the Charter.[5] The means of review and supervision provided by the 1966 Covenant, and their deficiencies, have already been remarked on elsewhere in this volume.[6]

It may be readily admitted that basic obligations in the Covenant are more qualified and ambiguous than in other human rights instruments. Excessive attention to this detail, however, when accompanied by like attachment to the dimension of individual rights and remedies, undermines the importance of the Covenant as a source of nevertheless binding obligations. The essential task remains to firm up those obligations, to give meaning and content to terms, and so to arrive at an international standard by which to assess the performance of States. Not only does the Covenant establish relations between the parties, but it also now gives certain domestic issues an international dimension. A State's policies and programmes, as well as legislative administrative and other measures, will be relevant in determining whether its international obligations have been efficiently and effectively implemented. What remains unclear, however, is the precise weight and role to be accorded to legislation as a means of ensuring rights or providing protection.

1. Obligations of Conduct and Obligations of Result

The general duty of a party to a treaty to ensure that its domestic law is in conformity with its international obligations has been frequently acknowledged, both in the jurisprudence of the International Court[7] and in the views of jurists.[8] Nevertheless, the principles declared do not include an obligation, *per se,* to incorporate the provisions of treaties or of general international law into domestic legislation.[9] The fundamental distinction is that between an obligation of conduct or means, and an obligation of result.[10] Though easier to declare than to apply, this distinction remains crucial in assessing a State's performance under its treaties. In practice, obligations of conduct are less frequent than obligations of result, and are most common where action is required in direct inter-State relations. Obligations of result, on the other hand, incorporating acknowledgement of the principle of choice of means, are most often found where states are required to promote or create a certain situation within their own legal system.

Article 22(1) of the 1961 Vienna Convention on Diplomatic Relations, for example, declares a clear obligation of conduct: "The premises of the mission shall be inviolable. The agents of the receiving state may not enter them, except with the consent of the head of the mission."[11] Here the internationally required conduct is that of omission by the organs of the receiving state; in other cases, positive action may be called for. Thus, states parties to the 1965 Convention on the Elimination of All Forms of Racial Discrimination agree, *inter alia,* "to amend, rescind or nullify any laws or regulations which have the effect of creating or perpetuating racial discrimination wherever it exists."[12] Similarly, the specific **enactment** of legislation may be demanded, as by Article 20 of the 1966 Covenant on Civil and Political Rights ("Any propaganda for war shall be prohibited by law").[13] In all these examples, the international obligation requires a specifically determined course of conduct; ascertaining that the obligation has been fulfilled turns on the simple question, whether the State's act or omission is or is not in fact in conformity with the internationally required conduct, the sufficient injury being the breach of legal duty.[14]

International obligations requiring the achievement of a specific result often expressly acknowledge the State's full freedom in its choice of means for implementation. Article 22(2) of the 1961 Vienna Convention on Diplomatic Relations declares the receiving State's "special duty to take all appropriate steps to protect the premises of the mission," but defines those steps no further. Article 10 of the ILO Migrant Workers (Supplementary Provisions) Convention 1975 (No. 143) obliges "Each Member for which the

Convention is in force...to declare and pursue a national policy designed to promote and to guarantee, **by methods appropriate to national conditions and practice,** equality of opportunity and treatment..."[15] The obligation of result is especially common in standard-setting and human rights treaties, where full freedom of choice may be implied from the terms of the treaty itself, or a preference be shown for legislative measures.Nevertheless, although legislation might be thought appropriate, even essential, it is evidently only one way in which the internationally required result can be obtained. It is not so much the letter of the law which counts, as actual compliance with the requisite conduct. Indeed, the International Law Commission has noted[16]:

"...so long as the State has not failed to achieve *in concreto* the result required by an international obligation, the fact that it has not taken a certain measure which would have seemed especially suitable for that purpose - in particular, that it has not enacted a law - cannot be held against it as a breach of that obligation."

2. Recent treaties and the bases of obligations

Two recent treaties require States to enact "such legislative or other measures as may be necessary"[17] to give effect to rights; and to "prohibit and bring to an end" certain conduct, "by all appropriate means, including legislation as required by circumstances."[18] In both cases the objective is clear, but the conduct/result distinction has become blurred. The context, however, is the protection of human rights and the elimination of racial discrimination, and this permits the inference that obligations of result are intended, which will have their effect within the domestic jurisdiction of States. At the same time, given the declared preference for legislative measures (or at least the adoption of rules), a State which elects to employ less formal methods of implementation may find it difficult to show, either generally, that it has fulfilled its international obligations; or specifically, that individuals intended to benefit from such provisions in fact possess effective remedies against their violation.

Words such as "necessary" and "appropriate" show that the State enjoys discretion in its choice of implementing measures, but the standard of compliance remains an international one. The question is one of effective or efficient implementation of the treaty provisions **in fact,** and in the light of the principle of effectiveness of obligations.[19] Just as taking the theoretically best appropriate measures of implementation is not conclusive as to the fulfilment of an international obligation, so failing to take such measures is not conclusive as to breach.

The same principle applies with regard to a State's adoption of a potentially obstructive measure, so long as the measure does not itself create a specific situation incompatible with the required result; what counts is what in fact results, not enactment and promulgation, but application and enforcement. This was clearly understood by the European Court of Human Rights

113

in its Judgement in 1978 in **Ireland vs. United Kingdom.** The applicant Government argued, *inter alia,* that the laws in force in the six countries of Northern Ireland did not specifically prohibit violation of Articles 3,5,6, and 14 of the European Convention. In so far as those laws authorized or permitted such violations the United Kingdom, apart from its obligations to individuals, was in breach of a separate inter-State obligation arising from Article 1.[20] The Court doubted whether a contracting State was entitled to challenge a law *in abstracto.* A breach, no doubt, might result "from the mere existence of a law which **introduces, directs, or authorizes** measures incompatible with the rights and freedoms safeguarded," but a challenge under Article 24 of the Convention (which enables inter-State applications) would succeed only if the terms of the law were "sufficiently clear and precise." Said the Court,[21]

"...the decision of the Convention institutions be arrived at by reference to the manner in which the respondent State interprets and applies *in concreto* the impugned text or texts.

The absence of a law expressly prohibiting this or that violation does not suffice to establish a breach since such a prohibition does not represent the sole method of securing the enjoyment of the rights and freedoms guaranteed."

The Court held that an examination *in abstracto* of the relevant legislation disclosed that it never introduced, directed or authorised recourse to torture or to inhuman or degrading treatment. It did find, however, that certain **administrative practices** violated Article 3 of the European Convention.[22]
In theory, at least, the test of implementation of an international obligation of result might appear as straightforward as that for an obligation of conduct: compare the result in fact achieved with that which the State ought to have achieved. Major problems of interpretation and appreciation can arise in practice, however, in view of the relative imprecision of the terminology employed in standard-setting conventions; the variety of the legal systems and practices of different States; the role of discretion, first, in the State's initial choice of means, and secondly, in its privilege on occasion to require resort to such remedial measures as it may provide; and finally, the possibility that the State may be entitled to avoid responsibility by providing an "equivalent alternative" to the required result, such as compensation for arbitrary detention.

The question whether a State has fulfilled an obligation of result must be examined therefore in the light of the initial means chosen for implementation, the remedies available in the event that an initially incompatible situation ensues, and the option, if permitted by the obligation, of substituting an equivalent alternative result in the event that the principal required result is rendered unattainable. In the field of standard-setting, local remedies are especially important, the beneficiaries of the obligations which affords them protection must obtain at the level of the internal law of the State in which they are active. Thus, the availability and effectiveness of local remedies will often determine the question of fulfilment or breach of obligation.[23] In principle, there is no reason why such remedies cannot be devised in order to

114

secure the implementation of economic rights.

Some of the problems in determining the precise scope of conduct required of States can be gathered from an examination of the phrasing of Article 2(2) of the Covenant on Civil and Political Rights, which requires states to adopt "such legislative or other measures as may be necessary to give effect to the rights recognized." This has been interpreted by one commentator as imposing "a conditional obligation" as to conduct, supplementing the parties' basic commitment to the obligation of result declared in Article 2(1), namely, "to respect and to ensure to all individuals within (their) territory and subject to (their) jurisdiction the rights recognized... without distinction of any kind..."[24] The provision in question nevertheless lacks the precision generally required of obligations of conduct, and clearly allows discretion in the choice of means. That discretion, however, is more closely controlled and structured than usual in statements of obligations of result, so that the practical choices open to States wishing to meet the demands of Article 2 are restricted by the inclusion of preferred means and declared objectives.

3. Articles 2 and 11 of the Covenant on Economic, Social and Cultural Rights

As noted above, economic, social and cultural rights, as well as the correlative States' duties, have been formulated in ways significantly different from those adopted for civil and political rights, which may conceivably affect the quality, (or length, breadth and depth) of the obligations assumed. It is worth reiterating, first, that in accepting obligations with regard to human rights, States necessarily undertake to implement them effectively and in good faith. In principle, the choice of means may well be left to individual States, which can opt between legislative incorporation, administrative regulation, informal and *ad hoc* procedures, or any combination thereof. In practice, however, freedom of choice may be confined by reference to specific objectives, and further structured in the light of declared methods proposed and preferred by the terms of the particular instrument. It will often be the case that legislative action is essential, not only for the purpose of sufficiently identifying human rights, a task important in itself, but also to ensure the availability of an effective remedy against violation. Such formal, legal provisions would be neither purely cosmetic, nor finally conclusive of a State's compliance with its international obligations. Whether in a given case such measures, together or alone, are sufficient conditions for effective implementation remains to be judged in the light of the actual workings of the municipal system as a whole. The standard of assessment is provided by international law and, in a formal sense, by the express terms of the treaty. The precise content of that standard may be self-evident, or remain to be filled out by other actors in the field - hence the increasing importance of the activities of rule and policy-making international organizations, as well as of supervisory machinery such as has been established by the I.L.O. or under universal and regional human rights institutions.

The statement of duties contained in articles 2(1) and 11[25] can be broken down into a series of related elements - the obligation as to conduct and the result to be achieved, the means to be employed and the qualifications relating to choice and achievement. Thus, under Article 2, States are bound to take steps to secure full realization of rights; the means to be employed include individual efforts, international assistance and co-operation and legislation, while States' action is limited to the maximum of available resources and to progressive realization. Under Article 11, states are bound, *inter alia*, to take steps to provide and ensure freedom from hunger; the means to be employed include international co-operation and special programmes; the former is qualified by reference to "free consent", and the obligation as a whole is subject to progressive realization.

The breadth of discretion remaining to States, as well as the various imponderables in the text, might lead one to suppose that little was left in the way of obligation. Nevertheless, in terms of international obligation, Articles 2, 11 and 23 all entail express recognition by States Parties of the importance of international co-operation for the achievement of the right to food.

It is in this context that the UN specialized agencies may be expected to make their contribution, and where some have already begun. One commentator, for example, has noted the work of the International Labour Organization in promoting the "Basic Needs Approach" to employment and growth;[26] and of the World Health Organization with regard to Primary Health Care.[27] For food and freedom from hunger, however, progress has been less than satisfactory.[28]

Despite the breadth of discretion, and notwithstanding the scope left for different types of international action, the core obligations to be derived from Articles 2 and 11 are clear enough: adequate food and freedom from hunger, with the latter described as a "fundamental" right. Given these basic international standards, the question next arises of implementation on the domestic level. Article 2 indicates legislative measures as possible method, although not as strongly as the corresponding article in the Civil and Political Rights Covenant. The nature of economic, social and cultural rights possibly entails different procedural demands by which to achieve effective realization, just as poverty cannot be excised by locking up the poor, so will hunger not be satisfied solely by legislation on the right to food. The overall role of such measures, however, cannot be summarily dismissed. A **fundamental** individual human right - freedom from hunger - is expressly recognized, effective, legal protection at the local level appears an essential if complementary element in the process of achieving this objective. The Covenant as a whole must be read as establishing priority for economic and social rights when it comes to the allocation of available resources.[29] In the absence of effective international supervision, States themselves are obliged to monitor levels of nutrition. Where starvation or hunger occur, the State's responsibility in international law will need to be judged in the light of the Covenant's overall objectives; the effectiveness, in fact, of the government's food programmes, if any, whether access to food supplies is available on a non-discriminatory basis, and whether other limitations apply; and whether effective legal or administrative remedies exist, at the domestic level.

Certainly, the assessment of State responsibility is a complex task, but so also in municipal law is the determination of the particular standard of care which is owed at large by those who engage in dangerous or hazardous activities. In both cases, however, the law provides an appropriate repertory of principle and policy by which to reach the relevant rule. As with all human rights, domestic legal remedies constitute an important protective and promotional tool, although what really counts for international law is how the system as a whole works out in fact, at the local level.

Notes

(*)The views expressed are the author's personal views.
(1) The general approach described below has also been applied by the present writer in The Refugee in International Law (1983), 140-8.
(2) Brownlie, Principles of Public International Law (3rd Ed., 1979), 572-3.
(3) Vierdag, "the legal nature of the rights granted by the international covenant on economic, social and cultural rights", 9 Netherlands Yearbook of International Law 69, 103 (1978).
(4) Trubek, "Economic, Social and Cultural Rights in the Third World: Human Rights Law and Human Needs Programs", in Meron, Ed., Human Rights in International Law, (1984), vol.1, 205, 231.
(5) European Social Charter, Approved Text in European Treaty Series, No. 35, Appendix, Part III.
(6) See Alston, Chapter 1, section 9, supra.
(7) See, for example, Treatment of Polish Nationals in Danzig, P.C.I.J., Ser. A/B, No.44, p.24, Greco-Bulgarian Communities Case, P.C.I.J., Ser. B.No.17, p.32, Free Zones Case, P.C.I.J., Ser. A, No.24, p.12, Ser. A/B, No.46, p.167, Article 27, 1969 Vienna Convention on the Law of Treaties.
(8) McNair, The Law of Treaties, (1961), pp. 78-9, Brownlie, Principles of Public International Law, (1979), pp. 36-8, id., System of the Law of Nations: State Responsibility, Part I, (1983), pp.241-76.
(9) The International Court has stressed that failure to enact legislation necessary to ensure fulfilment of international obligations will not relieve a state of responsibility, see Exchange of Greek and Turkish Population Case, P.C.I.J., Ser. B, No. 10, p.20.
(10) See generally, International Law Commission, Yearbook, (1977), vol. II, pp. 11-50, Brownlie, State Responsibility, pp. 241-76.
(11) Text in UN doc. A/CONF.20/13, Brownlie, Basic Documents in International Law, (1983), p.212.
(12) Article 2(1)(c), text annexed to UN General Assembly resolution 2106 (xx) of 21 December 1965, Brownlie, Basic Documents, p.302.
(13) Text annexed to UN General Assembly resolution 2200 (xxi) of 16 December 1966, Brownlie, Basic Documents, p. 270.
(14) Diplomatic and Consular Staff in Tehran, (USA v. Iran), I.C.J. Rep., 1980, pp. 3, 30-1. Cf. International Law Commission, Draft Articles on State Responsibility, arts. 16, 20: Yearbook, (1977), vol. II, pp. 10-11. In commenting on the irrelevance of harmful consequences actually resulting, the ILC suggests as one example that article 10(3) of the 1966 Covenant on Economic, Social and Cultural Rights ("...States Parties... recognize that... [child employment in certain circumstances]... should be punishable by law.") is breached by simple failure to enact legislation. This conclusion seems erroneous; article 2(1) of that Covenant refers expressly to "achieving progressively the full realization of the rights recognized", while article 10 alone in that instrument employs the ambivalent "should". The provision is thus rather an obligation of result, than of conduct.

(15) See also article 24, ILO Constitution, acknowledging the duty of every member State to secure "the effective observance within its jurisdiction of any Convention to which it is a party", text in Brownlie, Basic Documents, p. 49.

(16) ILC Yearbook, (1977), vol. II, p.23.

(17) Article 2(1) 1966 Covenant on Civil and Political Rights.

(18) Article 2(1)(d), 1965 Convention on the Elimination of All Forms of Racial Discrimination.

(19) See generally Brownlie, State Responsibility, also Lauterpacht, The Development of International Law by the International Court, (1958), pp.257, 282ff. Article 31(1), 1969 Vienna Convention on the Law of Treaties, McNair, The Law of Treaties, p.540f.

(20) Judgement of the Court, Ireland v. United Kingdom, (Application 5301/71), paras. 236ff. Article 1 of the European Convention provides: "The High Contracting Parties shall secure to everyone within their jurisdiction the rights and freedoms defined..."

(21) Ibid., para. 240, emphasis supplied.

(22) Ibid., paras. 241, 246.

(23) The local remedies rule was originally framed with regard to the standard of treatment of aliens, but is now increasingly applied, in human rights instruments, to all persons regardless of status.

(24) Schachter, "The obligations of the parties to give effect to the covenant on civil and political rights", 73 American Journal of International Law, 462 (1979), notes: "It is not enough for a party to say that it respects and ensures rights (the obligation of result); it must also carry out the obligation to use the specified means required by article 2 through its domestic legal system".

(25) The full text of these articles is contained in Chapter 1, supra.

(26) Trubek, (above, note 4), 231-42, see articles 6-9 of the Covenant, ILO, Employment, Growth and Basic Needs: A One World Problem (1976).

(27) Trubek (above, note 4), 242-5, see article 12 of the Covenant, WHO, Primary Health Care, (1978).

(28) See Alston, chapter 1, supra.

(29) Trubek (above, note 4), 215, cf Vierdag (above, note 3), 80ff.

118

Towards a System for Supervising States' Compliance with the Right to Food.

by
Gert Westerveen*

1. Introduction.

Supervision is a component of international law with the purpose of ensuring the observance of its rules. Supervisory functions are performed by those bound by the rules of international law, and with an interest that they are observed, primarily the States. Multilateral treaties often provide for supervisory mechanisms, establishing organs or organizations to supervise the performance of the States Parties to the particular treaty. The necessity for the creation of supervisory bodies for multilateral human rights treaties can be argued from the fact that those treaties put obligations on States in respect to their own citizens. With regard to the substantive provisions, such treaties do not contain reciprocal obligations between States. The lack of reciprocity of obligations, diminishes the urge for governments to see that obligations are kept; the need for monitoring the provisions of a human rights treaty is felt by governments to a lesser degree. Specialized supervisory bodies are needed to fill that gap.

Major human rights treaties, both universal and regional, have established their own supervisory body or bodies, like the Human Rights Committee, the Committee for the Elimination of All Forms of Racial Discrimination, the European and Inter-American Commissions and Courts of Human Rights. The African Charter of Human and Peoples' Rights and the Convention on the Elimination of All Forms of Discrimination against Women, which have not yet entered into force, follow the precedents of the establishment of specialized supervisory bodies. The type of supervision these organs and institutions perform varies between extremes of outright judicial supervision, e.g. the European and American Courts of human rights which give binding decisions, and non-judicial supervision, consisting of the consideration of State's reports by procedures combining factfinding and persuasion. The supervision of human rights treaties includes three distinctive functions: a review function, a correction function and a creative function. [1]

1.1 the review function.

Review is inherent in any supervision. It means "measuring" or judging something against a determined standard. In the legal context, the review consists of judging behaviour to determine its conformity with a rule of law. In international law, review can be performed by one or more States, or by an

* In the preparation of this chapter reference was made to an unpublished article by Philip Alston, reviewing experience to date in the implementation of the right to food under the Covenant.

international organ or institution created by a treaty. The review results in the determination whether the behaviour reviewed is in conformity with the rule of international law.

1.2 The correction function.

The correction function follows a determination of the behaviour evaluated to be contrary to international law. Its purpose is the correction of infringements of international law by persuasion of or pressure upon the State. In most national legal systems the correction function is highly institutionalised. Decisions of the judiciary are, if necessary, implemented by the executive branch of the government. In the international legal system, the efficient performance of the correction function is much more difficult because States themselves perform the functions of supervision. There is no international police force, and no international court with mandatory jurisdiction. Within the framework of international organizations the corrective measures available consist mainly in the withholding of benefits emanating from the membership in the organization. Within international human rights law the situation is somewhat different; there are few benefits to be withheld. Some supervisory bodies can award damages to the victims of human rights violations, like the European and American courts of human rights; other bodies can only make recommendations to the States whose behaviour is being evaluated, express their views, or make general observations. The preventive aspect of the correction function requires the discovery of violations of human rights not only to lead to redress, but also to act as an incentive to governments to avoid future violations.

1.3 The creative function.

The creative function involves more than an interpretation of legal norms, which forms part of any process of review. Since rules of international law are at times vaguely worded, and are related to issues of policy rather than to actual conduct, there will often be a need to elaborate on the rules, and fill the gaps. That function is sometimes known as "judge-made law". It is more than a mere interpretation of a norm, it comes close to the notion of progressive development.

2. Supervision of the International Covenant on Economic, Social and Cultural Rights.

A specific organ of the United Nations, the Economic and Social Council (ECOSOC), has been entrusted by the International Covenant on Economic, Social and Cultural Rights (ICESCR) to supervise the performance of the States Parties for "progressively achieving" the rights set forth in that treaty.

120

States Parties to the ICESCR have to report to the ECOSOC on how they have fulfilled their obligations, what measures they have taken to implement the rights set forth in that covenant. According to Art.16.2(a) the ECOSOC has to consider the reports submitted, and Arts.19, 21, and 22 specify what action the ECOSOC can take with regard to issues arising from the reports. The ECOSOC can transmit reports to the Commission on Human Rights, it can report to the General Assembly on the measures taken and the progress achieved, it can bring specific matters to the attention of other organs of the United Nations or to the specialized agencies.

The ECOSOC has not made use of these powers so far. The consideration of the reports by the sessional working group, which was established for that purpose in 1978, has not given much insight into the normative content of the right to food, nor into the degree of its implementation by the States Parties to the ICESCR. As supervision aims to measure the actual behaviour against a rule of law, it is necessary to know the content of the rule in question, more in particular the obligations embodied in that rule. According to the wording of Art.11 of the ICESCR, which asserts the human right to food, States Parties are obliged to take measures aimed at improving production, conservation, and distribution of food. No authoritative interpretation of Art.11 has been given so far, neither by the body from which such an interpretation could have been expected, the ECOSOC, nor by any other organ. A further exploration of the normative content of the right to food is certainly needed. Elaboration of the normative content of the right to food is important, but also the establishment of an effective supervisory mechanism is of vital importance for the implementation of the right to food.

It is not the right place here to dwell further on the possible contents of the right to food and correlative governmental obligations. At this moment the following fourfold distinction of governmental obligations is sufficient for a tentative description of a possible international supervisory mechanism. As with all other human rights, the obligations falling upon the States can be divided into four different obligations [2]: the obligation to respect, the obligation to protect, the obligation to fulfil, and the obligation to promote.

The obligation to respect requires mainly non-interference on the part of the State, whereas the other three require some kind of action or policy on the part of the State.

Art. 2 of the ICESCR requires each State Party "...to take steps...to the maximum of its available resources, with a view to achieving progressively the full realization of the rights recognized in the present covenant...". The main goal of the supervision process would be to determine whether a State takes measures aimed at achieving adequate food for all, and specifically the measures suggested in Art.11.2. With a view to the specification of the obligations mentioned above, supervision need not be restricted to measuring progress in time, the progressive achievement or the duty to fulfill or promote. The fourfold division of obligations applied to the right to food makes it possible to assert that States can violate the right to food by a breach of the obligations to respect and to protect, in a similar way as they can violate civil and political rights. This could be of importance for the mandate of a possible supervisory mechanism.

3. Supervisory Procedures.

The main existing procedures for the supervision of the performance of States in the field of human rights, are based on reports by States themselves, or the submission of complaints by States, individuals, or groups of individuals, or on a combination of both reporting and the submission of complaints.

3.1 Reporting.

Reporting can be an effective method for supervision. When submitted at regular intervals, reports can establish a dialogue between the bearers of the obligations and the supervisory body. A careful scrutiny of the performance of the bearers of the obligations over a period of time becomes possible on the basis of regular reporting. Such supervisory procedures are frequently provided for, both human rights treaties and constitutions of intergovernmental organizations. Human rights treaties which provide for a supervisory procedure based on reporting by States Parties are, *inter alia*, the International Convention for the Elimination of All Forms of Racial Discrimination, the International Covenant on Civil and Political Rights, the International Covenant on Economic, Social and Cultural Rights, and the European Social Charter. The UN specialized Agencies which provide for a reporting procedure in their constitution are, *inter alia*, the International Labour Organization[3], the Food and Agriculture Organization [4], the World Health Organization [5], and the United Nations Educational, Scientific and Cultural Organization [6].

These different reporting systems have been functioning with varied success. Among the UN specialized agencies only the ILO system has functioned more or less satisfactorily.[7] With regard to the FAO reporting procedure, it was said that the response of governments had been "less than satisfactory".[8] As far as reporting on health issues is concerned, it was pointed out that governments may be reluctant to report on their health problems for fear of excessive reactions by neighbouring countries, which might result in economic losses in trade and tourism.[9]

In the field of human rights the experiences of the Committee for the Elimination of All Forms of Racial Discrimination and of the Human Rights Committee with regard to State reporting are rather positive. Both committees have been able to establish a kind of dialogue with governments on their activities in the implementation of the rights proclaimed by the International Convention on the Elimination of All Forms of Racial Discrimination and the International Covenant on Civil and Political Rights respectively. Of course, problems such as delays in the submission of reports, reports containing insufficient information, or unwillingness of governments to participate in the consideration of reports remain unsolved.

The reporting procedure under the International Covenant on Economic, Social and Cultural Rights, has been disappointing so far. Three aspects of this reporting system have to be addressed here; the reports submitted by the States Parties, the participation of the specialized agencies in the supervision, and the role of the ECOSOC and its sessional working group of governmental experts.

A. Reports by States Parties.

The Secretary General of the United Nations, in consultation with the specialized agencies, drew up guidelines for the preparation of the reports to be submitted under Art.16 of the ICESCR. Those guidelines, which were reprinted as an annex to Un doc E/1980/6, suggested that "Governments should describe the basic conditions prevailing in their countries as well as the basic programmes and institutions relevant to the rights dealt with in Articles 10-12..." With regard to the right to food, the guidelines requested States to include in their reports information on the "principal laws, administrative regulations and collective agreements designed to promote the right of everyone to adequate food, and relevant court decisions, if any;". The guidelines further requested information on topics which follow the topics mentioned in Art. 11 of the ICESCR, however, without requiring to indicate what the effects have been on the enjoyment of the right to food. The result has been, even in the few cases where the States" reports follow the guidelines, an emphasis on technical issues. Although the reports on the right to food differ considerably, one report on the right to food being less than one page (German Democratic Republic, Un doc E/1980/6/Add.6), another having eleven pages on the right to food,(Norway, Un doc E/1980/6/Add.5), the general picture that emerged is as follows: difficulties affecting the fulfilment of the right to food were hardly mentioned;
very few States acknowledge the occurrence of hunger or malnutrition in their countries; statistical information is seldom given; most States mentioned legislation or administrative regulations, but only seldom referred to the practical effects of such legislation or regulations.
One government stated in its report:"there are no laws, regulations or agreements, nor court decisions bearing on the right of everyone to adequate food in the United Kingdom." (United Kingdom, Un doc E/1980/6/Add.16, par 21).

B. The specialized agencies.

According to the ICESCR, Arts.18-22, the specialized agencies can play a role in the supervision of the ICESCR. Under Art.18, the ECOSOC can make arrangements with the specialized agencies, in respect of their reporting to the ECOSOC on the progress made in achieving the observance of the provisions of the ICESR which fall within the scope of activities of these agencies. So far, such arrangements have been made with the ILO, the FAO, the WHO, and with UNESCO. Under Art.19 ICESCR, the ECOSOC can transmit reports of States Parties and of the specialized agencies to the UN Commission on Human Rights for study and recommendation. According to Art.20 ICESCR, the States Parties and the specialized agencies can react to recommendations made by the Commission on Human Rights under Art.19. In virtue of Art.21 ICESCR, the ECOSOC may report to the General Assembly of the UN, which reports may contain summaries of the reports made by States Parties and by the specialized agencies. According to Art.22 ICESCR, the ECOSOC may bring matters to the attention of, *inter alia*, the specialized agencies. In addition, ECOSOC resolution 1988(LX) provides that the specialized agencies shall be consulted by the Secretary General of the UN with regard to the drafting of guidelines for States' reports.

No action under Arts.19-22 has yet been taken, but the above mentioned specialized agencies have submitted reports in virtue of the arrangements made under Art.18 ICESCR.[10]

There are considerable differences between the various reports of the four specialized agencies. The ILO had the relevant parts of the States' reports considered by its Committee on the Application of Conventions and Recommendations, and submitted the comments of that body to the ECOSOC, in several reports.

The other specialized agencies submitted, as till 1984, only one report each, therein describing their own activities.

The report of the FAO follows the structure of Art.11 and the guidelines prepared by the Secretary General, in that it treats subjects as legislation, reform of agrarian systems, food production, conservation and distribution, etc. The report of FAO stresses that since the realization of the "right of everyone to be free from hunger...can be achieved, the adoption of all necessary measures...should be considered an obligation under international law." (Un doc E/1981/22 par 2) However, the FAO report refers to both "the right of everyone to be free from hunger" and "the right to adequate food", without attempting to explore the relationship between these norms, or the content of these norms. This aspect of the report, and the fact that it, unlike the report of the ILO, does not in any way refer to the reports of the States' Parties, or in any other way to activities undertaken by States, makes it doubtful whether the FAO report has helped the ECOSOC in assessing the progress made by the States Parties in implementing the right to food.

C. The role of the ECOSOC.

When the ICESCR entered into force in 1976, the ECOSOC adopted resolution 1988(LX), which outlined the procedures for the consideration of the reports which the States Parties had to submit. The resolution called for the establishment of a working group to assist the ECOSOC in the consideration of reports. The working group was established by ECOSOC decision 1978/10. It consists of 15 States, which are both members of the ECOSOC, and Parties to the ICESCR. The consideration of reports by the working group has, as yet, not led to any concrete results. The review function of the supervision has been performed superficially; the working group has not determined standards for the evaluation of reports, and it was not able to reach conclusions as to the compliance of the States Parties with the provisions of the ICESCR. The reports of the working group to the ECOSOC are merely listings of the States' reports considered.[11] Because of such a superficial performance of the review function, no attempt could have been made to perform the correction function. Till May 1984, the ECOSOC has not used the powers conferred upon it in the Arts. 19, 21, and 22 of the ICESCR.

The International Commission of Jurists, in a commentary on the 1980 and 1981 sessions of the working group, said: "The examination of reports has been cursory, superficial and politicized. It has neither established standards for evaluating reports nor reached any conclusions regarding its examination of reports."[12]

That assessment remains valid for the 1982 and 1983 sessions of the working group, despite some changes made in the structure of the working group in 1982. During the 1982 and 1983 sessions, again, no conclusions as to the performance of States Parties were made. ECOSOC decided by resolution 1982/33 that:

"(d) At the end of each of its sessions, the Group of Experts shall submit to the Economic and Social Council a report on its activities and shall make suggestions and recommendations of a general nature based on its consideration of reports submitted by States parties to the Covenant and by the specialized agencies, in order to assist the Council to fulfil, in particular, its responsibilities under articles 21 and 22 of the Covenant;".

Yet, the 1983 report of the working group did not contain such recommendations. In the chapter entitled "Issues arising from the consideration of reports by States parties to the covenant", the working group made remarks on the administrative arrangements for the working group, and on the form and content of the States reports. No substantive conclusions on the implementation of the provisions of the ICESCR by the States Parties were made.

It may be that the way in which the working group had been originally set up has contributed to its bad performance. First, supervision is performed by State representatives, instead of a body of independent persons. There is no guarantee that those State representatives have the necessary expertise, Additionally, the membership of the group was subject to change every year. Also, the time allotted to the working group was very short, only two weeks during the first regular session of ECOSOC. Difficulties further arose from the diversity of form and contents of States' reports, some reports not following the guidelines prepared by the Secretary General.

The awareness of the shortcomings in the working group induced the ECOSOC to attempt changes. In 1980, in its resolution 1980/24, ECOSOC decided to review the composition, organization, and administrative arrange-

125

ments of the working group. It requested the Secretary General to solicit the views of all States Parties to the ICESCR, and to submit a report thereon, including any comments he might wish to make. According to the report of the Secretary General, the replies received from 17 States vary between proposals to maintain the existing arrangements, and proposals calling for the establishment of a committee of independent experts. The Secretary General was of the opinion "that the Economic and Social Council will find it difficult to fully discharge its responsibilities under articles 21, 22 and 23 of the Covenant unless it devises more effective procedures for the consideration of reports..." [14]. The Secretary General referred to, *inter alia*, the need for expertise and continuity of membership in the working group.

By its resolution 1982/33, of 6 May 1982, the ECOSOC temporarily ended the review of the working group's composition, by introducing some changes. The most important were the following two: the 15 members of the group were to be elected for a renewable term of three years; the representatives designated by the member States had to be experts with recognized competence in the field of human rights. According to that resolution, the designation of States' representatives has to be effected in consultation with the Secretary General, and subject to the confirmation by the ECOSOC. Further, the group was to meet for a period of three weeks, beginning two weeks before the first regular session of the ECOSOC. Finally, the name of the group was determined as: "Sessional Working Group of Governmental Experts on the Implementation of the International Covenant on Economic, Social, and Cultural Rights". By the same resolution the ECOSOC decided to review the composition, organization, and administrative arrangements related to this group of experts again at its first regular session in 1985, and subsequently every three years thereafter.

Although these changes eliminated some of the previous shortcomings with respect to the working group, they did not result in a thorough improvement of the review function, that is, in the scrutiny of States' reports to determine whether States Parties live up to the requirements of the ICESCR.

3.2 Complaints.

The other major type of the supervisory procedures in the field of human rights, is based on complaints by individuals, groups, or States. At present, complaints procedures are provided for in the International Covenant on Civil and Political Rights, in an optional form, and in its Optional Protocol; in the International Convention for the Elimination of All Forms of Racial Discrimination, individual complaints being optional; and, with various forms of optionality, in the European and Inter-American systems for the protection of human rights. The ILO has several complaints procedures, especially through its machinery for the protection of the freedom of association; UNESCO has complaints procedures for the protection of human rights falling within its mandate; and the United Nations system for the protection of human rights recognizes complaints procedures, including the so-called "1503 procedure", which, however, only relates to cases of "gross" violations of human rights.

The advantages of a system based on complaints include the participation of the beneficiaries of the rights, in as much as they lodge complaints, and the possibility of a thorough investigation of factual and legal issues which are implied in an assertion of a violation of human rights. A major disadvantage of supervision based on complaints is that it can be set into motion only by the actual submission of a complaint by an affected party. The supervisory body cannot initiate any procedure on its own.

Practice shows that State complaints are rare. They have been lodged only within the framework of the European Convention for the Protection of Human Rights and Fundamental Freedoms. With respect to the International Covenant on Civil and Political Rights, only 15 States have made a declaration provided for by Art.41, recognizing the competence of the Human Rights Committee to receive communications by a State Party against another State Party. [15] Individual complaints are mandatory only in the American Convention on Human Rights, and in the ILO, and UNESCO. In all other human rights treaties, individual complaints are provided for on an optional basis.

Are complaints procedures feasible with regard to the right to food? Among most lawyers the general opinion seems to be that economic and social rights can only be implemented progressively, and that therefore complaints procedures would be impractical, since complaints could only relate to inadequate or insufficient programmes for the implementation of economic and social rights. However, the fourfold structure of the obligations relating to the right to food, as mentioned above, recognizes different types of obligations and gives a foundation for expanded possibilities to allege breaches of obligations. The obligations to respect and to protect could be implemented immediately, whereas the obligations to fulfil and to promote indeed contain elements of progressiveness. Theoretically, a complaints procedure could be envisaged to supervise the obligations to respect and protect.[16] It has been asserted that the real test of the effectiveness of a system of international protection for human rights is whether it provides an international remedy for the individual whose rights are violated.[17] From that perspective, possibilities for complaints by individuals are a necessary component of a future supervisory system related to the human right to food. In the light of the experiences of existing human rights complaints procedures, it is not to be expected that States will readily submit to a complaints procedure. Therefore, it is assumed hereafter that the feasible option for a supervisory body focusing on the right to food, is some form of reporting.

4. Composition and Powers of the Supervisory Body.

4.1 Composition.

The nature and composition of any supervisory body are of extreme importance. In a recent book, Sieghart writes: "Where that law (international

127

human rights law) assigns a supervisory function to an institution composed of governmental representatives, the results have so far ranged from the negligible, through the anodyne, to the blatantly political."[18] Government representatives in an international supervisory body, like at present in the Group of Experts of ECOSOC, act in a double capacity: as supervisors of an international instrument, and as representatives of their governments. It is clear that the latter may prevent them from exercising the supervisory functions in a proper way, if only because governments do not like to criticize other governments if they want to maintain friendly relations. Robertson argues that one cannot expect States to protect rights when they are *ex hypothesi* offenders.[19] There is obviously a need for independent persons performing the supervisory function in the field of human rights. Independence is a guarantee for objectivity and impartiality; without them no supervisory body can secure confidence and respect of governments.

Next to being independent, persons being members of a supervisory body should also have expertise in the fields covered by the mandate of the body. How can these conditions be met? One way to deal with the problem is to exercise proper care in the establishment of a supervisory body, with sufficient procedural guarantees. Members of the Human Rights Committee and of the Committee for the Elimination of All Forms of Racial Discrimination are elected by the States Parties to the respective treaty, whereas the experts of the Committee of Experts on the Application of Conventions and Recommendations are appointed by the Director General of the ILO. Would it be feasible, in the context of the right to food, to try to adopt some form of multiple structure to a supervisory body, resembling -for instance- the tripartite structure of the ILO and thus ensure representation by producers and consumers? The feasibility of such a proposal would depend to a large extent on the existence of "constituencies" on the side of producers and consumers, comparable to the constituencies of the ILO structure, trade unions and employer organizations respectively. Another way to introduce expertise into supervisory bodies is to enable representatives of the UN specialized agencies to participate in the proceedings of supervisory bodies. The possibility is already provided for in the ICESCR, and it has been used so far with varied success, as was already mentioned above. Nevertheless, such an approach can be useful in an attempt to bring expertise into in the supervisory processes. The technique is also used in the supervision procedure of the European Social Charter, where under Article 26 an ILO-representative can participate in the proceedings of the Committee of Experts.

Other issues which merit attention here include the question of secretarial support, and the frequency of the meetings of the supervisory body. Secretarial support to the supervisory body is of crucial importance; effective supervision depends on preparatory work, and on thorough research of the legal and factual elements of each case; without them no sound conclusions are possible. At present there are very few permanent supervisory structures. Experience shows that virtually all human rights supervisory bodies work under heavy time constraints. Would it not be advisable to create a permanent body, with salaried members?

128

4.2 Powers.

In an examination of the powers of a supervisory body, a distinction can be made between the powers to ensure adequate information in order to perform the review function of supervision, and the powers to persuade governments to remedy violations of human rights.

4.2.1 Powers to ensure adequate information.

Information is essential for any form of supervision. The experience of reporting procedures shows two major pitfalls: the non-submission of reports or their delays, and inadequacy or insufficiency of the information contained in the reports submitted. If the failure to submit a report is due to the unwillingness of the government, there are no remedies, except the possibility to publicize such instances in an attempt to mobilize shame. If, however, the failure to report is not due to unwillingness, but to a lack of familiarity with the obligations and procedures, or to a lack of trained staff, there are several ways to overcome these problems. An example, frequently used in intergovernmental practice, is to provide governments with guidelines or questionnaires for reporting. If necessary, the secretariats of supervisory bodies could give assistance to governments in the preparation of reports, e.g. by organizing training seminars for government officials.
Governments will not always provide detailed information on their conduct in the field of human rights, nor on the situation in the country. International supervision is at variance with national sovereignty. In this context one author[20] used the term "paper façade"; States describe the situation in their country in more favourable terms than reality would warrant, or give details only on legislation, and not on the practical impact of such legislation. For those reasons, supervisory bodies should have the power to verify, and supplement, the data contained in governmental reports. A supervisory body can be vested with powers to obtain sufficient and relevant data for the performance of the review function in different ways. One way is to empower the supervisory body to request additional information, on the lines set out in Art.9 of the Convention on the Elimination of All Forms of Racial Discrimination. Although the International Covenant on Civil and Political Rights does not contain a similar provision, the practice of the Human Rights Committee shows that States sometimes submit supplementary reports, to answer questions put to them by the members of the Human Rights Committee. Another method is to authorize the supervisory body to send reports, or parts thereof, to organizations competent to deal with the issues concerned, for comments or for action. Articles 18 and 22 of the ICESCR, and Art.40 of the ICCPR give such power to ECOSOC and the Human Rights Committee. Both bodies can submit State reports, or parts thereof, to the specialized agencies. As mentioned above, the participation of the specialized agencies in the supervisory process of the ICESCR has been of a different quality per agency. The very sending of reports to specialized agencies,

129

does not, of course, guarantee that the agencies will contribute useful comments or proposals. Yet another way to enhance the capabilities of supervisory bodies to obtain information, is to empower them to take into consideration information from other sources than governments. Such a competence is not self-evident under international law, and should be provided for expressly. At present, the reporting procedures for human rights treaties do not allow the supervisory bodies to consider sources other than government reports, however useful such additional information might be in breaking the "paper façade". Sources of additional information could be intergovernmental or nongovernmental organizations. With regard to the right to food, the accumulated knowledge and experiences of organizations like the Food and Agriculture Organization, or the World Food Council, could provide valuable information for the supervisory processes. It would be a major improvement for human rights supervisory bodies if they could, on their own initiative, make use of the information available within such agencies. Nongovernmental organizations could also be important sources of information supplementing States' reports. At present information from nongovernmental organizations cannot be officially used by any human rights supervisory organ in the context of reporting procedures, except in the case of the ILO. Yet, it is known that non-governmental organizations provide information to individual members of supervisory bodies on countries whose reports are under consideration.

Within the United Nations system, including the Commission on Human Rights, nongovernmental organizations having consultative status can submit information. A similar procedure might be elaborated with regard to the supervision of human rights treaties, including the ICESCR. It has to be recognized, however, that any such proposal will encounter the resistance of governments. During the drafting of the human rights Covenants, a proposal authorizing nongovernmental organizations to comment on the implementation of the Covenants, was rejected.[21]

An additional way to enhance the powers of a supervisory body to obtain information, is to give it the competence to conduct fact-finding inquiries in cases where State reports do not supply adequate information. Ideally, there should be an obligation for States to give *a priori* consent to such fact-finding. It is, however, unlikely that States would accept such a proposal. When the UN Commission on Human Rights recently completed the draft convention against torture and other cruel, inhuman or degrading treatment, one of the two provisions where no agreement could be reached upon, was article 20, which enables the envisaged supervisory body to initiate an inquiry if it receives reliable indications of torture being systematically practised in the territory of a State Party.[22]

4.2.2 Powers to persuade governments to remedy violations.

Once the review function has resulted in the ascertainment of a violation of a norm, the supervisory body has to carry out the correction function,

130

persuading governments to remedy the breach of the norm. Ideally, the supervisory body should have the power to formulate recommendations to the State Party concerned. Existing reporting systems in the human rights field show another picture. Of the UN sponsored treaties only the International Covenant on Civil and Political Rights and the Optional Protocol thereto, provide for the competence of the Human Rights Committee to address its recommendations and views directly to the State Party concerned. Art.21 of the International Covenant on Economic, Social and Cultural Rights, and Art.9(2) of the Convention on the Elimination of All Forms of Racial Discrimination stipulate that recommendations can be made to the General Assembly of the United Nations, but not directly to the States Parties.[23] A striking feature of the UN sponsored human rights treaties is the use of the adjective "general" in the provisions which deal with the recommendations to be made by the supervisory bodies. Such recommendations must not be specific.

The other instance during the drafting of the convention against torture, already referred to above, where no agreement could be reached dealt with the recommendations to be made by the envisaged supervisory body. To some States it was not acceptable that that body would be able to make "comments or suggestions"; they proposed that "comments" should be changed into "general comments". According to those States, the supervisory body should not be entitled to pass judgment on the measures taken by a State Party nor to recommend the adoption of additional or alternative measures.[24] This shows that there still is a tense relationship between international supervision and national sovereignty. It is not to be expected that this tension will erode quite soon.

This attitude towards international supervision adopted by some States raises the issue how the supervisory body for the right to food can ensure the cooperation of States in the performance of its duties. It should be kept in mind that realization of the right to food, especially the obligations to fulfil and to promote, may require the allocation of resources and (hu)manpower, and may only be achieved progressively. What sense does it make to recommend to a State to allocate more resources and (hu)manpower to the realization of the right to food in a case where a State hardly possesses such resources? In such circumstances, the supervisory body should be in a position to supply that particular State with assistance, in the form of money or technical assistance. In other words, the supervisory body should have a "carrot", to induce States to take the implementation of the right to food seriously. Only when the supervisory body for the right to food is in a position to create international solidarity, is it to be expected that States where the right to food is not yet realized will cooperate in the supervisory process of the right to food.

This proposition raises the issue of the place of a right to food supervisory body in the existing structure of intergovernmental organizations.

5. Place in the existing structure.

There are several theoretical possibilities which we might consider here. First of all, if ever a new international instrument on the right to food would be drafted, one might think of including in the draft a supervisory body along the lines of the Human Rights Committee, or the Committee for the Elimination of All Forms of Racial Discrimination. If such a supervisory body were to be established, it is hard to imagine how it could engage in providing technical assistance with regard to the right to food, which we stipulated to be a major requirement for such a body. Furthermore, in the light of the existence of already quite a number of international organizations dealing with either human rights or food issues[25], and already providing various forms of technical assistance, it seems superfluous to establish yet another organization. Seen from these perspectives, the existence of already a great number of organizations in this field, and the need of the ability to command international solidarity, indeed the ECOSOC, the present supervisory body of the ICESCR, comes to the fore as, in principle, a suitable organ. According to Arts. 62-64 of the Charter of the United Nations, the ECOSOC can make recommendations to the specialized agencies, and coordinate their activities, and under the provisions of the ICESCR, the ECOSOC can bring matters to the attention of the specialized agencies.

The reader may now be quite amazed to find, after the criticism of the working group of the ECOSOC which have been made in the previous pages, that the ECOSOC might provide a suitable organ for the supervision of the obligations relating to the right to food. But, in the author's opinion, there is no contradiction. Much of the criticism related to the composition and the working arrangements of the working group. Even under the terms of the International Covenant on Economic, Social and Cultural Rights, there are possibilities to change the character and composition of the working group. Since the ECOSOC has decided to review the composition and administrative arrangements regularly (resolution 1982/33), it can always decide to reorganize the working group along the proposals made above; a group of independent experts with sufficient time to meet and discuss States' reports, with adequate secretarial support, and with broad powers to secure information and the cooperation of States. At present there are already organs consisting of independent experts as subsidiary bodies of the ECOSOC, the UN Subcommission for the Prevention of Discrimination and the Protection of Minorities, and the Committee on Crime Prevention and Control.

As far as the powers to collect information and to react to violations are concerned, practice will then have to show whether such a group of individual experts will be able to use its powers as contained in the relevant documents in a dynamic and efficient way. The practice adopted to collect information could evolve along lines similar to the practice of the Human Rights Committee, additional information being requested of States to clarify issues which have remained obscure in the States' reports.

Although the ECOSOC, under the provisions of the ICESCR cannot make recommendations to States directly, the competence to address itself to various UN bodies and the specialized agencies seems to permit the infusion of right to food concerns into the work of these bodies and agencies.

6. Conclusions

In this short essay we have highlighted some aspects of the international supervision of the implementation of the right to food. The shortcomings of the present system of supervision of the International Covenant on Economic, Social and Cultural Rights have been touched upon, and possible improvements, either in the context of a new international instrument or in that of the present Covenant have been mentioned. If in a future instrument relating to the right to food, or in a restructuring of the present system of supervision of the International Covenant on Economic, Social and Cultural Rights, attention will be given to these issues, it will enhance the chance that a contribution to end the scourge of hunger and malnutrition will be made. But procedural improvements alone can never do the trick; it is absolutely necessary that consensus on the normative content of the right to food should be reached, before any supervisory procedure can function effectively. Absence of consensus on the normative content of the right to food will have a prohibitive effect on supervision; the supervisory body will not be able to set standards against which to measure States' conduct, and supervision will remain a futile exercise, regardless of the amount of powers conferred upon the supervisory body.

Notes.
(1) See the forthcoming book on supervisory mechanisms in international economic organizations by p. van Dijk (1984).
(2) See Shue, Basic Rights, Subsistence, Affluence and US Foreign Policy (1980) at 35-64.
(3) ILO Constitution Article 22.
(4) FAO Constitution Article IX.
(5) WHO Constitution Article 61.
(6) UNESCO Constitution Article VIII.
(7) See generally Landy, The Effectiveness of International Supervision, Thirty Years of I.L.O. Experience (1966).
(8) Dobbert, Some Aspects of the Law and Practice of FAO, in Schwebel (ed) The Effectiveness of International Decisions (1971), at 214-215.
(9) Roscam Abbing International Organizations in Europe and the Right to Health Care (1979), at 126.
(10) The reports of the ILO can be found in Un doc E/1978/27, E/1979/33, E/1980/35, E/1981/41, E/1982/41, and E/1983/40; the WHO report in Un doc E/1980/24; the FAO report in Un doc E/1981/22; and the UNESCO report in Un doc E/1982/10.
(11) ECOSOC resolution 1988(LX) established a reporting procedure in three stages. The first stage reports on the rights contained in Arts. 6-9 of the ICESCR had to be submitted initially on 1 September 1977, second stage reports on Arts. 10-12 had to be submitted initially on 1 September 1979, and third stage reports had to be submitted initially on 1 September 1981. Delays in the submission of reports is considerable: As of 1 March 1983, of the 46 first-stage reports due, 14 had not been submitted; of the of the 60 second-stage reports due, only 28 had been submitted; and of the 69 third-stage reports due, only 24 reports had been submitted. See Un doc E/1983/36. First-stage reports are reprinted in Un doc E/1978/8 + addenda, second-stage reports are reprinted in Un doc E/1980/6 + addenda, and third-stage reports are reprinted in Un doc E/1982/3 + addenda.

(12) The reports of the sessional working group to the ECOSOC are contained in Un doc E/1980/60, E/1981/64, E/1982/56, and E/1983/41.

(13) 27 ICJ Review, December 1981, 26-39.

(14) Un doc E/1981/6, par 11.

(15) Marie "International instruments relating to human rights, classification and chart showing ratifications as of 1 January 1984", 4 Human Rights Journal (1983) 4, 503-528.

(16) Interestingly, a Dutch court recently ruled that the rights laid down in the ICESCR could be directly applicable in cases where those rights had been realized. See 9 NJCM Bulletin 3 (1984) 245-252.

(17)Robertson, The Implementation System: International Measures, in Henkin (ed) The International Bill of Rights, 332, at 357.

(18) Sieghart, The International Law of Human Rights (1983) at 22.

(19) Robertson, loc. cit. at 358.

(20) Van Boven, Internationale instrumenten en procedures ter bevordering en bescherming van de rechten van de mens, in Rechten van de mens in mundiaal en europees perspectief, (1980) , 33 at 46-49.

(21) Landy, at 207 footnote 4, Un doc E/2573 at 12-13.

(22) Un doc E/CN.4/1984/72 par 52-56.

(23) Art. 40 International Covenant on Civil and Political Rights: "The Committee...shal transmit...general comments...to the States Parties..." Art.5(4) Optional Protocol: "The Committee shall forward its views to the State Party concerned..." Art.21 International Covenant on Economic, Social, and Cultural Rights: "The Economic and Social Council may submit...to the General Assembly reports with recommendations of a general nature..." Art.9(2) Convention on the Elimination of All Forms of Racial Discrimination: "The Committee shall report...to the General Assembly...suggestions and general recommendations..."

(24) Un doc E/CN.4/1984/72 par 49-51.

(25) Hopkins and Puchala, "Perspectives on the international relations of food" 32 International Organization 3 (1978) at 606, mention the existence of 89 multilateral intergovernmental organizations with food related objectives.

Human Rights Indicators: The Right to Food as a Test Case.

by
Katarina Tomaševski

1. Introduction

Quantifications are favoured in comparison with qualitative assessments because of their perceived objectivity and seeming neutrality. Numbers are considered to be "facts" or "proof" used as evidence for verbal statements, the latter are treated as "subjective evaluations" or "value judgements", and therefore in need of factual proof.

The "numbers do not lie" slogan spread into social sciences especially through indicators movement(s). There is currently hardly any area of social research left out of the use of quantifications, while computerization added to the spread of all-encompassing "mathematical barbarism". Human rights research has not escaped the use of quantifications. To prevent criticism of ideological prejudices or eurocentric bias, researchers resort to quantifications, implicitly asserting that those are objective and factual. States are often ranked by the criteria of ascertained human rights violations.

The terms "criteria" and "ascertained" bring up issues which are usually hidden behind the presentations of quantified results of research into the state of human rights. There is an implied assumption of a universal, or at least widespread, understanding of what a human rights violation is and what criteria for its ascertainment are. Computations presume an underlying conceptualization which is lacking more often than not.

It is easy to fall into the trap of seeming precision of reports and studies which substantiate their (qualitative) findings by figures and tables. Psychological reactions to statements like "there are millions dying of hunger" or "there are 862,739,501 people starving" are quite different. The latter invokes favourable reactions: the problem receives attention, as there is an entity ascertaining the exact figures and thereby the dimensions of the problem, and it can be presumed that something is being done about it.

An analogy with the existing quantifications of illiteracy in the world seems appropriate. We are quite used to reading statistics on illiteracy, even to quoting them ourselves. Divergencies in the conceptualization of illiteracy and in the method of estimating it are generally not visible from such quotations. Illiteracy is determined by the lack of any formal schooling or by the inability to read and write a simple text. Illiteracy is measured by asking the respondent whether he/she can read and write, or by testing the respondent's abilities. Results by variations of those four options are necessarily reflected in the quantifications given on the dimensions of illiteracy. Yet, they are not visible once the computations begin. The initial concepts are as a rule

135

not quoted any more. Figures are called facts and reported as such thereafter. [1]

The approach to human rights indicators has to take account of lessons learned in other fields of science. The often quoted statement of Albert Einstein should not be forgotten: "It is never possible to introduce only observable quantities into a theory. It is the theory which decides what can be observed." Applied to quantifications in social sciences, the basic rule amounts to the following: quantified results (data, indicators, tables) do not reflect reality, but theoretical assumptions of reality, and they cannot be interpreted without an insight into the underlying assumptions. A quotation from the book entitled Demystifying Social Statistics merits attentions:"... data are therefore conceived of as social products: statistics are not collected, but produced; research results are not findings, but creations". [2]

The use of quantifications does not make social research less biased than traditional methods are presumed to be. Indicators are construed according to a perception of what is important in the society (what is to be measured) and what an ideal society should look like (what is the yardstick for measurements, *i.e.* what is the perceived "reality" to be measured against).

The applicability of such a basic rule to the development of indicators for monitoring the realization of the right to food has to be used as caution against expectations that the use of indicators could amount to a breakthrough in the field.

Studies on the problem of world hunger inevitably begin with a statement on the dimensions of hunger in the world. Analyses of a human rights approach to world hunger quote in the introductions numbers - absolute or relative - of the hungry. Often, demands are addressed to relevant data-gathering agencies for more accurate figures; sometimes even expressions of disgust with the state of affairs: not even the number of the people starving is known, let alone how little is done to help them.

One can easily understand that people are dissatisfied - to say the least - by the lack of knowledge on dimensions of the world hunger. One can also agree with researchers who state that the precision of the assessment of the dimension of the problem has to be a basis for policies addressing it. Yet, would there be any change if the margins of error in estimates of the numbers of hungry in the world were smaller? Scott answers the question in the negative: "Whether poverty is globally 700 millions or 600 or 800 millions may have little practical importance, and it may not be worth spending a lot of money to find out which of these figures is correct." [3] He does give ideas on the development of monitoring schemes to determine the exact number of people deprived of food, water, shelter, employment, if there is a determined purpose connecting such data within a framework of policy changes.

Investments into a scheme which would yield precise statistics on the world hunger could be justified by a political commitment of the world community to alleviate hunger. The lack of such a commitment is common knowledge. More precise statistics would probably do little to increase it.

Which purposes could justify attempts to design and apply indicators for monitoring the realization of the right to food?

The first reason is the necessity to show that quite a lot of policies, measures, projects which are presented as solutions to the problem of hunger actually do not contribute to the alleviation of hunger. Monitoring changes over time is necessary and an identification of factors contributing to an increase or a decrease in the dimensions of hunger even more so. Yet, globalized impressionistic estimates contribute little to an insight of interplay of various food policies, economic policies in general, and their consequences on the fate of the individual when applied to a specific region, country or community.

An important aim of the human rights research is to supply evidence for allegations of governmental policies being (actually) against, instead of (as declared) in favour of the realization of human rights and the satisfaction of human needs. Research into actual policies (*e.g.* the relative priority of investments into food production for domestic consumption) as different, sometimes even contradictory to declared policies (*e.g.* the priority of the satisfaction of food needs of the population by increased food production) can be substantiated by the use of indicators.

Indicators are useful research tools when it comes to testing hypotheses on interlinkages within social systems. Assessment of governmental performance in the realization of human rights is generally linked only to identifying violations of human rights. One of the priorities in social research relevant for human rights is the determination of methods and measures for determining the over-all States" effort aimed at the realization of human rights. The identification of specific purposes of the utilization of available resources is one example. Another one, related specifically to food issues and insufficiently researched, is the interlinkage between patterns of land use and those of the satisfaction of food needs.

Ideally, human rights indicators should become quantified assessments of the state of the realization of human rights. That would imply the utilization of such indicators which treat the individual as the basic unit of observation. One does not need to explain how far away we are from such an ideal; it seems self-evident.

The Nation-State system is reflected in the current use of indicators by the adherence to national aggregate data for any issue (including estimates of the degree of satisfaction of food needs) and treating such aggregates as indicative of the state of the individual rights and needs. Countries which show the satisfaction of nutritional needs by 120% on the average will be treated as satisfying the nutritional needs of their people.

Also, getting beyond indicators related to things or their monetary value towards indicators relevant for the state of the people is far from easy. A conclusion of the study on social indicators relevant for the work of FAO reads: "...it is easier to collect statistics on commodities than on people, and ... it is more difficult to cut up statistics on population and living conditions into different sectors than it is to divide commodities." [4]

The first step which seems logical would be to compile whatever statistics there are on the state of the people, and extract those which deal with nutritional status. There are already indicators specifically designed for assessments of food consumption. However, this text claims that human rights indicators have yet to be developed, implicitly stating that the existing ones could not be just re-named into human rights indicators.

The explanation, given in the first part of the text, could be summarized in two following assertions: (1) the existing indicators jeopardize the universality of human rights by the adherence to the nation-state system. The individual is not treatcd as a human being, but as a citizen of a State, a member of a social stratum, or a part of a regional population, and (2) interrelatednes and indivisibility of human rights prevent the isolation of one human right, *e.g.* the right to food, and its analysis in a vacuum. Nutritional indicators cannot be treated as indicators on the realization of the right to food because the very satisfaction of nutritional needs is not the ultimate objective of the human right to food, only the essential condition for its realization. Nutritional needs can be met by the distribution of food packages while people receiving them cannot exercise their right to work. Nutritional needs can be satisfied to a large degree after a food harvest, but there can be a famine next season, because the majority of the population is dependent on the mercy of weather or, worse, that of landowners who could decide to grow export crops instead of food for domestic consumption. Nutritional needs of the whole population can be satisfied at the expense of the prevention of freedom of movement for peasants who have been tied to their lands for quite some generations.

Those few illustrations of situations which contain trade-offs unacceptable from a human rights perspective show that "dividing commodities", in the words of Nancy Baster, cannot be substituted for human rights indicators.

Yet, if one aims at the ideal, one could miss an opportunity of doing the possible. The fact that developing human rights indicators seems a remote vision should not prevent the development of proxy-indicators, *i.e.* of measures which cannot be named human rights indicators, but which come close to revealing the state of the realization of human rights.

An analysis of the existing indicators will show what is the dominant pattern of analysing ends and means of development from a human rights viewpoint, with a necessary focus on the right to food. The second step to be taken, designing indicators to spell out components of the human right to food which could be operationalized and quantified for data-gathering purposes, is more cumbersome. The conceptualization of the right to food is a pre-condition for such an endeavour and that is exactly the missing point in the current state of thinking on the right to food. However, the lack of a widely-accepted concept of the right to food is no excuse for the lack of attempts to generate it. Therefore, suggestions will be elaborated in the second part of the text.

138

2. The Right to Food and Development Analyses: Ends and Means of Development

There is a universal adherence to the postulate that the ultimate objective of development is the realization of human rights and/or the satisfaction of human needs. [5] While such a consensus exists only on a declaratory level and is of recent origin, the very fact that it could have been reached is a substantive progress of thinking about ends and means of development. Any survey of policy documents and literature on development for the last three decades would show a gradual, but definite shift towards human rights objectives from the initial ones.

The role of indicators is to provide quantitative assessments of the realization of determined objectives. The objectives are the necessary starting-point for the development of indicators, the nuclei of yardsticks to evaluate development. [6] If the realization of human rights is proclaimed as the ultimate objective of development, human rights can legitimately be introduced into development indicators for a determination of the degree of their realization within the process of development. The right to food has been singled out as an international development objective of a high priority rank, even if in its rudimentary form of the alleviation of starvation in the world.

A few steps backwards, into development planning of the previous decades, show that human rights objectives had not been treated as a development goal. The abundancy of literature on development issues permits only a brief and superficial survey to be done here, to illustrate the obstacles to an application of human rights indicators for evaluations of the earlier post-war development.

2.1. Focus on Economic Growth: People as Means of Development

Development is commonly understood as a process intended to lead towards a defined goal, whether it is an increased rate of economic growth, or elimination of illiteracy. Thus, the goal is an essential yardstick for the assessment of performance. The goals of the United Nations Development Decades changed substantially: The first insisted on economic growth of the developing countries, the second set forth equality of opportunity for countries and for individuals alike, the third (and the latest one) speaks about improvement of the well-being of the entire population. [7] Changes in development goal-setting were coupled, often preceded by changes in the measuring of development accomplishments. According to the aims of the First Development Decade, it should have been evaluated favourably for many of the middle income (or newly industrialized) developing countries. However, the conception of development changed in the meantime, placing egalitarian principles into the focus of new strategies for development. Thus, advocating fast economic growth came to be viewed as mixing up ends and means, good economic performance evaluated against existence and scope of absolute poverty, and differences in levels of living between and within countries. The generally increasing GNP would indicate progress, if the goals of the 1960s were taken as the yardstick. But, estimates of absolute poverty speak for the opposite conclusion. (It should be added that two contrary conclusions can be reached in this respect: if the relative numbers of undernourished and illiterate segments of the population are taken into account, they are decreasing; if absolute figures are calculated, they are increasing.) Development policy measures introduced during the Second Development Decade insisted on "human development" as a public investment which contributes to economic growth. People were treated as means of economic development. Investments into human resources and their efficient use were policy measures politically acceptable to international decision-makers and considered economically efficient by analysts. [8] Accordingly, education, health, nutrition, and fertility were given prominent place in policy recommendations. Consequences of structural changes which took place in many developing countries (particularly those with good economic performance), notably industrialization and urbanization, did not (yet) raise doubts on social costs of pursuing general development policies which had been recommended. Only proposals for alleviating some of the worst aspects of social costs of such economic growth were considered at that time (*e.g.* cheap housing and sanitary facilities for urban slums). [9] Achievements in human needs satisfaction were primarily measured by inputs (governmental expenditures devoted to specific social sector). First objections to such methods were voiced by analysts who proved that most of the inputs do not reach those whose needs have to be satisfied. The beginning of the 1980's was strongly marked by an orientation of U.N. policies towards human needs, the people's needs, rights, aspirations were proclaimed as the end of over-all development. Evaluations of successes and failures of the Development Decades were interwoven with radically new proposals, supported by empirical evidence of poor development performance by the criterion of the satisfaction of human needs in the past decades.

2.2. Focus on human needs: people as the ends of development

The Third United Nations Development Decade embodies the basic policy-shift towards satisfying fundamental human needs and emphasizes problems of those segments of the population below the existential minimum of nutrition, health care, access to safe water, shelter, literacy, *i.e.* the minimum level of living conditions deemed to be life-sustaining.

Economy is oriented towards means; from the human rights viewpoint it has to be treated as an instrument; therefore, the maximization of economic effects cannot be recognized as a social objective. [10] The priority attributed to economic growth over social development which has been an undisputed fact for a substantive period of post-war development still acquires influential advocates: the necessity of breaking the *circulus inextricabilis* of poverty, hunger, illiteracy and zero-growth requires fostering economic growth, which becomes treated as the priority, taking precedence over social development least in the time-frame. However, social costs which result from such a priority-setting demonstrate that fundamental human rights and needs have to be observed irrespective of "objective conditions". Otherwise the very achievement of economic aims is jeopardized by emerging social disturbances.

It is worth quoting here a conclusion reached in the United Nations Study on the implementation of economic, social, and cultural rights (hereinafter: the Ganji Report). [11] When projecting the future of the economic performance of the quickly-growing countries, it states: "In most cases, the chief problem in the continuing economic progress of such countries consisted of obstacles to their internal peace and political stability." [12] The ones the Ganji Report pointed out were unemployment rates and food insufficiency, specifically decreasing food production per capita and sky-rocketing food prices.

Two other studies point in the same direction as the Ganji Report. Olson stated, concluding his research on developing countries which achieved considerable economic success, that "until further research is done, the presumption must be that rapid economic growth, far from being the source of domestic tranquility it is sometimes supposed to be, is rather a disruptive and destabilizing force that leads to political instability". [13] More of the same is coming from human rights research. In one of the first attempts to design a scheme for cross-national empirical research of human rights implementation, Strouse and Claude concluded that there is "the negative influence of rapid economic development on political rights." [14]

Interrelatedness of human rights has thus been affirmed by empirical data, and the case for human rights strengthened by findings on negative impact of the neglect of human rights, or their widespread and continuous violations, on the continuation of economic growth.

It has been recognized, if not stated explicitly often enough, that the distribution of development benefits is an outcome of politics. Even if economic considerations were determining factors, investments into the people came to be viewed as necessary conditions for development.

Any scheme of indicators in regard to the realization of economic, social, and cultural rights has to include an assessment, and possibly an evaluation, of governmental performance. The adherence of a State to international legal instruments pertaining to human rights can be an initial indice of its commitment, the constitutional and legal provisions can be analysed as additional indices. However, the role of such legal instruments can in practice be depreciated to window-dressing for policies negating or violating human rights. The necessity of analysing the realization of human rights in a development context therefore requires the inclusion of the impact of governmental policies on the state of human rights as a subject-matter for inquiry. Such a need is expressed in the Ganji Report in the following terms: "...the need to plan development with a view to the fulfilment of the human rights of individuals and to establish methods for appraising the impact of development on individuals." [15]

141

Any such inquiry is a difficult task for a number of reasons. Suffice it here to mention just a few: (1) development priorities still focus on economic growth, thus neglecting its social impacts and costs, [16] (2) economic objectives are accorded priority over social and cultural goals, development analyses reflect such priorities by using economic indicators, [17] (3) the status of the individual is not an independent item either within development planning or development analysis, individuals arc lumped together into nations, countries, regions; statistical averages of their needs and their living conditions are used as indices of their actual condition, [18], (4) the global structure of power and wealth is clearly reflected in both the quantity and quality of the available information. [19]

There is an enormous diversity of development models, strategies, and policies, applied in a heterogeneous world divided by numerous criteria, but united - for our purposes - by the sole postulate of universality of human rights. It does not seem possible to design a unified system of indicators and apply it globally, yet there is a need to do so. Obstacles are tremendous: from great dissimilarities of development strategies, to divergencies in levels of development, and to insufficient numbers of ratifications of relevant human rights instruments. Common sense pleads for not using the same "measure" for Sweden and Somalia with respect to human well-being, while norms of international law speak against measuring the implementation of specific obligations for states which did not undertake them. Nevertheless, universality of human rights requires universal applicability of norms for their implementation. A currently used method for resolving such controversies is the adoption of universally applicable minimum standards for the implementation of human rights while leaving to each country the determination of what is "adequate", "appropriate", "desirable", and the like. In spite of the fact that a theory of rights is lacking, it was possible to achieve some consensus within the U.N. on the concept of fundamental human rights, on the principle of indivisibility and interdependence of human rights, and on priorities needed for their implementation. In the process of standard-setting little has been achieved in the domain of economic, social, and cultural rights, but significant developments occurred in the closely related area of measuring the satisfaction of basic human needs, i.e. human rights treated as priorities in terms of their survival relevance. The focus is on nutrition, health, education, and housing, implicitly asserting the right to life as the most fundamental human right and essential requisites for sustaining human life as principal areas of inquiry.

From a human rights viewpoint, there are justifiable objections to the use of indicators based on highly aggregated data for an assessment of the state of realization of individual rights. Their availability - while not acceptable for making judgements on the actual human condition - is a step ahead from the previous exclusivity of economic goals and economic indicators which treated human beings, at best, as "human potential", "human capital", or "human resources". [20]

Existing attempts to design universally applicable indicators are often blamed for eurocentric bias. Measurement techniques are not value-neutral, there is a danger of assuming universal validity of culture-specific and ideology-specific assumptions, values, and rules of conduct. The lack of precision in the relevant international instruments does not make such a task easier. [21] An evaluation implicit in any use of indicators follows the values of the development model which was taken as the starting-point for the determination of indicators to be used. The field of human rights, as applied research, has to promote human rights as a value.

It means that any evaluation has to assess the impact of policies, measures, activities on the enjoyment of human rights defined on the basis of their universality. For example, if analysing priorities of the resource allocation and ascertaining the place of human rights within it, one cannot take increased investments into food production as an indice of commitment to the implementation of the right to food; one has to use indices on the actual consumption or, better, improvements of the nutritional status. Even those are not satisfactory: aggregate national or regional data do not reveal existing inequalities. Nutrition policies might not (and generally do not) take into account more than average nutritional needs of "average" individuals, thus leaving out culturally determined patterns, and individual differences and preferences.

The dominance of aggregate indicators in the current usage is an instructive source of information on limitations of quantitative analyses with potential global coverage; the individual as the unit of measurement, or the individual-based standards have yet to be developed. Aggregate measurements are insufficient, sometimes even irrelevant for human rights research. [22]

3. Classifications of Countries: Analytical Tool or Jeopardy of the Universality of Human Rights?

A common approach in the development of indicators is categorization of countries of the world by various criteria. Issues of economic, social, and cultural rights would fit into categorizations by the criterion of the level of development. The most widespread one is dividing the world into the West (the developed market-economy countries), the East (developed planned-economy countries), and the South (the third world, developing countries, underdeveloped countries).

There are at least two policy issues supporting such divisions: States have the exclusive right to determine their development strategies and priorities, [23] and the realization of economic, social and cultural rights is regularly postulated as dependent upon the existing level of development.

The first policy issue is one of the stumbling-blocks of the international proclamation and protection of human rights - the balance between State sovereignty and international law of human rights. [24]

The second one is regularly invoked in analyses of the nature of human economic, social, and cultural rights: while their realization requires governmental intervention and investment, their genuinely political nature is often hidden behind statements on the "objective conditions" determining the

143

possible extent of the realization of human rights, or assertions of different development models adopted by States requiring re-defining of human rights.

In the words of Valticos, "nothing can be more dangerous for the protection of human rights than this sceptical relativism. Reasoning of this kind would lead to a denial of the recognition by mankind of certain common values which transcend differences of race, faith, political structure, culture and economic development and which are based on the equality, freedom, and solidarity of all men." [25]

Statistics and indicators follow the dominance of the nation-state system and accordingly utilize national aggregates as essential indices for determining the nutritional status of the people. Distributional indicators, revealing the pattern of access to food within countries and coming closer to information about the actual nutritional status of the individual do not exist for a number of countries. [26] Countries are the main units of measure for assessments of the satisfaction of nutritional requirements of the people. Annual statistical surveys are a starting-point in determining degrees of the realization of the estimated average nutritional requirements in the world. [27] The accumulated experiences teach us that the minimum nutritional requirements have to be exceeded by 15-20% on the national level (because of unequal distribution) to satisfy the initial presumption that a specific country meets - on the average - at least the minimum nutritional needs of its population.

The attention is focused on countries which annually reflect the aggregate satisfaction of nutritional needs below or just at the estimated minimum level. The identification of countries which belong to that group is complicated by the existence of several different categorizations in current usage: there are the least developed countries, most seriously affected countries, food priority countries, and low-income food-deficit countries. [28]

An example of the indices currently used is the FAO listing of selected developing countries according to the criteria of estimated per capita calorie intake and the estimated number of the undernourished in those countries. See the table: per caput calorie supply and percentage and number of individuals undernourished in selected countries 1969/71 and 1972/74.

An example of what is not available is given in the FAO estimate of shortfalls in per capita daily calorie supply and percentages of populations of selected developing countries with estimated calorie intake below the minimum. The latter is unknown for 14 out of the 50 countries listed. See the table: shortfall in per capita cereal consumption (1965 - 1977) calorie supplies and requirements (1972-1974).

144

	Calorie per 1969/71	Supply caput 1972/74	Critical limit (1.2 BMR)	Population with Calorie Intake below 1.2 BMR			
Country				Percentage		Number(1000)	
				1969/71	1972/74	1969/71	1972/7
Afghanistan	1947	2000	1548	43	37	7301	6774
Argentina	3342	3281	1631	2	2	475	494
Bangladesh	1945	1949	1512	38	38	25723	27026
Bolivia	1808	1860	1545	52	45	2486	2315
Botswana	2116	2025	1517	33	36	204	237
Brazil	2507	2538	1545	14	13	13329	13478
Burma	2184	2131	1487	19	22	5272	6555
Cameroon	2407	2383	1526	14	16	817	990
Chad	2088	1765	1526	34	54	1238	2063
Chile	2802	2736	1554	11	15	1031	1484
Colombia	2152	2164	1487	29	28	6402	6806
Dominican Rep.	2023	2158	1517	38	33	1650	1581
Ecuador	2062	2087	1507	30	30	1809	1995
Egypt	2676	2632	1557	7	8	2333	2866
Ethiopia	2168	2051	1512	26	38	6462	10174
Ghana	2273	2302	1498	22	20	1898	1866
Guatemala	2015	1987	1493	38	38	2013	2197
Guinea	2071	1994	1517	38	41	1490	1725
Haiti	1964	2029	1523	43	38	1821	1678
Honduras	2178	2052	1517	32	38	817	1075
India	2034	1970	1486	26	30	141214	175162
Indonesia	1965	2033	1507	34	30	40619	38742
Iran	2162	2326	1508	23	15	6523	4647
Iraq	2300	2392	1528	17	14	1591	1447
Ivory Coast	2608	2626	1517	9	8	388	371
Kenya	2241	2137	1517	24	30	2699	3722
Korea Rep.	2707	2749	1531	4	4	1255	1332
Liberia	1943	1976	1517	42	37	640	603
Libya	2553	2698	1526	13	7	252	149
Madagaskar	2463	2360	1517	14	17	970	1285
Malawi	2340	2414	1517	19	14	828	655
Mali	2056	1759	1526	38	49	1918	2656
Mauritania	1993	1867	1517	36	48	418	591
Mexico	2661	2693	1512	9	8	4528	4435
Morocco	2480	2593	1528	14	10	2118	1650
Mozambique	2019	1989	1536	34	36	2800	3173
Nepal	2041	2015	1486	27	29	3033	3499
Nicaragua	2417	2384	1523	17	18	335	391
Niger	1989	1857	1526	36	47	1446	2048
Pakistan	2148	2132	1512	24	26	14508	17223
Paraguay	2781	2723	1487	6	8	138	200
Peru	2312	2328	1526	23	23	3047	3326
Philippines	1945	1953	1517	35	35	13161	14550
Saudi Arabia	2361	2411	1534	14	12	1084	1014
Senegal	2229	2181	1526	25	25	981	1053
Sierra Leone	2311	2254	1498	20	21	529	596
Somalia	1874	1916	1492	42	40	1171	1202
Sudan	2096	2067	1526	30	30	4709	5153
Swaziland	2072	2118	1536	35	33	143	147
Syria	2462	2525	1536	12	10	750	683
Tanzania	1964	1958	1498	35	35	4646	5076
Thailand	2295	2315	1511	18	18	6434	7095
Togo	2164	2167	1498	24	24	470	510
Tunisia	2213	2378	1514	24	16	1233	877
Turkey	2833	2830	1577	7	7	2466	2655
Venezuela	2405	2399	—	7	7	739	806
Zaire	2022	1848	1504	34	44	7357	10244
Zambia	1980	2016	1517	35	34	1503	1600

Per Capita Calorie Supply and Percentage and Number of Individuals Undernourished in Selected Countries 1969/71 and 1972/74

Source: The Fourth World Food Survey
FAO, Rome, 1977, pp. 127-128

145

Shortfall in Per Capita Cereal Consumption (1965-77) Calorie Supplies and Requirements (1972-74)

Country	Consumption per 1 capita Adjustment Index (%) (1965-77)	Per capita daily calorie supply as percentage of requirements (1972-74)	Percentage Population with calorie intake Below 1.2 BMR (1972-74)
Africa			
Botswana	4.1	87	36
Cameroon	2.7	103	16
Central African Republic	10.3	103	N.A.
Chad	14.9	74	54
Benin	4.5	89	N.A.
Egypt	4.1	105	8
Ethiopia	6.0	88	38
Gambia	2.6	97	N.A.
Ghana	11.8	100	20
Guinea	2.7	26	41
Ivory Coast	3.5	114	8
Kenya	3.3	92	30
Lesotho	23.9	97	N.A.
Madagascar	2.0	104	17
Malawi	6.2	104	14
Mali	6.8	75	49
Mauritania	8.7	81	48
Mauritius	2.7	107	N.A.
Mozambique	3.7	85	36
Niger	13.0	79	47
Rwanda	6.7	91	N.A.
Senegal	2.9	92	25
Sierra Leone	3.6	98	21
Somalia	6.0	83	40
Sudan	6.8	88	30
Tanzania	3.1	84	35
Togo	6.3	94	24
Uganda	6.2	92	N.A.
Upper Volta	8.7	73	N.A.
Zambia	4.4	87	34
Zaire	2.1	83	44
Average	6.4	94.1	
Asia			
Afghanistan	3.6	82	37
Bangladesh	1.9	84	38
Sri Lanka	3.6	94	N.A.
India	8.3	89	30
Indonesia	5.5	94	30
Nepal	7.2	92	29
Pakistan	3.5	92	26
Philippines	2.4	86	35
Yemen A R	3.0	82	N.A.
Yemen D R	6.7	85	N.A.
Average	4.6	88.0	
Latin America			
Bolivia	2.5	78	45
Dominican R.	9.9	95	33
El Salvador	2.3	82	N.A.
Guatemala	3.7	91	38
Guyana	7.4	103	N.A.
Haïti	3.5	90	38
Honduras	6.0	91	38
Jamaica	8.8	118	N.A.
Paraguay	4.0	118	8
Average	5.8	96.2	

The index is calculated as the average of the rations of per capita shortfalls to actual per capita consumption in shortfall years.
Source: Calorie data from FAO, Fourth World Food Survey, 1977, appendices C and M.
Approaches to World Food Security FAO, Rome, 1983, pp. 127-128

3.1. Food Aid and the Human Right to Food

In terms of the essential provisions of the ICESCR, there is a division of obligations between States and the international community as to the realization of the right to food. The latter has been burdened by the task of developing a global system of access to food based on the criterion of need. The interpretation should be linked to the ICESCR determination of the essential obligation of States to implement policies and measures for the realization of human rights to the utmost of their available resources.

It would be a worthwhile endeavour to find out to which extent need is a determinant of development assistance; particularly food needs criteria for granting assistance, most relevant for its satisfaction. A human right perspective requires the inclusion of the notion of human rights by linking development assistance to human rights criteria. The promotion of human rights has been unanimously advocated as a goal, but without precise guidelines how the promotion could and/or should be accomplished in the practice of development assistance. The problem of an impact of the neglect for or violations of human rights by the recipient government on development assistance schemes is even more controversial.[29]

With respect to the right to food, analyses of the existing food-aid regimes merit attention, especially principles on which they are based. An essential issue of food aid from the human rights viewpoint is the determination of eligibility for food aid. The development of food-aid regimes gradually affirmed human needs as a determining factor, and introduced the notion of development needs into the criteria.

The Guidelines and Criteria for Food Aid reaffirm the basic criteria for food aid developed in the late 1970's (priority for low-income, food-deficit countries; lower priority for projects having envisaged benefits for the poorest segments of the population in other developing countries; special consideration for the commitment of the recipient country to self-reliant food policies)[30]. They are applicable not only to the multilateral food aid systems (the UN system and Food Aid Convention regime), but also to bilateral schemes. [31]

The aggregate estimates available raise an important question: should attention be focused on the number of countries which show the national average of per capita food supplies being below estimated nutritional requirements of their populations, or on the estimated numbers of people experiencing malnutrition? An example from the latest FAO World Food Report: "According to FAO estimates, about a quarter of the total population of all developing countries outside the Asian centrally planned economies cannot count on being able to consume an adequate diet. Most of the countries where malnutrition is widespread are in Africa, but the majority of malnourished people are in the more populous areas of Asia." [32]

The Guidelines single out low-income food-deficit countries as principal beneficiaries of food aid, adding as supplementary area projects intended to benefit the poorest segments of the population in other developing countries. There is an additional criterion envisaged:

147

"An important consideration in allocating food aid to the eligible countries should be a strong commitment on the part of their governments to development policies for achieving self-reliance, reducing poverty, and improving nutritional status particularly in rural areas." [33]

Such criteria bring back the underlying requirement of commitment to the goals specified (self-reliance, reduction of poverty, improvement of nutritional status) both on the part of donors and of recipients of food aid. If such a commitment existed, food aid would not be a marginal measure for marginalized people. Yet, if such a commitment did not exist at all, there would be no food aid. Food aid is one of the current topics of heated debates. Attitudes vary between the extreme range of treating it as a panacea for world hunger, and the opposite one of discarding food aid as acceptable means of satisfying either nutritional or developmental needs of actual or potential recipients.[34]

An integration of the right to food approach and food aid problems requires a re-evaluation of food aid from the right to food viewpoint. An easy way would be taking the right to food in isolation from other human rights, and conceptualizing it as the right to get adequate food (*i.e.* "the right to be fed"). Such an approach induced severe criticism, drawing upon a right to food approach to food aid. Collins writes: "The right to food should not and cannot be addressed in terms of the right to charity, the right to be a recipient, the the right to so-called food aid, the right to surplus of some nations or farmers."[35] Even common sense would plead against a "right to be fed", as the very term implies a humiliation of those who are being fed. There are, of course, factors justifying the food aid regimes in their current state. The first one is the origin: food aid was initiated as surplus disposal, therefore the supply-side still takes precedence over the demand-side, that is, the decisive factor is not human needs. The second reason is the evident need of food aid within disaster relief systems (whether for natural or man-made disasters), but also for the continuation and increase of food aid until food-deficit countries could introduce and implement changes needed for their eventual food-sufficiency. [36] It has to be kept in mind that some of them do not have sufficient natural resources for achieving ever food-sufficiency.

The need to introduce a right to food approach into analyses of food aid brings back the necessity to abolish single-issue approaches within a human rights analysis. The evolution of conceptualizations of food aid (from surplus disposal, over meeting of nutritional needs, to providing a favourable development impact) demonstrates the increased awareness of interlinkages within global and national development policies and between their specific objectives. [37]

It took the food aid regime two decades to incorporate the interrelationship of the criteria of surplus disposal and the requirement of fostering indigenous development into its guiding principles; the same process does not have to be repeated now with respect to human rights requirements (*i.e.* those enabling individual development). Experiences already accumulated can be used for a design of comprehensive schemes integrating the distribution of surpluses (the obligation of the international community as a whole to provide for world food security) into the framework of national food strategies (an integrated approach to the food system as a whole with a main objective to satisfy nutritional needs of the people by mobilizing all the available resources).

It is being increasingly realized that neither nutritional needs should be separated from other human needs, nor the right to food can be isolated from other human rights. Research into effects of nutrition interventions proves that such measures can be accepted only temporarily and exceptionally. [38] Research into human rights proves that the postulate of indivisibility of human rights has to be taken as the guiding principle.

Within such a framework, proposals for solving food problems could acquire the requisite comprehensiveness, including linkages within and between human rights and development. The World Food Council proposals aimed at ensuring higher food availability stress the need of their integration with "schemes to generate employment, incomes, and assets specifically to the poor." [39]

Nutritionists have begun to include the human rights perspectives into their development of policy proposals. An account of a workshop on food and nutrition policy includes an explicit statement on the human rights aspect of nutrition: "if the poor were considered the subject of the goal-planning process rather than the object, then food-related goals would be formulated as only one of many human rights."[40] (emphasis added)

An important issue of the development of human rights indicators is the rejection of the implication of the often-used divisions of the world into regions and countries by whatever criteria, thus making the nature and scope of human rights dependent upon the status of the individual within the existing structures, the determining factor being the position within the nation-State system. Different sets of the divisions of the world have already been accused of advocating "sub-standards for sub-humans" or "global apartheid" if applied to human rights.

The significance of the establishment of universal standards for the realization of human rights cannot be over-emphasized. It does not amount to requiring the impossible, that is, the immediate and full realization of the whole range of human rights for all irrespective of actual possibilities. The ICESCR cautiously spells out the "progressive realization" requirement. Yet, the universally applicable standards have to be upheld, even if their observance can today be required for no more than the minimum degree.

4. Towards Universally Applicable Indicators: Minimum Nutritional Standards

If one reads either scholarly works or international instruments dealing with nutrition, enough proposals can be found as to the necessity of developing a scheme for the assessment of the nutritional status of the people. The World Food Conference, held 10 years ago, referred to the problem of the lack of information and suggested an approach to its solving. The Conference recognized that "information on food consumption patterns and on their consequences for the nutrition and health status of the majority of the population in developing countries is insufficient and inadequate"; therefore, the primary task envisaged was the assessment of the character, extent, and degree of malnutrition. It also agreed upon an ambitious plan of setting up a global nutrition surveillance system by recommending:

"That a global nutrition surveillance system be established by the Food and Agriculture Organization of the United Nations, the World Health Organization, and the United Nations Children's Fund to monitor the food and nutrition conditions of the disadvantaged groups of the population at risk, and to provide a method of rapid and permanent assessment of all factors which influence food consumption patterns and nutritional status".[41]

Such a global system does not exist, but even if it had been established, it would remain questionable whether equating the realization of the right to food with estimates of the nutritional status of the population were acceptable. The right to food, as already emphasized, means something different from getting sufficient quantity and quality of food, from "a right to be fed." [42]

The awareness of the insufficiency of calorie / protein measurements and of economic indicators for the assessment of the status of the individual has entered current thinking on indices for monitoring development. A rather extensive quotation from the regulations pertaining to the evaluation of development projects by the International Fund for Agricultural Development merits attention:

"The main objectives of the Fund - to reduce rural poverty, improve nutrition, and increase food production - cannot be judged or analyzed in terms of pure economic indicators, such as food production or agricultural growth rates. Certainly Fund projects must meet reasonable standards of economic viability, but such standards cannot suffice either to select future IFAD activities or to evaluate their results. Even attempts to extend the traditional cost-benefit criteria from economic to social objectives, by assigning weights to certain social objectives like income distribution and employment, fall short of measuring the Fund's broad development objectives - to satisfy the basic needs of the people in developing countries in a self-reliant and positive social environment. The Fund would attempt to evolve, over a period of time and in the light of its own experience and that of other agencies concerned, new indicators and analytical techniques that take account of the objectives of the Fund. [43]

An estimate of the extent of nutritional deprivation is a necessary condition for designing and implementing policies for the eradication of hunger. It is far from easy, as those who have to be target groups - the hungry - are the most difficult to reach, whether by statistical surveys or by nutrition intervention measures. Statistics on world hunger reach different results: there is no exactness in the numbers of the hungry in the world supplied by the relevant data-gathering agencies.

It might seem superfluous to attempt to establish precise statistics: the fact of world hunger being widespread is common knowledge. An editorial in

CERES emphasizes negative aspects of such endeavours:

"Academic squabbles about the methodology for estimating the extent of undernourishment can, especially if oversimplified and dramatized in mass media, begin to create doubts about the validity of any estimates. The fact that there is an enormous range in these estimates, reflecting, among other things, differing assumptions about what constitutes an adequate intake of food, should not be permitted to obscure that even conservative estimates indicate that nearly a quarter of the total population of the developing regions of the world... do not have access to food to provide for their minimum energy needs." [44]

An issue to be addressed could be stated as follows: there is sufficient food produced globally to prevent starvation; yet, access to food (access to land to produce it or access to work to earn it) does not follow requirements of human needs, but those of the power structure.

It was argued here that universality of human rights demands universal criteria for their observance; an application of different criteria for different parts of humanity cannot be tolerated. Nevertheless, the existing differences in the actual implementation of governmental obligations with respect to human rights have to be taken as facts. In addition, possibilities of the observance of human rights and obstacles to their recognition and respect have to be included into such an analysis, also as facts. It would be ideal, but it is therefore impossible, to demand full and immediate realization of the right to food for all from all States. Such a demand would immediately encounter the obstacle of actually existing possibilities; common sense pleads for a gradual approach, which is backed by the wording of Article 2 of the ICESCR. Its text requires each State to take steps:

"to the maximum of its available resources, with a view to achieving progressively the full realization of the rights recognized in the present Covenant by all appropriate means."

Progressive achievement of the full realization of the right to food could be interpreted as including the elimination of starvation as a minimum level, based on the proclamation of freedom from hunger as the fundamental human right.

There is a lot of disagreement in the current literature on the determination of minimum nutritional needs, and consequently on the number of people who experience nutritional deprivation. [45] Lawyers are not qualified to enter such debates. If a norm defining the minimum level of the realization of the right to food for all is to be established, a universally applicable minimum standard of the satisfaction of nutritional needs has to be determined for monitoring its observance.

The proclamation of the right to adequate food for all as the full-fledged human rights norm does not preclude the determination of a minimum standard which should become an internationally accepted and binding principal benchmark for obligations as to the observance of the right to food and of human rights.

Any attempt to summarize results of the work already done towards an establishment of universally applicable minimum standards for nutrition has to begin with widely accepted - if also widely criticized [46] -calorie/protein requirements. As they already gained acceptance in reports on the state of nutrition in the world, perhaps the best approach is to elaborate upon them. While such requirements are insufficient from the human rights viewpoint, they could be accepted as minimum targets for demanding universal realization of the minimum scope of the right to food.

An assessment of nutritional impact of any policy which aims at the eradication of hunger is an essential tool for its evaluation. An improvement or a deterioration of the nutritional status of the population, in aggregate data, does not reveal the status of the enjoyment of the right to food at the level of the individual. It also does not reveal the effort of the particular government to implement its obligations relating to the right to food.

5. The Development of Right to Food Indicators

5.1. Indicators of States' Performance

The universality of human rights provides the foundation for conceptual unity within the conceptual framework of the recognition and observance of human rights. The advantage of quantifications is their requirement of uniform and precise definitions of what is to be measured. The development of human rights indicators, in such an early stage, cannot supply answers which would claim universal applicability; formulating questions has to be dealt with first.

Abstract notions have to be operational to be amenable to empirical investigation. The use of quantitative methods demands the formulation of hypotheses which are later tested by the use of quantitative methods.

Human rights research is dominated by lawyers and they are hesitant to involve themselves in quantitative methods. Yet, the role of lawyers in developing and clarifying the normative standards related to human rights is indispensable. To clarify what is required to realize the human right to food means to operationalize the general postulate of "progressive realization" and to make possible investigations whether such requirements are in practice realized, neglected or violated.

There seems to be a misunderstanding as to the notion of the human right to food, culminating in assertions of governments realizing human rights for their people. Governments are obliged to create conditions for the realization of human rights, and it is the people who realize their rights. Such a clarification is necessary for the explanation of dual requirements upon human rights indicators: they have to "measure" governmental effort to implement its obligations relating to human rights, and the state of the actual realization of human rights.

For practical purposes it is essential to prove the existence of the international law norm relating to the right to food, and to confine any proposed indicators for monitoring its realization to the scope of the norm.

An explicit norm on the right to food is the necessary basis for elaborating its content, for demanding its realization, and also for monitoring it.

Obligations which are necessary for the implementation of the right to food could be specified along the structure outlined in the scheme below.

A basic agreement on the insufficiency of normative standards for economic, social, and cultural rights in the ICESCR has been shared by all researchers who attempted to operationalize those rights in order to find out to what extent their realization could be monitored and degrees of their observance supplied by empirical evidence.

More precise normative standards have to be extracted from constitutional and legislative enactments of the particular country. While one might say that constitutional guarantees do not give any insight into the degree of the realization of a specific right, such guarantees have to be taken to represent the nature and the scope of norms and standards defining a particular human right. [48] There is a difference between constitutional and/or legal provisions which just proclaim a specific right, and those which spell our guarantees for its realization. A similar difference can be established between those provisions recognizing a particular right as a human right, and those providing for indices for its monitoring and mechanisms for its protection.

The obligation to recognize the right to food means to include it into human rights law, first, by the adherence to and incorporation of provisions of the ICESCR into national law, and/or by the introduction of the right to food into constitutionally guaranteed human rights. [47]

The obligation to promote the right to food includes the requirement of the enactment of national legislation leading towards progressive realization of the right to food. This is a complex topic to define *in abstracto*, as it requires taking account of a wide range of issues having an impact on the right to food- from the need for agrarian reforms, to the necessity of matching the calorie/protein requirements with the protection of cultural rights by favouring culturally satisfactory diets. The complexity of issues to be dealt with is aggravated by differences with respect to actual possibilities of states to implement obligations relating to the right to food.

The achieved state of the satisfaction of nutritional needs has to be assessed by the use of the principal criterion of resource availability. The general international law norm requiring progressive realization of the right to food can be interpreted as demanding governments to incorporate specific targets aimed at progressive realization of the right to food into their development plans, so that their realization could be monitored by the use of indicators. Particular objectives of States cannot be expressed by any universal norm. A State cannot be expected to achieve the same nutritional level for its population as one which starts from a previously higher level, but each is required to make an effort to improve the state of the realization of the right to food for its people. Envisaged objectives can be subsumed under three levels: (A) to raise nutritional levels, *e.g.* by incorporating quantified objectives into the development plans and provisions for monitoring their realization, (B) to eradicate hunger and malnutrition, that is, to identify target groups and adopt appropriate intervention measures to eliminate hunger,

153

A SCHEME OF OBLIGATIONS NECESSARY FOR THE REALIZATION OF THE HUMAN RIGHT TO FOOD

Types of obligations	content of specific obligations
to recognize or respect	to include the right to food into human rights law (the ratification of the ICESCR, the inclusion of the right to food into constitutionally guaranteed human rights, etc.) to include the realization of the right to food into development objectives (the incorporation of the goal of adequate food for all into objectives of the development strategy, the adoption of a national food strategy, etc.) to enact legislation aimed at progressive realization of the right to food (to enact legislation leading towards equal access to food production resources, i.e. to design and implement agrarian reforms, to enact stimulative measures for food production destined for domestic consumption, etc.)
to promote	to incorporate specific targets leading towards progressive realization of the right to food into development plans, categorized according to the criterion of resource availability, into three levels of the implementation of the right to food: (1) To raise nutritional levels (the incorporation of quantified objectives concerning the state of satisfaction of nutritional needs into development plans) (2) To eradicate hunger and malnutrition (the identification of target groups and the adoption of appropriate measures for the elimination of hunger) (3) To ensure adequate food for all (the establishment of a system of guarantees of the ull and immediate applicability of the right to food, including complaints and remedial procedures)
to protect	to refrain from, and to enact and enforce, prohibitions of any acts resulting in deprivation of food, to establish mechanisms for the supervision of compliance with the obligations undertaken, to establish entities empowered to monitor the realization of the right to food,
to fulfil or to ensure	to adopt national food legislation and national food strategy securing the progressive implementation of the right to food or full and immediate application of right to food, depending on the availability of resources, to establish a system of monitoring and complementary interventionary measures to identify and eliminate widespread nutritional deficiencies.

154

and (C) to ensure adequate food for all which means to apply fully and immediately the right to food for all by establishing a system of guarantees for its realization, including remedies in case of an alleged violation of the right to food.

The obligation to protect the right to food entails the obligation of the State to refrain from any act which might result in deprivation of food for a large number of people, and to enact and enforce prohibitions of acts and activities resulting in deprivation of food and/or impossibility of the realization of the right to food. International obligations concerning the protection of human rights provide for prohibitions of gross and systematic violations of human rights. Nevertheless, they cannot be automatically applied to the right to food, as this does not enjoy the same level of protection as those human rights requiring abstention from activities jeopardizing them. The right to food entails obligations for its progressive realization, but there is no general norm securing its universal applicability. However, purposeful starvation of the people is already prohibited by international humanitarian law.

To protect the right to food implies the obligation to establish systems for the supervision of compliance with obligations necessary for its realization and for monitoring. Two separate, but mutually related mechanisms have to be envisaged for the following reasons: the supervision of compliance with obligations focuses on the identification of policies and measures undertaken to implement the right to food. Therefore, it is the governmental activity (*i.e.* effort), which is the object of inquiry, and not results in terms of immediate, short-term changes in the level of the satisfaction of nutritional needs of the population. Assessments of development performance from the viewpoint of their impact on the realization of the right to food have to be separated from procedures for the assessment of compliance with international obligations. Indicators relating to nutrition, which are widely used and should be developed further, insufficiently reflect the actual governmental effort to promote the realization of the right to food or its neglect to do so.

Finally, the obligation to fulfil includes interventionary policies and measures necessary to provide for the needs of those people who are unable to do so for reasons beyond their control. It consists of a set of rights and obligations with respect to the identification and alleviation of structures and processes which result in jeopardies of basic human rights and needs. Interventionary measures are considered to be a supplementary, exceptional means for the realization of the right to food, as they regularly create or strengthen dependence at the expense of self-reliance, and jeopardize other human rights while fulfilling the right to food in the sense of "a right to obtain food". The ultimate objective of provisions relating to the right to food is the elimination of the obligation to fulfil, and a conceptualization of the right to food as a system of guarantees of equal access to resources, including guarantees of freedom, so that every individual is enabled to provide for his/her own needs.

One of the fundamental tasks of the human rights approach to development is the correction of distorted development priorities. While there is universal verbal agreement on human rights being the ultimate ends and means of development, the practices vividly demonstrate that actual priorities frequently, often irreparably, negate human rights. Cases of arms race and armed conflicts and deprivations of food are sufficiently known as such examples.

The realization of the right to food requires extensive investments of a country's overall resources. Therein, nutritional needs have to compete with security needs and as a rule they do not win. As Ruth Leger Sivard concludes: "Judged by a variety of measures of national and global welfare, budget priorities show a persistent slant toward military strength to the neglect of other needs that are vital to society's well-being and its security." [49]

Not only food has to compete for resources with other issues of human survival, but the human right to food has to compete with other usages of food. The problem of cash crops is an illustration of such a state of affairs: food is not produced for the consumption of the indigenous population, but for export. It has been stated long ago that "agricultural exports must provide the bulk of foreign exchange earnings for the import of capital goods required for industrialization". [50] Another illustration are recent experiences of the utilization of arable land for growing sugarcane and producing alcohol for fuel. [51] Such plantations are recommended solutions for energy-deficient countries; however, many of those are at the same time food-deficient.

The development of indicators of States' performances with respect to the realization of the human right to food presupposes the recognition of the right to food as a national objective, and the commitment of a State to its realization.

One has to take account of changes in the strategy adopted on the international level as a recommended course for States to realize the goals commonly agreed upon. It means that an evaluation of the performance of a State has to follow the course which was at that time suggested as "adequate", "appropriate", or "recommended" by the international community. For that reason, inter-temporal comparisons with respect to the States' implementation of obligations relating to the right to food do not seem possible for the whole post-war period.

Twenty years ago the usual policy recommendation tied the problem of world hunger to population growth. The FAO Freedom from Hunger Campaign was set up "to alert the world to a fundamental problem facing mankind: maintaining the balance between the world food supply and its population" [52]. It was later ascertained that population growth was a consequence of underdevelopment or maldevelopment, and not the cause of it.

While some twenty years ago the eradication of hunger had been treated as an objective of development, in the 1970's the elimination of poverty and hunger was proclaimed an essential condition for development.

Later, and still widespread, the advocacy of increasing food production in developing countries emerged as a panacea for resolving food problems, including the realization of the right to food. It did not take long to ascertain that neither development as such, nor increased food production, have beneficial effects on the realization of the right to food. The crucial issue of distribution became tied to that of food production. The Universal Declaration on the Elimination of Hunger and Malnutrition proclaimed: "It is a fundamental responsibility of Governments to work together for higher food production and a more equitable and efficient distribution of food between countries and within countries." [53]

Essential objectives of policy-recommendations for the eradication of hunger are alleviation of hunger by satisfying nutritional needs of the undernourished, and prevention of occurrences of widespread hunger in the future by encouraging sustainable growth of food production and by developing a pattern of distribution adapted to the nutritional needs of the population. Such a complexity of necessary changes to be accomplished by policy measures requires comprehensive and coherent planning and monitoring. Mutual influences of various policies and interrelatedness of their effects have been an object of research for years and the knowledge gathered is increasingly reflected in development planning. Yet, as research results of the International Institute for Applied Systems Analysis show, effects of various policy measures on crucial objectives of development (growth, equity, stability, and sustainability) can be outlined in abstracto, but extensive studies adapted to the national framework and conditions are needed for meaningful analyses. [54] The positive effects of public food distribution on equity, for example, have to be weighed against their negative effects on the growth of food production.

5.2. Indicators of the Realization of the Right to Food

The flexibility of the progressive realization norm can be assisted in its interpretations by the use of indicators. The ICESCR requirement of the governmental effort to the utmost of the available resources can be empirically investigated to prove the frequent assertion that it is not the lack of resources, but their misallocation (from a human rights viewpoint) which hampers the realization of human rights.

The other side of the coin, the effects of governmental policies on the state of the realization of individual rights, is more difficult to "measure". There is knowledge of the information needed for the development of indicators, but it stops short of applicability to those parts of the world which lack resources. Any proposals for wider application of indicators meaningful for an assessment of the realization of human rights have to be supplied by schemes for international assistance for their application. The feasible solution seems to advocate case-studies instead of suggesting globally applicable indicators without providing for their implementability.

The existing range of various social statistics is useful for human rights research to a limited degree. There is an evident need for wider use of distributional indicators, especially for those which represent universally desirable attributes which should extend to the entire relevant population. The state of the realization of human rights is too abstract a notion to be translated into a synthetic indicator, but the human right to food could be operationalized by singling out its components and applying them within a monitoring scheme.

It has to be kept in mind that "what you see depends on where you stand". A change of focus of inquiry is the first step towards the development of human rights indicators.

The illustration of striking similarities between the proclamations of specific human rights in the ICESCR and the social statistics, or indicators, which are regularly used is given in the scheme on the following page. The underlying idea of the need to change the focus of inquiry can be expressed as follows: possibilities for secondary analyses of the existing social statistics from a human rights viewpoint are limited, but nevertheless underutilized. The existing limitations do not prevent analyses of social sectors from the viewpoint of output instead of input, for example. [55] They are not possible for a large number of countries, and cross-national comparisons might be misleading, but case-studies are increasingly being done and they could be attempted in the right to food field. [56]

The fact of economic, social, and cultural rights resembling the existing classifications of social statistics is by no means a coincidence. It reflects the universal adherence to basic postulates of governmental obligations towards the population.

The development of indicators has to follow the requirements of applied research - it has to demonstrate in quantitative terms the legitimacy of demands for the realization of human rights. It has to supply evidence for requests addressed to authorities to change policies considered to be unacceptable from a human rights perspective. The requirements of governmental performance can be substantiated by the interpretation of international obligations and by the additional standards into country-specific schemes, thus evaluating each country against its own achievements from the past and objectives for the future.

Some Indicators in Current Usage Relating to the Subject-Matter Addressed by the ICESCR Provisions
1. arable land per capita (Global 2000)
per capita water availability (Global 2000)
national disposable income per capita (UNRISD)
investments per economically active person (UNRISD)
public expenditure per capita in education, health,
nutrition, and water (Sivard)
national poverty estimates (UN)
2. dependency ratios (UN)
economically active population as per cent of the total
population (UN)
unemployment rates (UN)
3. percentage distribution of governmental expenditure by social sector (UN)
coverage of social security schemes - estimates (UN)
4. calorie/protein daily supply per capita (FAO)
percentage of undernourished population (FAO, IBRD)

Economic, Social, Cultural Rights: Standards for Monitoring Compliance (the ordering and definitions follow the ICESCR)		Some Indicators in Current Usage Relating to the subject-Matter Addressed by the ICESCR Provisions
1. right of self-determination	1.1. control over natural wealth and resources 1.2. prohibition of the deprivation of means of subsistence	1. arable land per capita (Global 2000) per capita water availability (Global 2000) national disposable income per capita (UNRISD) investments per economically active person (UNRISD) public expenditure per capita in education, health, nutrition, and water (Sivard) national poverty estimates (UN)
2. the right to work	2.1. opportunity of gaining one's living by work 2.2. freedom to choose and accept work 2.3. policy of full and productive employment 2.4. just and favourable conditions of work 2.5. equal pay for work 2.6. right of trade unions	2. dependency ratios (UN) economically active populations as per cent of the total population (UN) unemployment rates (UN)
3. the right to social security	3.1. the right to social insurance 3.2. protection and assistance for the family, mothers, and childeren	3. percentage distribution of govermental expenditure by social sector (UN) coverage of social security schemes - estimates (UN)
4. the right to an adequate standard of living	4.1. adequate food, clothing and housing, 4.2. continuous improvement of living conditions	4. calorie/protein daily supply per capita (FAO) percentage of undernourished population (FAO,IBRD) physical quality of life index (UNICEF) level of living index (UNRISD)
5. the fundamental right to freedom from hunger	5.1. improving the production, conservation, and distribution of food, 5.2. equitable distribution of world food supplies in relation to need	5. food production per capita (FAO) share of food production in public investment (?) index of consumer process of food (Ganji) expenditure on food as per cent of total private consumption expenditure (UNRISD) food security indications (FAO)
6. the right to the highest standard of health	6.1. the reduction of infant mortality, 6.2. the improvement of hygiene, 6.3. prevention of diseases (preventive and curative health care)	6. life expectancy at birth (UN) infant mortality rate (UN) child death rate (IBRD) access to safe water (WHO)
7. the right to education	7.1. fully available and compulsory primary education, 7.2. generally available and accessible secondary education, 7.3. equally accessible higher education, 7.4. freedom of choise of education for children	7. adult literacy rate (UNESCO) educational enrolment ratios (UNESCO)
8. cultural rights	8.1. the right to part in cultural life, 8.2. enjoyment of benefits of scientific progress and its application, 8.3. freedom of scientific research and creative activity, 8.4. protection of scientific and artistic production, 8.5. development of international contracts and co-operation.	8. newspapers and books, radios and television per capita (UNESCO) personnel in research and development per 10,000 population (UNRISD)

physical quality of life index (UNICEF)
level of living index (UNRISD)
5. food production per capita (FAO)
share of food production in public investment (?)
index of consumer process of food (Ganji)
expenditure on food as per cent of total private
consumption expenditure (UNRISD)
food security indicators (FAO)
6. life expectancy at birth (UN)
infant mortality rate (UN)
child death rate (IBRD)
access to safe water (WHO)
7. adult literacy rate (UNESCO)
educational enrolment ratios (UNESCO)
8. newspapers and books, radios and television per capita (UNESCO)
personnel in research and development per 10,000
population (UNRISD)

The task is far from easy. It requires the establishment of a conceptual link between food issues, which are regularly dealt with in economic/technical terms, and human rights issues, dealt with by abstract objectives and principles. To establish such a link means to re-evaluate the "objective" indicators from a human rights perspective and to translate the "subjective" requirements into quantifiable aims.

The issue of States' performance has already been singled out as a priority topic. It is not difficult to re-analyse the existing data on resource allocation and establish some measures of governmental effort to implement its obligations relating to the human right to food. The essential governmental obligation - progressive realization of the right to food - could be monitored by the evaluation of the over-all governmental effort, by some form of a human rights audit of governmental performance. [57]

The current system of reporting relating to the ICESCR requires self-evaluations by governments, with a possibility of an impartial assessment of States' performance by UN specialized agencies. Such a possibility would become feasible if standard-setting advanced to a stage of actual existence of standards and if the relevant international bodies could connect the role of supervisors with that of assistance generators. An unfavourable evaluation of the performance of a country would not be beneficial for the realization of the right to food unless a redress mechanism existed. The attribution of blame would not assist the cause of the right to food unless a viable option for meaningful changes was provided for. Therefore, a more active role in monitoring and supervision for international bodies has to be coupled by possibilities to remedy the jeopardy or violations of the right to food. [58]

To make the human right to food operational and amenable to empirical investigations, one could structure the full norm on the right to food into three degrees of its realization. The lowest degree, freedom from hunger, would require the use of all available data to identify instances of widespread

160

starvation as violations of the fundamental human right. Such a data-gathering activity could be meaningfully used only within a mechanism providing remedies, and one could envisage its link to the UN food aid scheme. It was asserted here that food aid does not follow food needs as the principal criterion of eligibility for aid, and such data-gathering could prove or disprove such a hypothesis.

The requirement of progressive realization of the right to food implies a medium-level degree, which could be provisionally entitled to the right to food. Such a level could be linked to the existing indicators of quantity and quality of food available and consumed (the usual calorie/protein "measures"), which exist for a large number of countries. It has to be emphasized that those are only components of the right to food and by no means sufficient indicators from a human rights perspective. Yet, any re-analysing of the existing indicators implies the utilization of those which are readily available.

The right of everyone to adequate food, as the full-fledged norm, demands the entire scope of human right to be reflected in proposed indicators. It has already been stated that three components have to be identified - quantity, quality, and the respect for cultural rights. Narrow interpretations of the right to food, and of economic and social rights in general, frequently neglect the interlinkage between the rights component and the freedom component, which should not be separated. It is inconceivable to monitor the full-fledged norm of the right to food without taking account of freedom of movement and freedom of association, to mention just two striking examples.

An essential requirement for indicators relating to the right to food is their affirmation of the indivisibility and interrelatedness of human rights. It means that indicators for "measuring" the realization of the human right to food include, but are not confined to, measures for the satisfaction of nutritional needs.

Theoretical assumptions on interrelatedness of human rights are affirmed by practice. Studies on causes of hunger without exception warn that access to work and income represents a condition for the realization of the right to food. Suffice it here to quote one: the FAO asserts that "the basic cure for malnutrition is to raise the income levels of the poorest, while ensuring that there is food available". [59]

The two components, the demand side and the supply side, have dominated the research into food issues for quite a long time. As early as 1943 the objective of the supply side was determined as secure, adequate, and suitable supply of food for every person. Variations in terminology and in collection and presentation of information on food supplies did not change the basic line of reasoning.

Research into access to food regularly asserts as the crucial issue of the realization of the human right to food the demand side. Whether it is called "access to food supplies", "food entitlements", or "food security", it addresses the notion of distribution and essential principles regulating who-gets-what.

161

The use of indicators is not necessary to demonstrate that food supplies are today not distributed by the criterion of food needs. It is common knowledge.

Notes

(1) Gillette & Ryan, "Eleven issues in literacy for the 1990s", Assignment Children, 1983, no. 63/64, 19

(2) Irvine et al. (eds.), Demystifying Social Statistics (1979) at 3

(3) Scott, "Poverty monitoring in developing countries", 10 Development and Change (1979) 445 at 445.

(4) Baster, Social Indicators and Social Statistics in the Context of FAO's Concerns, FAO doc. ESS/MISC/78-5 (1978) at 65.

(5) The relationship of human needs and human rights can be explained in the following way: "International human rights are those human needs that have received formal recognition as rights through the sources of international law." Marks, "Emergencing human rights: new generation for the 1980's?" 33 Rutgers Law Review (1981), 435 at 436.

(6) The importance of linking development goals and development indicators can be explained in the following manner: "In fact, the designation of development goals is the most important part of the whole research process; studies on the indicators of social development are characterized not by how they go about measuring things but what they attempt to measure." Mokrzycki, "The negative indicators of social development", The Polish Sociological Bulletin 1980, No. 1, at 19.

(7) Cf. the main United Nations resolutions concerning the Development Decades: the General Assembly resolution 1710 (XVI) United Nations Development Decade - A Programme for International Economic Co-operation of 19 December 1966; General Assembly Resolution 2626 (XXV), International Development Strategy for the Second United Nations Development Decade of 24 October 1979; and General Assembly Resolution 35/56, International Development Strategy for the Third United Nations Development Decade of 5 December 1980.

(8) Estimates of successes and failures of the Second Development Decade without exception concluded that social aspects of development - and the realization of human rights could be subsumed under that heading - could not have been evaluated because of the lack of data for assessing social problems. Cf. Economic and Social Progress in the Second Development Decade. Report of the Secretary-General U.N. Doc. Sales No. E.77.A.11., (1977); Social Development and International Development Strategy, UNRISD (1979).

(9) Henry de Soos calls such policies "marginal measures for marginalized population" and adds: "Because the Fourth World has remained outside politics, it has remained without human rights." Soos, A Theoretical Approach to the Violation of Human Rights at the Foot of the Social Ladder. In: Human Rights in Urban Areas UNESCO (1983), 61 at 76.

(10) Economists are extremely skilful in planning and evaluating development by using solely technical-monetary indices: "Place any economist in the capital city of any underdeveloped country and give him the necessary assistance and he will in no time make a plane... No sociologist, psychologist or anthropologist would ever think of trying to do such a thing." Myrdal, -The challenge of world poverty: A World Anti-Poverty Programme in Outline (1970) at 2.

(11) Ganji, The Realization of Economic, Social and Cultural Rights: Problems, Policies, Progress, UN doc. Sales No. E.75.XIV.2, (1975) (hereinafter cited as: Ganji Report). para 61.

(12) The Ganji Report singled out the developing countries having the fastest rate of annual growth of the GDP, and pointed out the strong positive correlation between GDP growth and export earning. In assessing the negative aspects of the growth achieved, the Report emphasizes high unemployment rates for some of the countries which furnished the data (the highest ranking being Trinidad and Tobago, Singapore, Philippines, South Korea, Sri Lanka, Panama, Mauritius, Argentina, and Chile); data on changes in food production and food demand is supplied afterwards, adding to them increases in food consumer prices (the worst rating

162

ascribed in that respect to Brazil, Uruguay, Chile, Argentina, Congo, Indonesia, Laos, Vietnam, and South Korea). The Ganji Report has no analysis of political rights, such as the assertion of political instability as an obstacle to development; yet, some direction of the line of reasoning of the author is offered by his emphasizing unemployment and food shortages as main causes of political instability.

(13) Olson, "Rapid Economic Growth As a Destabilizing Force", 23 The Journal of Economic History (1963), 529.

(14) Strouse and Claude examined the relationship among three groups of indicators (indicators of political stability, social and economic development) for 122 countries. The basic data were taken from Taylor & Hudson, World Handbook of Political and Social Indicators and supplemented by the Freedom House survey of civil liberties and the status of freedom. Strouse & Claude, Empirical Comparative Rights Research: Some Preliminary Tests of Development Hypotheses, In: Claude (ed.) Comparative Human Rights (1976), 51-67.

(15) The Ganji Report, at 30.

(16) The principal criterion for evaluation is the impact of any change on economic growth. The World Bank states: "Increases in average calorie supply appear to have a clear, positive effect on economic growth; but the possibility cannot yet be ruled out that this may reflect the effect not of nutrition but of agricultural output." World Development Report 1980 (1981) at 38.

(17) "Although how distribution works is essentially a technical economic question, the rules under which it provides incentives and distributes costs and benefits reflect political judgements." McLaughlin, -The United States and World Development. Agenda 1979, (1979) at 5.

(18) Not even quality of life indicators take individuals as units of observation:
"...in its actual application as a social research concept, quality of life is a collective attribute that adheres to groups or categories of people, not to individuals".
Szalai, -Whence "Quality of Life"? IN: Szalai & Andrews, (eds.) - The Quality of Life. Comparative Studies (1980) at 16.

(19) James Grant asserts that malnutrition is a consequence of social injustice and a factor of its maintenance. Injustice is reflected in the research field as well: Grant claims that "probably no more than 1% of the world's research into food and agriculture is focused on the problem of the hungry." The State of the World's Children 1982-183, UNICEF, (1983) at 3 and 5.

(20) Cf. Gostkowski, Towards a System of Human Resources Indicators for Less Developed Countries. A Selection of Papers prepared for a UNESCO Research Project (1978).

(21) A good example of the requirement of flexibility for setting forth any definitions of standards with intended global applicability is the ILO concept of basic human needs.
"Basic needs include two elements. First, they include certain minimum requirements of a family for private consumption: adequate food, shelter and clothing, as well as certain household equipment and furniture. Second, they include essential services provided by and for the community at large, such as safe drinking-water, sanitation, public transport, and health, educational and cultural facilities.
It is important to recognize that the concept of basic needs is a country-specific and dynamic concept. The concept of basic needs should be placed within a context of a nation's over-all economic and social development. In no circumstances should it be taken to mean merely the minimum necessary for subsistence; it should be placed within a context of national independence, the dignity of individuals and peoples, and their freedom to chart their destiny without hindrance".
The World Employment Conference (1976) Programme of Action, art.1, paras 2 and 5.

(22) National aggregate data should not be discarded as indices of the existence of widespread threat of starvation in a country.
"... The mere fact that even the average calorie and protein intake in many of these (developing) countries is below universal standards, taking into account specific climatic conditions and the inequality in income distribution, indicates the insufficiency of nutrition levels in low-income groups."
The Ganji Report, at 79.

(23) Relevant U.N. instruments related to development frequently emphasize the exclusive right of each State to set its development goals and define strategies for their attainment. Just one example:

"the new international development strategy should duly stress the need for each country to define within the context of its development plans and priorities an appropriate social development policy taking account of its socio-economic structure and its degree of development."
G.A. res.33/48 World social development of 14 December 1978, para 7.

(24) "One of the most striking contradictions of the present situation is the simultaneous discrediting of the nation State as incapable of coming to grips with the challenges it faces; the renewed insistence on self-reliance and the right of the nation State to choose its style of development free of external pressures; and the continued proliferation of new States."
Wolfe, Elusive Development (1981) at 173.

(25) Valticos - The role of the ILO: present action and future perspectives, In: Ramcharan, (ed.) - Human Rights Thirty Years after the Universal Declaration (1979), 211 at 213.

(26) "It has to be remembered that the countries that most need information for selecting priorities for the allocation of limited resources are usually those that are least able to obtain the information precisely because of the limitation of resources and inadequate data collection mechanisms. A balance has to be struck between the allocation of resources to information collection for making priority decisions about alternative strategies and action and the allocation of resources to the programmes themselves." Development of Indicators for Monitoring Progress Towards Health for All by the Year 2000, WHO (1981) at 14.

(27) World Development Reports use two food-related indicators: the average index of food production per capita, and daily per capita calorie supply (the percentage of requirement). In its annual State of Food and Agriculture reports FAO is using food production and consumption data, while the World Food Surveys include estimates of calorie / protein supply and numbers of the undernourished.

(28) The least developed countries include the following States, listed by region:
Africa: Benin, Botswana, Burundi, Cape Verde, Central African Republic, Chad, Comoros, Ethiopia, Gambia, Guinea, Guinea-Bissau, Lesotho, Malawi, Mali, Niger, Rwanda, Somalia, Sudan, Tanzania, Uganda, and Upper Volta.
Asia: Afghanistan, Yemen Arab Republic, Bangladesh, Bhutan, People's Democratic Republic of Yemen, Laos, Maldives, and Nepal.
Pacific: Samoa.
Caribbean: Haiti.
The category was established without applying food-related criteria. See: General Assembly resolution 34/203 of 12 December 1979, and Report of the U.N. Conference on the Least Developed Countries, UN Doc. A/conf. 104/22 (1981)
The most seriously affected countries were declared as a separate category, in need of emergency assistance because of requirements of importing food. The list comprises the following countries:
Afghanistan, Bangladesh, Benin, Burma, Cape Verde, Central African Republic, Chad, Democratic Yemen, Democratic Kampuchea, Egypt, Ethiopia, El Salvador, Gambia, Guatemala, Ghana, Guinea, Guinea-Bissau, Guyana, Haiti, Honduras, Ivory Coast, Kenya, Laos, Lesotho, Madagascar, Mali, Mauritania, Mozambique, Nepal, Niger, Pakistan, Rwanda, Samoa, Senegal, Sierra Leone, Somalia, Sri Lanka, Sudan, Uganda, United Republic of Cameroon, United Republic of Tanzania, Upper Volta, Yemen Arab Republic.
See: General Assembly Resolution 3202 (S-VI) of May 1, 1974, section X.
FAO lists low-income food-deficit countries as a separate category in its statistical surveys of the global food situation, and it comprises the following countries listed by region:
Africa: Botswana, Cameroon, Central African Republic, Chad, Benin, Egypt, Ethiopia, Gambia, Ghana, Guinea, Ivory Coast, Kenya, Lesotho, Madagascar, Malawi, Mali, Mauritania, Mauritius, Niger, Rwanda, Senegal, Sierra Leone, Somalia, Sudan, Tanzania, Togo, Uganda, Upper Volta, Zambia, Zaire.
Asia: Afghanistan, Bangladesh, Sri Lanka, India, Indonesia, Nepal, Pakistan, Philippines, Yemen A R, Yemen D R.
Latin America: Bolivia, Dominican R., El Salvador, Guatemala, Guyana, Haiti, Honduras, Jamaica, Paraguay.
Cf. Approaches to World Food Security, FAO (1983) at 115-117.
The WFC suggested the establishment of a category of food priority countries, by the application of the following four criteria:
(1) seriousness of their food problems,

(2) economic or resource limitations for solving them,
(3) being victims of frequent natural calamities,
(4) potential for increasing their food production.
Cf. Manila communique of the World Food Council, U.N. Doc. A/32/19, part 1, para. 1.A.1.

(29) A link between international development assistance and promotion or violations of human rights by the beneficiary government is far from clear even on a high level of abstraction. Two contradictory policy-attitudes are cited here as illustrations of the current thinking on inter-governmental and governmental levels. A U.N. document envisages that "...in extreme cases involving gross and consistent violations of human rights, it might be appropriate for States and the international community as a whole to seek to protect human rights through the adoption of measures relating to aid and trade."
U.N. Doc. E/CN.4/1488 (1981) para. 185.
The attitude of the Dutch Government is exactly opposite:
"The Government rejects the idea that aid should be used to reward countries which respect human rights and conversely withheld to punish countries which disregard those rights. Aid should relate to the needs of the people and not to the conduct of governments."
Quoted from: Baehr, P.R. - Concern for development aid and fundamental human rights: The dilemma as faced by the Netherlands. Human Rights Quarterly, vol. 4, No. 1, spring 1982, pp. 39-52, at p. 45.

(30) Guidelines and Criteria for Food Aid, World Food Programme, Committee on Food Aid Policies and Programmes U.N. Doc. WFP / SL/ 144 of 5 October 1979.

(31) As a document of the U.N. Committee on World Food Security explicitly stated:
"It is uncertain to what extent these principles have been followed in practice by bilateral donors".
Director-General's Report on World Food Security:
A Reappraisal of the Concepts and Approaches
U.N. Doc. CFS:83/4 1982

(32) World Food Report 1983, FAO, 1983, at 15.

(33) Guidelines, para. (d)

(34) Suffice it here to quote two contradictory opinions. James Ingram states: "Food aid is, in fact, an additional resource for development which benefits directly poor people while simultaneously addressing the causes of their poverty."
Ingram, "Food for development (an interview)"
Development, special issue: The Fight against World Hunger (1982) No. 4, at 18.
Tony Jackson claims just the opposite: "Food aid is the prime example of an available commodity determining aid policy... It is a commodity-oriented programme which starts with food and then has to devise projects through which to distribute it... Distribution not development becomes the overriding factor."
Jackson & Eade - Against the Grain. The Dilemma of Project Food Aid, (1982) at 92.

(35) Collins, -The Right to Food and the New International Economic Order, UNESCO Expert Meeting on Human Rights, Human Needs and the Establishment of a New International Economic Order, (1978) Doc. No. SS-78/CONF. 630/6, at 11.

(36) "Many countries will take one or more decades before they can satisfy their internal food requirements, and enough food must be available to them while they are building up their domestic capacity. North-South: A Programme for Survival (1980) at 101.

(37) "...both general condemnation and general advocacy of food aid is pointless. Food aid provides an opportunity to promote growth or reduce poverty in poorer countries; this opportunity may be taken or it may be wasted. That depends on the way food aid is being given and the way it is being absorbed. It depends on the purposes of the donor countries and even more so on the policies and efficiency of the recipients."
Clay & Singer, Editorial to the special issue of the IDS Bulletin Food as Aid: Food for Thought (April 1983) at 1.

(38) Experiences from reconceptualizations of the appropriate treatment of refugees as beneficiaries of international assistance can be cited as an example of a change of the concept of aid. Not long ago, humanitarian aid was formally separated from human rights issues: relief had been treated as non-political and accorded on the basis of needs. However, perhaps most drastically expressed at ICARA II, the separation between humanitarian and development as-

165

sistance was rejected. Omar Bakhet (UNHCR) says with respect to assisting refugees: "We are out there to save lives, but there is the danger we can make them captives of our own help. While our point of departure is the peoples" needs, our goal is their self-sufficiency."

Bakhet, "Beyond Survival", Refugees (October 1983) at 10.

(39) Food Security for People - Direct Measures to Reduce Hunger, The World Food Council UN Doc. WFC/1982/6 of 3 March 1982, para 45.

(40) Wallerstein, "Inter-Disciplinary Dialogue on World Hunger: A Summary of the Workshop on Goals, Processes and Indicators of Food and Nutrition Policy" Food and Nutrition Bulletin (1978) 16-23, at 19.

(41) The World Food Conference: Policies and Programmes to Improve Nutrition (resolution 5), preamble and operative paragraphs 1 and 13. Report of the World Food Conference, Rome, 5-16 November 1974, UN Publ. Sales No. E. 75.11.A.3

(42) An illustration of what can be taken to mean the satisfaction of human needs, while being detrimental for human rights, is taken from an OECD study. It cites assertions that "basic needs once they have been identified and measured by experts, have to be provided by some sort of delivery system on the moral grounds that every man, woman and child has a right to minimum standards of living."

Quoted from: Alberti, Basic Needs in the Context of Social Change: The Case of Peru, OECD (1981) at II.

(43) International Fund for Agricultural Development: Lending Policies and Criteria, UN Doc. IFAD /8/ Rev. 1, (1978) para 30.

(44) The nutritional element, 16 CERES (March-April 1983) at 50.

(45) Problems involved in assessments of the nutritional status, from conceptual issues to practical constraints of funds and time needed, result in confining the actual projects to small scale endeavours. "Methods for an assessment of improvements of the nutritional status of those vulnerable groups which are targets of specific supplementary feeding programmes are applicable within those projects only."

Cf. Measuring Change in Nutritional Status. Guidelines for Assessing the Nutritional Impact of Supplementary Feeding Programmes for Vulnerable Groups, WHO, (1983) at 1.

(46) Briefly, major objections are the following: there is no satisfactory theoretical framework, the development of calorie / protein requirements ignores individual variances, they also disregard the interlinkage with cultural rights neglecting the requirement of food being culturally satisfactory.

Cf. Shrivasen, Malnutrition: Some Measurement and Policy Issues, (1980).

(47) Comparative analyses of national constitutions show that the right to food has not been explicitly recognized in such a number of constitutions as to make it statistically relevant on the global level. Cf. Maarsseveen & Tang, Written constitutions. A computerized comparative study (1978).

(48) The reason for not disregarding constitutional provisions as irrelevant for an analysis of the actual state of the realization of human rights is stated well by Hernan Santa Cruz:

"... the very fact of the inclusion of provisions prohibiting discrimination or ensuring equality before the law in the constitution or the fundamental law of a country is of paramount importance, as such provisions establish a mandate to followed by all public authorities in the exercise of their functions."

Study of Discrimination in the Matter of Political Rights, U.N. Doc. E./CN.4/Sub.2/213/ Rev.1, at 43.

(49) Sivard, World Military and Social Expenditures. An annual report on world priorities, (1983) at 23.

(50) Agriculture and Industrialization. Freedom from Hunger Campaign Basic Study No. 17, FAO/FFHC (1967) at 3.

(51) Cf. Gray, Food Consumption Parameters for Brazil and Their Application to Food Policy (1982).

(52) Quoted from the UN survey of the state of the realization of economic, social and cultural rights, in: The United Nations and Human Rights, (1978) at 78.

(53) The Universal Declaration on the Eradication of Hunger and Malnutrition, para 2.

Another resolution adopted by the World Food Conference (resolution II: Priorities for agricultural and rural development) in its preamble emphasized self-reliance as "the fundamental approach to the solution of the food problems of developing countries"; by self-reliance it means: "striving in accordance with each country's respective conditions for the maximum possible degree of self-sufficiency in basic foods".

(54) Parikh & Rabar (eds.). Food for All in a Sustainable World: The IIASA Food and Agriculture Program (Summarizing presentations at the IIASA Food and Agriculture Program Status Report Conference, February 1981) (1981) at 4-8.

(55) "... the per capita proportion of those basic goods and services to which the members of the poorest working groups of the country have finally access is determined mainly on political grounds."

Harari & Garcia - Bouza, Social Conflict and Development: Basic Needs and Survival Strategies in Four National Settings, OECD, (1982) at 16.

(56) Previous treatment of economic, social and cultural rights as a-political, or non-political is increasingly refuted by the social reality. A good example is given by demands of the workers' movement in Poland in 1980s, which focused on problems of food and health. Cf. Sokolowska, "Health as an Issue in the Workers' Campaign" Sisyphus, Sociological Studies, vol III: Crises and Conflicts - The Case of Poland 1980-81 (1982) at 91.

(57) Limitations of an application of any monitoring system for the realization of economic, social and cultural rights are clearly expressed in the following attitude of the Inter-American Commission on Human Rights:

"(the IACHR) recognized the difficulty of establishing criteria that would enable it to measure the state's fulfillment of their obligations. It has also seen the very difficult options that the governments face when allocating resources between generations, consumption and investment, and hence, between current and future generation. Economic policy and national defense policy are closely related to national sovereignty."

The lack of progress is exemplified by the fact of the IACHR, in its report for 1982-1983, quotes the above statement from its report for 1979-1980.

Annual report of the Inter-American Commission on Human Rights 1982-1983, OEA/Ser.L/V/11.61 of 27 September 1983 at 36.

(58) There is already plenty of scholarly literature dealing with the attribution of responsibility for violating the right to food, and occasional NGO reports possible cases of violations. Just one example:

"The luxury buildings of the Voix du Zaire, a second international airport at Kinsangani, a satellite telecommunications system are only part of an endless list of the prestige undertakings of a regime under which the population is dying of hunger, poverty has led to the return of certain epidemics thought to have been eradicated, and corruption has become a system of government. The result: the terrifying destitution of the population, for more than 50 per cent of Zairians currently suffer from malnutrition, while bacterial, viral and parasitical diseases proliferate... Infant mortality is catastrophic (one child in two does not reach the age of five), and the birth rate has dropped to alarming levels".

Communication submitted by the International League for the Rights and Liberation of Peoples, a non-governmental organization in consultative status, under the agenda item "Question of the realization in all countries of the economic, social and cultural rights contained in the Universal Declaration of Human Rights and in the International Covenant on Economic, Social and Cultural rights, and study of special problems which the developing countries face in their efforts to achieve these human rights", UN Doc. E/CN.4/ 1984/ NGO/4, 8 February 1984, at 3.

(59) World Food Report 1983 (1983) at 15.

Part IV:
Implementing the Right to Food

Right to Food for Peoples and for the People: a Historical Perspective

by
P. Spitz

"Take a barren year of failed harvests when many thousands of men have been carried off by hunger. If at the end of the famine the barns of the rich were searched, I daresay enough grain would be found in them to save the lives of all those who died from starvation and disease, if it had been divided equally among them."

Sir Thomas More UTOPIA, 1516

"That people are starving for lack of food is because there is grain hoarded in storehouses of the rich instead of in government granaries (...) If the ruler fails to take heed, then traders wander in markets and take advantage of want among people."

Kuang Chung
First Minister to the Duke Huan of the Feudatory of Ch'i, 650 B.C.

1. Economic Rights and the Right to Food

To recognize economic rights and to devise legal instruments to enforce them is, in this second half of the 20th century, to recognize that the so-called "natural laws of the economy" such as "market laws" work in such a way that some countries, social groups and peoples, are deprived of the basic necessities while others are accumulating surplus wealth. It is also to recognize that the co-existence of extremes of poverty and wealth calls for some corrective measures. If such measures are designed to protect economic rights they must take some legal form. This in turn implies recognition that such rights are threatened by forces which take advantage of the present international economic order and, at the national level, of the status quo. To recognize economic rights is to recognize the existence of conflicts of interest both between and within nations between those who have and always want more and those who have not. For these reasons the adoption of legal instruments to enforce economic rights is opposed by those countries and social groups which take advantage of the status quo. A pessimistic response would be that it is impossible to devise legal instruments, either internationally or nationally, which could ensure economic rights. A less pessimistic response would be that while it might be possible to reach some consensus the resulting laws will not be enforced.

I do not share these pessimistic views because history has demonstrated the strength of utopian ideas, ideas which by definition and etymology are "nowhere" -i.e. nowhere near the concrete world in which we live. In the last analysis pessimists, in invoking realism, defend the status quo.

Positive social transformations have been achieved by social forces which have been able more easily to gather their strength around utopian ideas (such as "Liberté, Egalité, Fraternité" in the French Revolution) than around "realistic" analyses of the forces that they were struggling against.

The right to food is the most concrete of the economic rights; it has an immediate appeal to deeply-rooted human feelings because food is a matter of life and death. It is therefore quite in order to start trying to define a legal framework for the right to food before dealing with other economic rights. Among the necessities of life, food has a number of distinctive features, some of which are so mundane that one tends to forget them.

The need to eat every day gives food a special time dimension. As one cannot live many days without food (six or seven weeks at the most in hunger strikes) and certainly cannot perform manual work during a long period of fasting, food has to be obtained within much stricter time constraints than other necessities of life (clothing, shelter, etc.) This daily anxiety has been voiced billions of times in many languages in the Christian prayer "Give us this day our daily bread". Food obviously also has a nutritional dimension since some nutritional elements should be part of the diet, in certain quantities and proportions, if not every day then at least over a short period of time, as the body does not effectively store many elements. In addition, food has a socio-cultural dimension as not everything edible and nutritionally satisfactory is socially, culturally and psychologically acceptable. Last but not least it has an economic dimension as most of the food items consumed are available in the market at a price. Food thus has a dual nature: for the producers it has both a use value (self-provisioning) and an exchange value on the market.

This dual nature is reflected in pairs of opposites at different levels of reality and analysis such as: commodity and basic needs; forces of extraction and forces of retention [1]; market and self-provisioning; extortion practices by some social groups (landlords vs. tenants and sharecroppers; farmers vs. agricultural labourers; traders and usurers vs. people in need at some time of the year etc.) and redistribution, within certain social configurations (kinship groups; local communities; patron-client systems); exploitation and solidarity; economic realism and moral outrage; economic laws and human rights.

Before seeking to identify the major processes of deprivation which characterize the 1980's, it is useful to recall, through a few examples, the approach which has been taken to the right to food in earlier times.

2. The right to food: an historical background

Before the development of a state apparatus in pre-capitalist societies, the

170

right to food was imbedded in social relations within each society through a variety of redistributive mechanisms. Each society was in fact setting its boundary conditions in recognizing, usually implicitly, the right to food and to life, for its members. Those who were denied these rights were de facto outsiders or foreigners and for that reason their houses, granaries, boats, fields or lands could be preyed upon. The right to food and to life was therefore mainly threatened by outsiders. By contrast, within each society, athough the situation was not egalitarian or idyllic a la Rousseau, sharing food within a kinship group or a local community was generally positively valued by existing social norms. In these pre-capitalist societies the state apparatus emerged most often through the simultaneous development of a military and a fiscal system both of which gave important impulses to the development of a monetary system. In such agricultural societies the fiscal system was mainly geared to agricultural commodities, and took the form of food extracted from the producers, as taxes, levies, tributes, etc.; other fiscal measures included control over the production of and trade in salt (an essential food item) and metal (for instance iron, for which military demand preceded its use in agriculture).

Military, fiscal, monetary and food systems were intertwinted. Within each state the fiscal system could support army expendidures and feed soldiers with less disruption than by letting them live off the land. In ancient Morocco the same word - makhzen[2] - was used to mean both granary and government. Measures of grain or heads of cattle (in Latin pecus from which derives 'pecuniary') were used as monetary units until the increasing complexity and dimensions of the transactions (particularly in connection with the payment of soldiers) made them too cumbersome and were responsible for the development of metal coins. Against a background of important year-to-year fluctuations of agricultural output, taxation, whether fixed or proportional to output, could leave the smaller producers without sufficient food for their families' own use until the next harvest. The military (later police) system began to be used for the recovery of fiscal dues in times of scarcity. Thus in the process of development of the state in pre-capitalist societies, with the concomitant development of coercive fiscal and military systems, the right to food was progressively denied by the state itself to many of its own subjects, and particularly to those who were producing food, while food was guaranteed to non-producers, such as soldiers, priests, and civil servants.

The early rulers of agricultural societies, although trying to maximize fiscal revenues, were nevertheless keen to avoid the social trouble and disruptions that enforced tax collection during a famine situation could trigger. In all the societies of which records are availble this dilemma was very early recognized and reflected upon and was at the root of the development of political economy. It is in ancient Chinese writings that the most extensive and elaborate thinking can be found. If, in Confucius' Great Model of the Canon of History, food was listed as the first of the eight responsibilities of government, it was not so much out of recognition of the right to food but rather because it was considered to be the most difficult responsibility to face. The challenge was to strike a balance between prosperity in terms of public finance and the maintenance of social order, between food availability and low prices for the consumers on the one hand and self provisioning of food and remunerative prices for the producers on the other.

Li K'uei, counsellor of Duke Wen of Wei (about 400 B.C.) formulated this dilemma very clearly: "If grain is very expensive, consumers suffer and their families are scattered and emigrate; if grain is very cheap, the producers suffer and the state is impoverished. Whether the price is very high or very low, the prosperity of the state suffers".[3]

His solution was to stabilize prices through state purchase of grain in years of plenty and sale at controlled prices in years of scarcity.

Although Li K'uei was, to our knowledge, the first to build a quantitative model of food price stabilization and one which was much more sophisticated than the biblical granary of Joseph (a fact entirely ignored by ethnocentric western histories of economic throught), public granaries had already been established much earlier.

Thus the annals of Chinese history tell us that a great famine led the legendary Emperor Shun (on a date fixed by some scholars at arround 2000 BC) to appoint a minister of agriculture, ranking first among other ministers, whose task was to control the production and distribution of grains. Confucius himself, according to some of his disciples, was, in his youth, in charge of a public granary. Food price equalization and stabilization schemes as well as public grain policies have therefore been discussed and implemented with varying results in China for nearly 4000 years. Throughout the annals the same questions keep repeating itself: how to guarantee food in bad years? Should it be: through state or village granaries; through tax exemptions in difficult years; through regulating trade; through attacking the problems at the roots by implementing egalitarian land reforms, through redistribution of income or assets; through egalitarian policies ensuring basic needs and forbidding luxuries or through an economism which stresses the dynamic role of inequality; through an emphasis on agriculture or crafts, on food crops or cash crops?

All schools of thought in ancient China have taken sides on these questions, including the anarchist Taoist school. For instance, in the famous "Debates on Salt and Iron" (81 BC) the arguments exchanged between confucianists and legalists could be summarized under four headings: "(1) civil "cultivation" versus military achievement, (2) agriculture as the basic activity versus crafts and commerce, (3) benevolence and righteousness versus utilitarian advantage, (4) penal measures versus ethics"[4]. Beyond the debate on the abolition of the state monopoly over salt and iron, it was a one on war and peace, on the right to food of a people threatened by military expenditures.

Whatever the period and the school of thought, food, war and peace have always been linked in Chinese political economy. In a document relating to the western Chou dynasty, prior to the eighth century BC, a nine-year period during which it was possible to store enough grain for three years' consumption was called a "period of maturity" (teng). A period of eighteen years (two tengs) providing for six years of reserve was called a "period of

172

peace" (p'ing). Three successive teng periods, constituted a "period of great peace" (t'ai-p'ing).

The Imperial Secretary Sang Hung-yang, representing the legalist school in the Debates on Salt and Iron, justified State intervention in the following way:
"The (wise) ruler stops the flow of natural wealth, interdicts (its movement through) customs barriers and markets, maintains regulations and enforces time requirements, ad uses price management to control the people. In a year of plentiful crops when the harvests are collected, he accumulates stores in preparation against shortages; in a bad year of poor harvests he administers the sale of commodities and transports goods from places of excess to adjust deficiencies . . . In the past when money and goods were insufficient, the soldiers might not receive their pay. Now (under the managed economy), should Shantung suffer a disaster or famine appear in Ch'i or Chao, we can depend on the equalized distribution from stores and the accumulations in our warehouses and granaries; the soldiers thus receive their pay, and starving people thus are given aid. Therefore, the goods subject to equalized distribution, like the wealth accumulated in treasuries and warehouses, do not represent profiteering at the common people's expense for the sole purpose of supporting the army, they also are the means for bringing aid to the distressed and the impoverished, and are a preparation against disasters of flood and drought."[5]

This attemp to reconcile fiscal, military and food systems required many laws and regulations, particularly in relation to private trade in food. To the Imperial Secretary's argument, "When commands are strict the people become circumspect; when laws are established evil is barred", the Confucian scholars answered: "Now, today the regulations and commands run to over a hundred articles; their text is voluminous and the crimes they define carry heavy penalities . . . The texts of the regulations and commands lie gathering dust and being eaten by bookworms on the office shelves. The officials cannot read them all, and all the less the simple people do so". To the Confucian arguing for teaching moral conduct to the people instead of imposing laws, the Imperial Secretary answered that "people's characters are fixed by natural endowment and cannot be altered". He said: "Hustling and bustling, all the world goes after profit . . . merchants are not ashamed of disgraceful conduct if it brings them lucre."[6]

In another civilization which left us a wealth of written material on politics and ethics, food traders were subjected to severe laws and regulations. In Greece, in the fourth century BC, the grain trade was, unlike other trades, governed by special laws and supervised by special magistrates.

"(Officials regulating the grain trade), unlike the officials who controlled the sale of all other commodities in Athens, were subject to the death sentence for serious faults in the exercise of their office. What was pardonable for metals, textiles and even oil was not so for wheat." In 386 BC, some wheat traders who had bought from importers more than their authorized quota were brought before the Council of Athens. Lysias demanded that they be condemned to death, and his speech is a classic accusation of the wheat traders by the people: "When do they make the biggest profits? When the news of a disaster enables them to sell at high prices. Your misfortunes are so welcome to them that sometimes they hear of them before anyone else, sometimes they invent them (...) And their hostility goes to the extent that, in critical periods, they conspire against you, exactly like your enemies. When wheat is most in demand, they buy it up and refuse to sell it, so that there will be no discussion on the price - we shall be only too happy to buy it, however high the rate, rather than return home empty-handed: sometimes, even in peacetime, it is as though we were besieged by them."[7]

It should be observed that it is easier for public authorities to denounce the excesses of the grain traders and to take measures to curb their power than to denounce excessive inequalities in the distribution of wealth and particularly of land ownership. It is easier to lower food prices or even to distribute food free than to implement a land reform, (as the history of Rome demonstrates[8], and easier to distribute income than to distribute assets. In the rich eighteenth century French literature on food policies no one has better expressed these conflicts of interests in terms of conflicts of rights than Necker.

"The Landowner sees wheat merely as the fruit of his labours and the product of the land belonging to him; he wants to treat it like any other income. (...) The Trader sees nothing more in this commodity than an item that is bought and sold; he wants to be able to acquire it and resell it as he pleases. The People (...) think of wheat as an element necessary for their survival. They are in the world and they want to live there. They want to be able to ensure their subsistence by their own work. (...) The Landlord invokes the rights of property; the Merchant, those of freedom; the People, those of humanity . . . Within this continual clash of interests, principles and opinions, the Legislator must seek out the truth."[9]

By means of the 1789 revolution the French bourgeoisie wanted to secure freedom of trade and get rid of all feudal and old regime restrictions on the movements of commodities. During the preceding fifty years, the French 'Physiocrats' and others had argued that free trade was the only way to avert famines and thereby ensure the people's right to food. This approach did not conflict with property rights once ownership had been transferred to the bourgeoisie. The 1789 Declaration of the Rights of Man and the Citizen insisted on the right of ownership and was no different in this respect from the American Declaration of Independence of 1776. But when food crises started to develop in 1792 and particularly in 1793 the right of people to a decent livelihood and particularly to food became a central issue. As the French Constitution of 1793 was never put into practice it is sometimes forgotten that its preamble is more explicit than the better known 1789 Declaration. In this preamble, entitled "Declaration of Rights", article 21 states that "society has the duty to ensure the sustenance of the poor either by providing them with work or by giving the means of livelihood to those who are unable to work". Article 35 states "when government violates people's rights, insurrection is for the people . . . the most sacred of its rights and the most obligatory of its duties". The 1793 Declaration of Rights and the Constitution were adopted not only after heated arguments by those who wanted to abolish, limit, or strengthen the rights of ownership, but also after practical legal measures had been taken against the excesses of the food traders and hoarders, against food price rises through the setting of price ceilings ("loi du maximum"), and in favour of the establishment of public granaries, state foodgrain monopolies, etc. Much of this was reminiscent of the Confucian debates (particularly Robespierre's insistence on educating the people in order to make them virtuous) as well as of Thomas More's recommendation that "laws might be made that no one should own more than a certain amount of land or receive more than a certain income".

It is interesting to note that, although not explicitly dealing with the right to food, the 1789 Declaration was invoked against the food speculators in 1792-93 through an interpretation of its Article 4: "Freedom consists in doing that which does not harm others". The priest Jacques Roux was the most eloquent on the subject: "Equality is only a ghost if the rich man can exercise the right to life and death over his fellow-men. Freedom is only a ghost when one class can starve another class with impunity". The conflict between "formal freedom" and "real freedom" was thus emphasized and the right to food of each individual was explicitly recognized.

In the 19th and 20th centuries famines and severe food crises disappeared gradually from the now industrialized countries. Food issues lost their specificity. Socialist movements and trade-unions fought for decent wages which would permit, *inter alia*, a "sufficient" diet for workers and their families. They also struggled for unemployment benefits, old age pensions, education grants, health benefits, housing, etc.

In developing countries today, food is still a central issue for the rural poor with insufficient land and for the urban poor with insufficient food purchasing power and often with neither work nor unemployment benefits. The definition of a right to food for these people raises many of the issues referred to above and debated for centuries. But is also raises new issues since today's industrialized countries have reached their present stage of development in which the right to food as such has ceased to be central issue through a process of depriving other peoples and nations of their rights to food: For example, the British industrial revolution and its Poor Laws are inseparably linked to the 19th century Indian famines. The right to food for peoples is therefore an entirely new concern in the context of the present international economic order.

3. Counting the hungry in the 1980's

In most countries of Africa, Asia and Latin America some people have, over the last decade, died for lack of food. How many is anybody's guess: the order of magnitude is ten million a year for some commentators, two or three times the number for others. There is no arithmetic scale for moral outrage. One starvation death can no more readily be tolerated than one million starvation deaths in the world of the 1980's, where such great riches have been accumulated, and so much knowledge and technology generated. There are probably more than one million starvation deaths every year, roughly three times the population of Geneva. This provides a sufficient indication both of the scale of the scandal and of the relatively small percentage of world resources which would theoretically be needed to avoid such deaths, even for a population ten or twenty times greater than present. Comparisons with arms expenditures have often been made and need not be repeated here.

If thousands of inspectors monitor poverty and deprivation on a world scale, in much the same way as the 19th century inspectors of the British Poor Law Board, we could know month by month, with age and sex specified, the exact number of persons deprived of their means of livelihood and susceptible to death from hunger as well as the actual number of deaths from starvation. We would be able to estimate the cost of food relief projects but still not be in a position to know how to deliver it or how to avoid a recurrence of deprivation. In order to intervene effectively we have to understand the processes we want to modify.

After two centuries of social science development, we should be in a position to draft legal instruments concerning the right to food having in mind their likely consequences on social processes. We should learn the lesson from what happened in England after the Poor Law Amendment Act of 1834: the New Poor Law, once drafted and enacted, required for its implementation statistics on the poor. The Statistical Society developed rapidly and its Journal "provided a quantitative commentary on the trends of social change and the social incidence and running costs of expansive industrialism"[10] But, in turn, it was realized that processes leading to poverty and destitution had to be understood: this was what such pioneers as Charles Booth, Seebohm Rowntree and Henry Mayhew attempted to do. It is why the Statistical Society encouraged the formation in 1857 of the National Association for the Promotion of Social Science, whose annual sessions frequently devoted themselves to the discussion of poor relief.[11]

The Poor Law Medical Officers' Association was also set up, and through its periodical, "Lancet", exposed the state of sick wards in a number of London Workhouses in 1865. Humanitarianism was blended with the necessity of social control; nutrition studies developed largely in response to the central question of the industrial revolution, which was how to keep wages as low as possible without jeopardizing the conditions of reproduction of the labour force. It is against this historical background that we must assess the strong statement by the first Director-General of FAO, Lord Boyd Orr, at the Quebec Conference in 1945: "The hungry people of the world wanted bread and they were given statistics . . . No research was needed to find out that half the people in the world lacked sufficient food for health"[12]. As one of the heirs to the British tradition of socio-medical enquiry into the situation of the poor, as brilliantly illustrated by his 1936 work *Food, Health and Income,* Boyd Orr was particularly qualified to criticize the trend which is still so strong today, of counting the poor and their calories. He also understood the difficulty of ensuring the right to food for peoples. His proposed World Food Board was opposed in 1946 by the Truman administration, whose secretary of Agriculture said to a Congressional Committee: "Some people are going to starve. We're in the position of a family that owns (sic)a litter of puppies: we've got to decide which ones to drown".

Fortune [13] commented on this statement as follows: "While half a billion people in Europa, Africa and Asia faced hunger and possible death by starvation, Americans continued to eat about 20 per cent more food (measured in calories) than nutritionists recommend as a healthy diet. The U.S. was short of wheat in a time of world famine because the government had deliberately planned for scarcity".

More detailed statistical knowledge cannot help when such powerful political processes are in motion. One of the most difficult tasks in analyzing food and develeopment issues, once the analysis of functional linkages has been completed in an interdisciplinary and systematic manner, is to establish the hierarchies to be found in the different processes.* If this is not done we run the risk of, for instance, advocating perfectionism in statistical reporting or the establishment of "nutritional surveillance" schemes in a country whose political system is such that the end result will be a reinforcement of oppressive and repressive mechanisms. An alternative approach in such a case, although less rewarding for foreign (bilateral and multilateral) aid agencies and experts, would be to bring pressure on the government to allow greater freedom of association, so that the people themselves could voice their needs through their own organizations instead of being the passive objects of enquiries. Counting the poor and hungry in the name of their right to food might, in certain circumstances only lead to further deprivation of their rights of expression, assembly and association and, ultimately, jeopardize their right to food itself. Experts and intellectuals who have the power to express their opinions and sometimes to be heard should therefore be conscious of their responsibilities in peddling their wares. They should help those who have difficulties in being heard to voice their demands more forcefully rather than silence them.** People who are starving for lack of food do not need to be told how many calories and proteins they should have. The people's right to food is, first and foremost the right to resist those who are depriving them of food.

In a booklet on the famine then devastating Russia, Tolstoy wrote (in 1893):

"Feed the people! Who then has taken it upon himself to feed the people? It is we, the civil servants, who have taken it upon ourselves to feed the very men who have always fed us and who go on feeding us every day . . . It can be said that bread, not to mention all other forms of wealth, is produced directly by the people . . . How is it then that this bread is to be found, not in the possession of the people, but in our hands, and that, by a peculiar and artificial process, we have to return it to the people, calculating so much for each person? . . . Must we delude ourselves by saying that the people are poor merely because they have not yet had time to adjust to our civilization, but that, come tomorrow, we shall set about imparting all our knowledge to them, concealing nothing, and that then they will doubtless cease to be poor . . .? Do not all enlightened folk continue to live in the towns - for what they claim to be a very exalted purpose - and to eat in the towns the sustenance which is

177

brought there and for want of which the people are dying? And these are the circumstances in which we have suddenly started to assure ourselves and everyone else that we are very sorry for the people and that we want to save them from their wretched plight, a plight for which we ourselves are responsible and which is indeed necessary to us. Here is the cause of the futility of the efforts made by those who, without changing their relationship with the people, wish to come to their help by distributing the riches which have been taken from them."[14]

4. Identifying processes of deprivation in the 1980's

(a) The extraction/retention dichotomy

We have referred earlier to the dual nature of food, which is subjected to the conflicting forces of extraction for the market on the one hand, and of retention for self-provisioning on the other. Retention forces, in an uncertain universe of relative prices, tend to ensure food security by self-provisioning. Extraction forces are by nature composite reflecting *inter alia* consumption needs, tax payments for farm rent, and farming inputs. As we have seen from a few historical references, direct taxation of agriculture in developing countries was once an important means by which resources were withdrawn from rural areas, peasants being required to make cash sales or deliveries of grain that would otherwise have been kept in reserve. In some places (in West Africa for instance) taxes which for administrative convenience were placed on local granaries, led to their disappearance. Such taxation has generally declined in importance, however, and, with the commercialization of village life, is being replaced by pressures for cash income needed by agriculturalists in order to purchase consumption items and new farming inputs. The poll tax nevertheless still puts a burden on some African farmers, obliging them to sell crops on the market, and direct taxation of cattle is also still significant in some African pastoral cummunities.

The credit system, whether traditional or modern, is another example of a mechanism that can in effect extract food from reserve supplies: small peasants producing just enough, or not enough, food for their needs until the next harvest are often compelled to sell or deliver some of their food after the harvest in repayment of loans at usurious rates. Then, when their own stocks are exhausted, they are obliged to buy food later at a higher price. Their consumption is thus maintained at a low level in normal years and those who might have the possibility of storing a surplus for balancing off bad years and meeting famine threats are unable to do so because of the squeeze caused by usurious practices.

The tenancy system may provide another example of an extractive mechanism, when rent consisting in, say, half of the produce must be paid to the landlord even when the half left to the producer does not cover his subsistence needs. The tenant is prevented from accumulating reserves for himself and his family, while reserves accumulate in the landlord's barns. The land-

178

lord is able to release these at a high price in times of scarcity. While the landlord's reserves may provide some immediate relief for the tenants from famine conditions, it is likely to put them in debt to him. They will then be forced to sell at harvest time to repay their debts, thus prolonging the predicament in which they are obliged to liquidate stocks to make debt repayments. The holding of reserves by the landlord at the local level may substitute constant hunger for acute famine.

(b) The impact of pricing policies

In general, the transfer of resources through barter, selling and exchanges on the market as well as through taxation, tariffs, etc. is a function of the relative bargaining power of the groups involved, and groups vulnerable to famine are likely to have little such power. Nomadic pastoralists who need to buy grain do not generally have such command in good years over the prices they receive for their own products, and under scarcity conditions this bargaining power is reduced even more.

Historically, direct taxation of agriculture represented a rather brutal mechanism through which resources were squeezed out of the countryside to finance castles and temples and to feed rulers, priests and soldiers. When direct taxation clearly denied the right to food of, *inter alia*, the food producers themselves, people could not only identify the reason for their starvation but also identify those responsible for it, from the king to the tax-collectors. Indirect taxation, relative prices, terms of trade, inflationary processes in a context of increased monetarization, commercialization of farm produce and of farm inputs are the more recent means of extraction of resources from the agricultural sector. These mechanisms for denying the right to food to the most vulnerable are thus more elusive than were their forerunners. Similarly, the identification of the parties responsible has become much more difficult since many of them are sitting in far-away banks, stock exchanges or ministries.

Price setting mechanisms for food commodities are of course largely governed by the relative bargaining power of the large farmers vis-a-vis the most influential groups of urban consumers (often middle classes at a time when the industrial working class was still in its infancy).

Most prices of basic food commodities, in less developed countries, are determined by the State, which attempts to strike a balance between the conflicting demands of food producers and non-food producers. Lowering the prices paid to producers has a disincentive effect on production while raising them in order to stimulate production undermines the food purchasing power of increasing numbers of poor consumers. Governments have to face on one side the discontent of large famers (who most often play an important part in the political make-up of the social basis of governments) and on the other the social protests of consumers, protests which, in the cities, carry all the more weight because cities are the seats of political power.

(c) Processes of Deprivation of the Rural Poor.

The rural poor, who have to buy staple foods because they do not produce enough, are also hurt by an increase in food prices. Very often they make up more than half of the rural population. They include not only the landless but also those who have some means of production (land, agricultural implements, livestock, boats) but do not produce enough food for their families during the whole year and have the greatest difficulties in making ends meet by the sale of their products. This group includes small farmers, tenants, sharecroppers, livestock raisers, fishermen, craftsmen. Family income very often has to be supplemented by sporadic wage earning. In many countries, most of these families are indebted in a manner which precludes productive investments, which are also discouraged by insecure tenure or sharecropping systems. Events such as bad harvests, animal losses, or poor fish catches show up the instability of these fragile survival systems. Large producers, traders and money lenders take advantage of this situation to evict tenants and to acquire land and other productive assets at distress prices. In other words, it is in crisis situations (sometimes caused by climatic events) that the forces working within society towards increased control of the land by a few and the dispossession of marginal peasants (who are then forced to migrate to cities) find an opportunity to expand.

Protection of the right to food of those small producers requires: land reform legislation; security of tenure; fairer share-cropping systems; re-distribution of landholdings exceeding a certain size to benefit the most deprived; regulating the use of common pastures; equitable allocation of fishing rights etc. It also requires the adoption of laws curbing usurious practices and the creation of more liberal agricultural credit systems. In addition credit and marketing systems organized along cooperative lines supported by an adequate legislation could help small village craftsmen who have not yet been eliminated by colonial policies and international competition to increase their production and competitiveness thereby safeguarding important sources of seasonal enployment and income. However all these laws will be ineffective if the potential beneficiaries do not have the right to organize themselves in order first to contribute to the drafting of such legislation and secondly to guarantee its enforcement.

Those who have lost their land or their craft and do not own any means of production, but still live in rural areas, depend entirely for their livelihood on the sale of their labour. The main source of employment being agricultural work, they have to rely on seasonal incomes. Off season they have to make do with whatever other work is available in the area or might have to migrate temporarily. Landless agricultural labourers have emerged as a growing category especially at risk wherever collective or communal land tenure systems have broken down and inequalities in land distribution have increased.

Large numbers of them, especially in Asia and Latin America, and to a lesser extent in Africa, are between two worlds. The old systems which afforded, although at a low level of subsistence, a certain security during lean periods[15] have broken down and protective welfare systems (providing un-

180

employment benefits, social security, old age pensions, etc.) have not yet emerged. And these systems might never emerge if existing trends continue, particularly in relation to technological choices in agriculture. In this connection it should be kept in mind that the volume of available employment and its seasonal distribution depend on the production techniques used, but the choice is not made according to the needs of the majority but to the power of the dominant groups. It is patterned after the Euro-North American model of agriculture combining two distinct Post-World War II trends, both of which originated in the mid-19th century. In North America the trend was towards increased productivity of labour through mechanization (since land was abundant and labour scarce); in Europa it was towards increased productivity of land through improvement of agronomic practices and fertilizer use (since land was scarce and labour abundant). In the latter case, which was the most favourable for labour absorption in agriculture, we should remember that even with the development of European industries in a period of world market dominance, sixty million Europeans had to leave their continent between 1840 and 1920, out of a population of about 300 million in 1900. Even without mention of the high energy cost of the Euro-North American model (which precludes its application in most developing countries) and its impact on the fragile tropical environment, it is clear that this model cannot absorb labour, particularly in the demographic conditions prevailing in developing countries. In these countries the absorbtive capacity of industrialization processes is, in addition, even lower than in the 19th-century Europe.

Technological choices in agriculture should therefore be made only after full account has been given of their potential impact on the right to food of landless agricultural labourers and small producers, and should in particular ensure remunerative employment in all seasons.

(d) Policy implications in rural areas

In rural areas, resource flows and food availability are structured by time (by seasons) not only for agricultural producers and labourers but also to a large extent for rural artisans, craftsmen, rural industrial workers, traders, etc.

In this and other respects the situation of the rural poor is very different from that of their urban counterparts. For example, in rural areas it is possible to foresee the consequences of poor weather or a bad harvest. Moreover the smaller size of the groups involved in social inter-relations facilitates a response in times of seasonal crises, although it may sometimes take the form of exploitation rather than solidarity. Protection against destitution was greatly diminished with the disappearance of pre-capitalist relations although the persistence of such relations in some situations has made it difficult for workers to organize themselves, and has facilitated the maintenance of bonded labour and comparable practices. In bonded labour situations the labourer enjoys a right to a minimum of food but at the expense of personal freedom.

181

With the evolution of capitalist relations, marked for instance by the replacement of wages in kind by wages in cash, agricultural labourers have lost even this minimum insurance. The personal freedom, which they have gained is more often than not a freedom to be unemployed and to starve, since they have not yet gained enough collective bargaining power. It is therefore essential that the people's right to food be better protected, and that processes of destitution are attacked at their roots particularly through land reform, appropriate technological choices (in agriculture as well as in industry) and the stimulation of remunerative employment in the countryside, thus stemming the flow of the rural poor towards the cities. Curbing the abuses of landlords, traders and usurers clearly requires limits to rights of ownership and freedom of trade today, just as it did centuries ago. In summary, realization of the right to food for small rural producers and landless workers requires respect for the right to organize (already recognized in several ILO conventions):
- for land reform including security of tenure, and fair sharecropping systems;
- for fair agricultural credit, price and marketing policies;
- for minimum wages legislation and its enforcement; and
- for appropriate technological choices in agriculture.

This last requirement has consequences for, *inter alia*, agricultural scientists and extension workers, who should drastically change their current priorities and, instead of working for a minority of large farmers in well-endowed areas, should devote their creative energy to understanding, through a two-way process, the needs of small farmers and agricultural labourers and thus help the majority to improve their food security.

Technological choices, agricultural research priorities and extension models are, of course, shaped by social and political forces which are heavily weighted in favour of large farmers, livestock raisers, plantation owners and agribusiness interests in chemicals, machinery, seeds etc. at the national and international level. Realists/pessimists might say that nothing can be changed, given such power relationships. The most they will expect from attempts to operationalize the right to food is the development of a system of experts/inspectors whose limited task is to count the poor and their calories in order to better distribute food aid, i.e. a redistribution at the international level of the same nature as the one criticized by Tolstoy at the national level.

We have made our position clear from the outset by quoting Thomas More: The definition of a right to food has to do with social utopias; it requires an emphasis on the processes of deprivation and the means to achieve more social justice and equite.

(e) Food insecurity among the urban poor

In urban, as compared to rural areas, the time dimensions of food insecurity, as well as social relations, are of a different nature.

As non-food producers, the urban poor depend entirely on the distribution through time of their earnings on the one hand and on food availability and prices on the other. Although there are some employment opportunities linked to the season (construction activities, road repairs and processing of agricultural products), their earnings are generally erratic and not time-bound and their livelihood depends on makeshift arrangements.

For the most vulnerable urban groups, often made up of recent immigrants from the countryside, there exist of course no unemployment benefits. Prolonged unemployment periods, resulting from the lack of work opportunities, bad health, or just bad luck, might lead to starvation and death, unless it is possible to have some access to welfare centres or hospitals (most often overcrowded) or to rely on begging, or on some other expressions of solidarity. The latter are not easily found in large cities. Credit is not easily obtained in the absence of security. As a result, deaths occur in large cities of poor continents, with each death surrounded by its own peculiar circumstances. The atomistic nature of these individual tragedies is such that their sum does not constitute a collective phenomenon equivalent to a famine in rural areas.

The food purchasing power of the urban poorest is not only constantly threatened by the instability of employment and income opportunities, but also by periodic food shortages and price increases. For this group the general tendency is towards anomy, in Durkheim's sense, with wages mostly fixed at the individual employer's will and with other income from chance profits in petty trade or begging, stealing etc. in an everyday struggle for individual survival.

On the food availability side, there is, for the whole society, a strong structuring by time, linked to market arrivals and price fluctuations: food scarcity and price increases both affect consumer groups, although to varying degrees, and trigger temporary solidarity between classes in order to bring pressure on the government. Entrepeneurs, knowing the likely impact of food price increases on wages, use their political influence on the government as does the middle class, for whom food expenditures are still an important budget item. Trade unions organize protests, or spontaneous demonstrations occur. It is only when such street demonstrations cannot be kept under control by the police, that inter-class solidarity weakens.

The threat of food riots is generally sufficient to induce public authorities to carefully watch the food situations in cities and to take the necessary measures, particularly with respect to food subsidies and food imports which are mainly intended for city dwellers.

Thus we can say that the right to food is better-protected for the urban than for the rural poor, mainly because those who hold political power will not risk the development of an urban famine situation (at least in peacetime) which could threaten their own existence.

Urban circumstances therefore provide a certain degree of protection against collective starvation. This protection should be strengthened at the popular organizational level as well as the state level through appropriate employment and technology policies, fair price shops etc. We should not forget that in the industrialized countries of today, social achievements are not the natural outcome of economic growth; they have been reached through social struggles, through people's organizations and trade unions inspired by "utopian" ideas such as social justice.

Conclusion

Third World governments seeking to ensure the right to food of its peoples should adopt policies following the suggestions made above.

Such a benevolennt state would, of course, face many dilemmas between the interests of producers/consumers, short-term/long-term, consumption/investment etc., as well as the fundamental dilemma between a strong central State power and people's organizations. A prerequisite is, of course, that the power of the dominant groups be sufficiently eroded in favour of the majority to enable food deprivation to be attacked at its roots through internal redistribution of assets and political power. A corollary is that the State has enough bargaining power at the international level to obtain fairer terms for its international financial transactions, etc. To recognize the right to food for peoples and for the people is to recognize the necessity for nations whose food security is still at risk, to carry out internal structural changes, as well as to seek changes in the present international economic order. All those, dominant social groups or States, whose economic and political privileges are thus threatened, tend to limit the right to food to food aid, in particular if they are food exporting States. Continuing food aid, year after year, can be inducive to postpone structural political changes, but it can also be used in a very positive manner during a transition period in which structural changes are carried out. Yet, precisely when such changes are being initiated, as in Chile in 1972, food aid is withdrawn, development aid dries up and economic retaliation begins. In the gradual responses to structural change the next steps are disguised military interventions as in Nicaragua today, and then outright war. As this progression has unfortunately been well established during the last quarter of a century, nations attempting to ensure their people's right to food through policies of structural change have been forced to enter into economic and political alliances and to build up their military capacity. This is only possible by diverting economic and human resources from development tasks and making policies aimed at autonomy more difficult to carry out.

If there were only one justification for defining right to food policies it would follow from the recent policies of the International Monetary Fund, intended to bring pressure to bear on governments of African , Asian and Latin American countries to reduce food subsidies, in the name of economic realism. This invocation of market laws against the right to food of the poor caused food riots in Cairo and Tunis, in the cities of North East Brazil, and in the Dominican Republic. Those who have died in these riots have been deprived of their right to live in the name of "economic realism" taught in quiet university classrooms to students who can get the highest degrees and honors in Economics without having ever heard of words such as human dignity

184

or exploitation. The most sincere among the economists, including those at the IMF who propose policies which deny to the poorest of the poor countries their citizens' right to food, might feel they are taking rational technical decisions in the best interests of those countries. They may not perceive that if "the house has to be put in order", it is because disorder has been brought about by the existing international economic and political order which most strongly supports regimes that pose no threat on the status quo and that are not therefore not dealing with the real causes of poverty and hunger. We would suggest that future decision makers be exposed during their university years to the history of peoples' struggles for the recognition of their right to food so that when they take decisions, they do so "en toute connaissance de cause", as clearly as a soldier knows the result of pulling a trigger. Denying the right to food to peoples and to the people in the name of economic realism is naive ignorance on the part of some, or cynical realpolitik on the part of others. Through a campaign for the right to food, which focuses the limelight on peoples' history and their rulers' policies, let us educate the former and expose the real motives of the latter.

As Ernst Bloch wrote "human dignity is not possible without economic liberation, economic liberation is not possible without human rights (...) No genuine human rights can be established without the end of exploitation. No genuine end of exploitation can be arrived at without human rights".[16]

Notes

(1) For an elaboration of this concept see Spitz, "Drought and Self Provisioning", in Ausubel and Biswas (eds), Climatic Constraints and Human Activities, (1980).
(2) This word, taken from the Arabic Khazana, meaning "to store", is the root of the French "magasin", the English "magazine" (in its meaning of store) the Spanish "almacen".
(3) Chen Huang-Chang. The Economic Principles of Confucius and his school, Columbia University, New York 1911.
(4) Kung chvan Hsiao, A History of Chinese Political Thought (1979) Vol. 1, 458.
(5) Ibid, 460.
(6) Ibid, 465.
(7) Lysias, Discours, Volume II, Les Belles Lettres, (1926).
(8) See Spitz, "The Public Granary", CERES, Nov.-Dec. 1979
(9) Necker, Sur la legislation et le commerce des grains, (1775) also in Oeuvre Completes (1820-21).
(10) Beales, "The Making of Social Policy in the Nineteenth Century, Hobhouse Memorial Lecture (1946)" in Rose (ed.) The Relief of Poverty 1834-1914 (1972), 17.
(11) Rose, op.cit., 24.
(12) Boyd Orr, As I Recall (1966) 162-63.
(13) The Food Scandal, Fortune, May 1946.
(14) Tolstoy, La Famine, Editions Perrinot, (1893).
(15) We have referred above to redistribution along kinship or community lines patron-client relationships (in the latin-american form or the indian "Jajamani" form) etc. Gleaning rights were pre-capitalist forms of food rights. Increased monetarization and commercialization have restricted the access to wild produce, food and fuel, formerly freely collected. Some of these resources might appear quantitatively negligible but today often play a strategic role at particular times of the year to tide over periods of scarcity. The prohibition of access to forests at the end of the Middle Ages sprovoked revolts in Europe - similar measures in Asia, Africa and Latin America have been a source of great tensions.

(16) Bloch, Droit naturel et dignité" humaine, Payot, Paris, (1976), 13.
(*)This is the general approach taken by the Food Systems & Society programme of research carried out by UNRISD.
(**)These issues are among others dealt with in the Participation Programme of UNRISD.

The Right to Food and Agrarian Systems: Law and Practice in Latin America.

By
Roger Plant

1. The Problems Today: an Overview

In April 1984, rioting over massive increases in food prices in the Dominican Republic led to a death toll of some 52 dead. In one of Latin America's few "democracies", the army reacted quickly and savagely to spontaneous demonstrations in the capital city of Santo Domingo and elsewhere. The social democratic government, not previously tainted with the brush of repression, was determined to keep order after promulgating a series of austerity measures that raised the price of beans from 30 to 65 cents a pound, and a gallon of cooking oil from 9.75 to 25 US dollars. These measures, as the *International Herald Tribune* reported, had been demanded of the Dominican Republic by the IMF in order to end the nation's financial difficulties.

While the immediate catalyst to the April 1984 killings may indeed have been the IMF-imposed austerity measures of that month, the roots go further back. The Dominican Republic is a classic example of the one-crop export economy, of a small Caribbean Republic whose economy has been dominated by export-oriented sugar production since the late nineteenth century, and which has seen more and more of its best agricultural land given over to the production of cash crops for export in recent decades. Since the 1950's there has been a steady growth in cotton, coffee, and meat exports, together with sizeable amounts of land taken up with tobacco cultivation. As the price of sugar plummeted on the world market, from an all-time zenith of 65 cents per pound in the mid 1970's to an all-time nadir of 4.9 cents in mid 1984, the Dominican government was saddled with an enormous and growing debt. In 1982 the incoming social-democratic president, Dr. Salvador Jorge Blanco, affirmed that his government would pursue a policy of stimulating agricultural exports, together with the necessary austerity policies. The results, predictable enough, are now being seen. The carnage around the April food riots may be only the beginning.

The Dominican example is by no means unique. All over Latin America, similar patterns can be detected. In many countries, the land area under subsistence crops has declined sharply over the past one or two decades, and the area under export crops has correspondingly increased. The number of absolutely landless rural workers, or of "semi-proletarians" (small peasant farmers with too little land for their subsistence requirements) has meanwhile increased immeasurably. A few statistics can give some idea of the general patterns in the 1970's and 1980's. In Guatemala, the acreage under basic grain production actually declined from 969,000 hectares in 1970 to 719,000 hectares in 1978, while the acreage under export crops increased by some fifty per cent during this same period [1]. And in the Brazilian province of Sao Paolo, the acreage under traditional food crops similarly fell by 28 per cent, while the area under industrial and export crops was up by 53 per cent [2]. In the light of such statistics, it comes as no surprise that the Economic Commission for Latin America (ECLA) estimated in 1978 that 62 per cent of the rural households in Latin America could not satisfy their minimal subsistence needs.

In some areas, climactic factors have added to the structural problems. The north east of Brazil, for example, has suffered from a five-year drought that has, undoubtedly, had very adverse effects on food production. But, as a recent OXFAM publication has pointed out, climactic factors alone do not reveal why the price of beans rose by over 700 per cent during 1983 alone. The essential problem, as elsewhere in Brazil and the rest of Latin America, is that the marked growth in export-oriented commercial enterprises has led to a rapid decline in the labour force regularly engaged in agriculture. [3]

The severity of the problems does certainly vary from one country to another, and one cannot generalise for the whole of the Latin American continent. As a general rule one can say that, the earlier and the more comprehensively agrarian economies of these Republics were integrated within the world market, the greater the concentration of land today became, and the larger the percentage of the absolute landless rural population. The small Central American and some Caribbean Republics, which first developed one-crop export economies (sugar, coffee, or bananas) in the late nineteenth century, then diversified partially into other export crops after the second world war, tend to have the most acute structural problems at the present time. The countries which possess a larger land area, and whose agrarian economies have been less comprehensively dominated by export agriculture, proved more amenable to land reforms in the 1960's and 1970's. By the mid 1980's, however, some similarities can be found in the pattern of the majority of Latin American Republics. Saddled with enormous and growing private and public international debts, the governments of these countries are desperate for foreign exchange earnings. To bring in foreign exchange, they protect and encourage the agro-export sector, and exempt the agro-exporters from expropriation within land reform programmes. The international financial institutions (IFI's), likewise concerned with the balance of payments and the servicing of the burdensome foreign debt, place a similar emphasis on export-oriented development models, while exercising strong pressure on the Latin American governments to eliminate food subsidies for the marginal urban and rural poor. For the Latin American poor, it becomes an exceptionally vicious circle. The subsidies are cut out, cheap food policies are progressively eliminated, and lands for subsistence cultivation are progressively less available. And when the price of the export products falls dramatically on international commodity markets - as has happened with coffee, cocoa, cotton, and most markedly with sugar in recent years - the costs are passed into the work force in declining real wages. To attempt to protect themselves against the militant unionisation of rural workers, the agro-exporters make increasing use of contract labour that does not enjoy trade-union rights. During the harvest season, when the labour requirements of commercial farmers may increase by four or five times, recourse had traditionally been had to cheap seasonal labour. But in recent years landowners have tended to make increasing use of non-unionised contract labour even outside the harvest season.

As the percentage of the population without direct access to the land increases, and as the relative price of food rises, the problems of hunger likewise grow throughout Latin America. The right to food is violated, and measures are urgently needed to redress the situation. The mere proclamation of the right to food is of course not enough. Most Latin American Constitutions already proclaim the right to be free from hunger. Manifold structural changes are necessary, including land reform more genuinely adapted to the needs of the small farmer, tenant farmer, and landless labour than the tentative agrarian reform experiments of the 1960's and 1970's; and radical changes in credit, marketing, and pricing mechanisms in order to favour the interests of the small producer of food crops for domestic consumption rather than the large agro-export producer. And one obvious point is that enjoyment of the right to food is closely related to the rights of use and ownership of the land itself. The next section examines the nature of this relationship.

2. Land Rights in International Law

Food is essentially produced on the land, and is a prerequisite for human survival. International law may proclaim the right of everyone to be free from hunger. However, if all persons need access to the land or its resources in order to survive, one might expect to find some articles on land questions in the most important international human rights instruments. In fact, the only international instrument to deal specifically with **land rights** as such is the ILO's Convention 107, on the protection and integration of indigenous populations. It stipulates that the right of ownership, collective or individual, of the members of indigenous populations over the lands which they traditionally occupy shall be recognized. [4]

The Universal Declaration of Human Rights stated only that no one shall be deprived arbitrarily of his property: and that everyone has the right to own property alone as well as in association with others. This article, however, does not appear in either of the two human rights Covenants subsequently adopted by the United Nations - not surprisingly so, as the question of the ownership of property (in its private, communal, collective, or national forms) is perhaps the major source of ideological disagreement in the contemporary world.

What one does find, however - in the resolutions and declarations adopted by the United Nations over the past two decades - is a gradual but decisive movement away from private property notions, and towards acceptance of the principle that property has a social function. Thus property which does not fulfil this function is liable to expropriation in the national interest. The International Covenant on Economic, Social and Cultural (ESC) Rights has little to say on the matter. It contains only the somewhat general statement on agrarian policy that the States Parties to the Covenant, recognising the general right of everyone to be free from hunger, shall take individually, and through international co-operation, measures ... "to improve methods of production, conservation, and distribution of food by making full use of technical and scientific knowledge of the principles of nutrition and by developing or reforming agrarian systems in such a way as to achieve the most efficient development and utilisation of natural resources" (Art.11.2).

Thus in Article 11.2 - as indeed throughout this particular instrument - the language of the ESC Covenant lays more stress on the need for international cooperation to achieve a more equitable share of global resources than on the need for structural change at the national level. While mention is made of the need to reform agrarian systems in the interest of efficiency, there is no mention of the concept of equity within individual States. The emphasis is on the provision of technical skills in order to improve methods of food production, and on the need for mechanisms to improve food distribution at the international level. The pressing need for the redistribution of existing resources within those States with the most skewed patterns of land ownership is altogether overlooked.

The ESC Covenant was drafted in the 1950's, and reflects the trickle-down attitude to development that was so widespread at that time. In the three decades since then there has been a more noticeable trend within UN Declarations and Resolutions to emphasise the social dimensions of development; and to stress that the obstacles to meaningful development within poorer countries lie in unjust social structures at the national as well as the international level. Thus certain international instruments have stressed the importance of redistributive measures, not least with regard to the use and ownership of land. For example, the Declaration on Social Progress and Development, adopted by the UN General Assembly in 1969, endorses the social function of property, calls for the ownership of land and of the means of production which preclude any exploitation of man, and urges land reforms in which the ownership and use of land will be made to serve best the objectives of social justice and economic development. And in 1974 the UN World Food Conference adopted its Universal Declaration on the Eradication of Hunger and Malnutrition, which again stresses the need for structural changes in order to remove the obstacles to food production, and to provide proper incentives to agricultural producers. For the attainment of these objectives, it noted the need for "effective measures of socio-economic transformation by agrarian, tax, credit, and investment policy reform and the reorganisation of rural structures, such as the reform of the conditions of ownership...".

Similar conclusions and recommendations were adopted at the FAO's World Conference on Agrarian Reform and Rural Development (WCARRD), held on July 7, 1979 and attended by 145 Member States. The Conference adopted a detailed Declaration of Principles, together with a Programme of Action for the FAO itself and the other specialised agencies, which was later adopted by the UN General Assembly. While the language

190

in these documents is cautious - as might be expected from a declaration approved by almost every government in the world - the overall trends in the conclusions are clear enough. Agrarian reform policies in individual countries must aim at growth with equity, at the redistribution of economic and political power, at ceilings on the size of private landholdings; they must arrest trends towards unequal privatisation of rights and absentee ownership, and protect the right of small cultivators and nomadic populations; there must be greater local participation in agrarian reform and rural development programmes: security of tenure for tenant farmers must be enforced; and rural labour legislation should be enacted and enforced in order to protect rural workers from exploitation.

The issues of agrarian reform and land ownership have also received attention in the reports of the UN Secretary General on the "Right to Development". His 1981 report on the national and regional dimensions of the "Right to Development" mentions the need for agrarian reforms aimed at the requirements of social justice, as a precondition for the adequate realisation of those ESC rights enshrined in the Universal Declaration of Human Rights and in the International Covenant. It is once again emphasised that "the reality is that the desired transformation of agrarian society in most cases requires a change in the structure of political and economic power, both local and national".

To summarise, a number of United Nations declarations over the past fifteen years have reaffirmed that governments have the duty to reform inequitable and inefficient agrarian structures; and that landless workers and tenant farmers have the corresponding right to benefit from these redistributive agrarian reform policies and programmes.

Translating these standards into concrete and positive action proves to be a difficult task. Indeed, as it is generally accepted that the foremost obstacles to meaningful agrarian reform are political ones, it should come as no surprise that land reforms tend to be insignificant, and to have little effect on overall patterns of tenure, except in those cases where land reform programmes have been enacted after radical or revolutionary changes in government. But within the United Nations system itself, there has to date been inadequate attention given to the drafting of specific conventions which might lead to improved international monitoring of agrarian reform issues and other land-related human rights. For example, Article 23 of the ESC Covenant reads that the States Parties to this Covenant agree that "international action for the achievement of the rights recognised in the present Covenant includes such methods as the conclusion of Conventions, the adoption of recommendation, etc..". Article 2.I of the ESC Covenant, moreover, affirms that the steps taken at the national level to the rights enshrined in this instrument should include "particularly the adoption of legislative measures".

In other words the ESC Covenant does provide ultimately for the elaboration of specific and enforceable legal rights. Conventions should be adopted at the international level, and they should provide the general parameters by means of which agrarian legislations, as well as other aspects of economic and social policy, should be adapted to the requirements of human rights and social justice.

Unfortunately the FAO, the UN specialised agency charged with responsibility for food and agrarian questions, has devoted practically no attention to the vital issue of standard-setting. In the area of labour rights, the ILO has been extremely active in the standard-setting area, in formulating clear international labour standards through its 150-plus Conventions, in having these incorporated within municipal law as justiciable legal rights, and in providing for certain enforcement procedures through its complaints machinery and the work of its two Committees on the Application of Conventions and Recommendations. When ILO Conventions have been ratified, ratifying Member States have an immediate obligation to ensure that domestic law and practice is in conformity with the international standards. The ILO's successful experience in this area is doubtless due to its tripartite structure, in which representative employer and worker organisations in addition to government representatives form part of its governing body, and participate in its annual international labour conference where the Conventions and Recommendations are drafted.

The FAO's experience is markedly different. Its Charter, no less than the UN's Covenant, encourages it to draw up Conventions in its specific areas of concern. However, unlike the ILO, it is essentially an inter-governmental body with no specific procedures to allow for representation by the members of peasant and rural worker organisations, or even to facilitate a regular flow of information from non-governmental organisations. There is thus no pressure on the organisation to respond to specific grievances from below. The voices of peasants and rural workers are generally not heard, and play no part in the FAO's deliberations. The upshot of this is that the FAO has interpreted its standard-setting obligations in a highly technical manner, ignoring the structural problems that surely constitute the primary obstacle to adequate food production. As international lawyer Philip Alston has observed, not only has the FAO (together with WHO) so far produced no human rights-oriented Convention, but "..Even more disturbing than this past record of inactivity is the fact that, as far as can be ascertained, neither organisation intends to take advantage of such opportunities in the near future - despite the entry into force of the Covenant... There is no inherent justification for this neglect".[5]

The establishment of firmer criteria at the international level - perhaps through the adoption of specific Conventions focusing on the importance of redistributive land reform policies in the areas of greatest inequality and hunger, on the basic rights of tenant farmers and landless labourers, etc. - would also make it far easier to monitor the role and performance of multilateral and financial donors who can themselves have a decisive impact on agrarian policy. Policy analysts **within** the international financial institutions (IFI's), for example, may recognise the need for redistributive land reforms in the interests of both economic efficiency and social justice, but may be reluctant to dabble in internal affairs of aid-recipient countries which are construed by them as political rather than strictly economic. One such example

192

is the World Bank, where there seems often to be an immense gap between the rhetoric of its policy and the reality of its lending operations. In its publications, the World Bank has endorsed verbally a basic human needs concept of development and has stressed that its projects should be geared towards the requirements of the landless and the rural poor. In the mid 1970's, in the book *Redistribution with Growth* published jointly by the World Bank and the Institute of Development Studies in Sussex, some of the basic policy and practical dilemmas were described. The authors stressed that in the Latin American context they saw "an effective land reform as a necessary condition for the kind of strategy propounded in this volume", and noted in this regard that "the immediate problems are political rather than economic". They then argued the need for firmer general criteria for redistributive policies on which the Bank's individual country strategies could be based. First, they stressed the need for a firm endorsement by each of the international agencies of the importance of redistributive policies. Then, as a second step, they pointed to the vital need for the development of criteria to assess the extent and effectiveness of a country's "redistribution with growth" policies. Noting that objective criteria would be necessary if international agencies were to move more explicitly in support of such strategies, they asserted pertinently that:

"More objective criteria might also help take some of the ideological heat out of the debates and evaluations involved in decision-making... Indeed land reform is so crucial a measure for peasant welfare that it should be given central importance in any criterion of growth and redistribution policies. The adoption of such criteria would also help to legitimise the concern of international agencies - and possibly donor governments - with redistributive policies, sometimes argued to be matters solely of domestic concern" [6].

It has sometimes been suggested that the IFI's, which should take their decisions on strictly economic considerations, cannot be bound by the human rights instruments of the UN system. It is a specious argument, not only because the IFI's are themselves affiliated to the United Nations, but also because there is no such thing as a politically neutral economic decision. The problem, of course, is that the bulk of IFI funding comes from private banking sources, which are generally concerned to see a rapid and safe return on their investments. Hence the pressure in the IFI's to support those undertakings which are likely to prove most profitable in the short run, and which in current circumstances are most likely to consist of export-oriented initiatives in the rural sector. However, an important precedent was set in 1981 when a World Bank paper on the protection of tribal peoples recognised explicitly that the Bank must take cognisance of the requisite international human rights standards in dealing with projects that might have an adverse effect on tribal peoples' land rights. It noted in this regard that "The Bank, as an affiliate of the United Nations, should prudently be assured that those borrowers who are signatory to the UN Charter are complying with the spirit of the United Nations Charter, international covenants, treaties and agreements when it lends for projects affecting tribal people" [7].

In sum, there would appear to be a general acceptance within international fora that structural reforms are a precondition for meeting the requirements of human rights and social justice, including the production of adequate food to provide for domestic consumption needs. But the acceptance can be found in the "soft law" of innumerable declarations and resolutions by the UN, its specialised agencies, and other international bodies. There are no binding agreements - binding on either governments, IFI's, bilateral donors, or others - to support policies and projects that give precedence to redistributive reforms or food-first schemes rather than to the proliferating export-oriented agricultural enterprises. These problems are accentuated when foreign enterprises and transnational corporations develop an important stake in agribusiness within the developing countries. As the Sixth United Nations report on "Progress in Land Reform" observed pertinently in the context of Latin America:

"The best agricultural lands, usually plantations or large agricultural enterprises, are used for growing export crops. The crops produced on these lands earn foreign currency and the trade and balance-of-payments position of the country depends on them. This dependence has given the landlords additional power to prevent changes, on the pretext that changes would endanger their ability to meet international trade and monetary obligations and thus weaken the whole economy. This means that in many countries the best agricultural lands are excluded from any agrarian reform programme; sometimes the Governments themselves support or protect the latifundia used for the cultivation of export crops. The problem of protecting these large enterprises becomes more acute when the owners are foreign individuals or corporations. International market fluctuations and conditions forced the national landowners to associate themselves with foreign concerns; gradually they were absorbed into these foreign-owned commercial enterprises".

3. Land Rights and Land Reform in Latin America

Latin American republics, almost without exception, have agrarian reform laws technically in force today. The principle of the "social function of property" is generally enshrined in the Constitution. Many countries have a ceiling on the amount of land that can be held by individuals. And the legislation of most countries stipulates that land which does not fulfil its social function, which is left idle or inefficiently cultivated, is liable to expropriation with or without compensation, depending on the circumstances. The general principles behind the land reform laws of the last two or three decades have been summarised in the Declaration of Punta del Este, adopted by the Organisation of American States in 1961:

"To encourage, in accordance with the charactheristics of each country, programs of comprehensive agrarian reform, leading to the effective transformation, where required, of unjust structures and systems of land tenure and use; with a view to replacing latifundia and dwarf holdings by an equitable system of property so that, supplemented by timely and adequate credit, technical assistance and improved marketing arrangements, the land will become for the man who works it the basis of his economic stability, the foundation of his increasing welfare, and the guarantee of his freedom and dignity".

Since the early 1950's all Latin American countries with the exception of Argentina and Haiti have had some kind of agrarian reform programme. While these have generally been based on the principles of the Punta del Este Declaration, and have had such limited objectives as the abolition of semi-feudal labour systems and the abolition of the unproductive traditional ha-cienda, some have been far more radical. This has been particularly the case when land reforms have come in the aftermath of a social revolution, rather than being piecemeal reforms with the essential aim of **averting** social re-volution. Thus the Bolivian social revolution of 1952 was followed by an agrarian reform programme that nationalised all traditional haciendas in the *altiplano* region, and distributed the former estate lands to the former la-bourers and tenant farmers. Then came the Cuban revolution of 1959, bringing yet more radical land reform laws which confiscated large and for-eign-owned plantations, abolished tenancy and share cropping systems, and eventually provided for the expropriation of all farms over 40 hectares in size.

But the experience in many other Latin American countries, where land reform legislation had been enacted without such political upheavals, shows the limitations of law when the political will to enforce it is absent. In fact, long before the 1960's, when most of the "reforms from above" took place, a number of Latin American countries already had some kind of reform law on the statute, or labour legislation which placed certain limitations on the absolute ownership of rural property. Between the 1920's and the 1950's social legislation including labour codes, generally based on the new forms of social legislation adopted in Mexico after its 1917 revolution, were enact-ed in almost every Latin American country. It is worth examining the implic-ations of this legislation, and the relative rights and duties enshrined within it, in some detail. To appreciate the significance of the Mexican legal tradi-tion on economic and social rights, and its implications for legislative models subsequently adopted in other Latin American countries, one has to provide some historical perspective. The analysis must begin with the Spanish colo-nial legacy, for the reason that post-revolutionary Mexican land law aimed to restore certain forms of communal land ownership that were first legally recognised in the colonial era.

During the colonial era, relatively uniform patterns of land and labour distribution could be found throughout Latin America. The Spanish Crown attempted to safeguard the traditional farming systems of the indigenous po-pulations, and protect their communal lands against encroachment by the Spanish colonists. The Crown was concerned with the exaction of tribute, sometimes in cash but usually in kind by means of agricultural surplus. Moreover, the indigenous peoples were required to perform regular forced labour on the colonists' estates. The colonists, for their part, did their utmost to secure a permanent Indian labour force, through the introduction of the

195

debt-peonage systems that were later to become so widespread after independence. Land was in abundant supply, labour was scarce, and the land was considered valueless without sufficient labour. Historians have argued that this factor accounts for the early concentration of land in a few hands, even though the bulk of it was left idle; influential landowning colonists strove hard to limit the total number of landowners, in order thereby to reduce competition for the scarce Indian labour supply. Nevertheless, thanks to the endeavours of the metropolitan authorities, a significant amount of indigenous communal lands did survive intact by the end of the colonial era.

Upon independence in the early 19th century, the protection of Indians broke down. Liberal notions of property rights, recognising only private forms of ownership, replaced the mixed systems of the colonial era. By the mid-nineteenth century Civil Codes had been adopted in almost every Republic, providing for the abolition of communal forms of ownership, and the registration of individual property titles. In theory the Indians could register their lands with private title. In practice they rarely managed to do so. They ended up either on inferior lands in the more isolated mountain regions, or (in the majority of cases) as debt-peons on the proliferating haciendas. The nineteenth century saw the consolidation of the semi-feudal hacienda, autonomous and often producing little for the market.

From this time onwards the agrarian systems of Latin America began to evolve on different lines, depending on the extent of their integration within the world market. In the Central American Republics, the emphasis on large-scale coffee cultivation for export led to strong pressure on communal lands, and a high demand for labour on the new plantations. Thus laws abolishing communal farming systems were stringently enforced. Forced labour laws were also enacted, requiring former *comuneros* and other landless labourers to work on the plantations. Specialised rural police forces, created to enforce the laws and represent the landowners' interests, paved the way for the repressive militarisation that has dominated such countries as El Salvador and Guatemala up to the present day. In many Andean countries, where no single export crop dominated the economy at this time, there was far less pressure on the land, partly because the available land areas were so much greater, and partly because there was a smaller incidence of cash-crop farming for export with its concomitant demands for seasonal and plantation labour. Thus the letter of the law in the classic liberal era had a less fundamental impact on agrarian structures. Traditional *comunidades* survived alongside the large haciendas, even if not recognised in law, until the exclusively liberal notions of property rights were revised in the early twentieth century. In Brazil too, there was little pressure on the land in the nineteenth century. Much of the population resided in the north-east of the country, by the large sugar plantations previously worked by negro labour until the abolition of slavery. Labour was provided by squatters and tenant farmers on the large estates, who had no legal rights and were technically subject to eviction at any time. But such squatting was generally tolerated and encouraged, as long as the squatters provided personal services to the landlords and cheap labour during the harvest season.

196

It was in Mexico, perhaps even more than Central America, that the alienation of Indian land was widest at this period. By the time of the Mexican revolution in 1910 some half of the rural population were tied labourers on vast plantations, over a hundred of them over 100,000 hectares in size. But the Mexican revolution - the social principles of which were eventually to form the basis of agrarian reform and labour codes elsewhere in Latin America - then brought an end to the absolute liberal era. It brought a new legal tradition based on the principles of equity, recognition of communal land ownership through its *ejido* system, the social function of property, limitations on land ownership. The Mexican Labour Code of 1924 was also the first to recognise the labour rights of rural workers. It provided for the abolition of personal services and semi-feudal labour systems, for minimum wage legislation, and a series of welfare rights in which the obligation to provide social benefits (health care, housing, social security, etc.) fell not on the State but on the individual landowner in the countryside.

Labour codes based on the Mexican precedent were to be enacted in almost every Latin American country over the next three decades. The national codes discriminated at first against the rural sector. Many of them contained articles explicitly denying the right of association, or minimum wages, to hacienda and plantation workers. Others contained restrictions on the right to strike during harvest time, or restricted rural unions to farm enterprises that employed more than 15 or 20 workers. But militant pressure from rural worker organisations, to support demands that the labour laws be extended to rural areas, ultimately had their effect in many countries. From the perspective of the rural worker, these labour and welfare rights were seen as being of equal importance with the right to land itself. As one author has written on this issue:

"Labour legislation may be considered part of the rural property system itself. When such legislation exists (minimum wages, health codes, social security, tenancy law, unionisation provisions), it imposes legal limits on proprietorship, which must be considered, from the point of view of the landowner, as impositions on the scope or domain of the authority vested in him as proprietor of rural land ... Political capability of farmers to extirpate rural labour movements without resort to the coercive capacity of the nation state is a critical measure of the strength of rural proprietors as an autonomous class and of their ability collectively to control the countryside."[8]

By the 1960's the traditional latifundio - with its vast underutilised land area, its large number of tied labourers, and poor use of capital - had been earmarked by social reformists and agrarian capitalists alike as the main obstacle to progress in Latin America. It was also seen as a source of peasant unrest. The peasant *colonos* - the tied labourers and debt peons on the large estates - were paid well below the minimum wage, and were permitted to cultivate small parcels on the estates in exchange for the provision of labour. The excesses of the system had led to the Bolivian revolution of 1952, and to the short-lived land reform in Guatemala between 1952-4. Then the Cuban revolution of 1959 proved to be the major catalyst that ushered in the reforms "from above" in the following decade.

But with or without the Cuban revolution, the balance of power in much of Latin America would anyway have been propitious for the limited land reforms that were promulgated during this period. After the second world war, rapid industrialisation in certain countries was increasing the need for marketable, cheap food to cater for the needs of the rising urban population; political power was increasingly dominated, at least in the Andes, by a new entrepreneurial class who saw the unproductive hacienda as anachronistic; there were new opportunities for commercial and capital-intensive farming, with the expansion of export agriculture; and, most importantly, population increase and changing agricultural patterns meant that there was no longer a labour shortage in rural areas. By the 1960's there were already the first signs of the labour surplus which was to increase dramatically over the next two decades.

Perhaps the major deficiency of the average land reform law in Latin America is that, whatever its declared aim, its real objective was rarely to give land to the landless. Rather, the aim was to rationalise and modernise production methods, and replace semi-feudal and servile labour systems by more strictly capitalist ones. Thus the land reform laws, interpreting the social function of property by the criteria of efficiency and productivity alone, declared that uncultivated land was liable to expropriation. Except in such cases as the Chilean one (where a progressively lower ceiling was placed on retainable private land under the Allende regime before the land reform was altogether aborted by the 1973 military coup), the land ceilings were kept high, and landowners were usually given a period of time to bring the land under active cultivation. In both the Peruvian and Ecuadorian land reform programmes, the enforcement of labour legislation was an important criterion. Landowners who could be shown to have violated the provisions of labour law (on minimum wages, and other welfare provisions) were deemed liable to expropriation. In Ecuador, for example, landowners who had violated minimum wage provisions were given the choice of providing backpay to make up the difference, or giving land parcels in lieu. But the major point is that the reforms were premised not so much on the **rights** of the landless as on the obligations of the **landed**. In many cases, landowners who could prove that they were good and efficient capitalists, who abided by the provisions of labour law, were generally deemed to fulfil their social function and to be eligible to keep the land. Except in Peru, where very significant land distribution took place between 1968-75 and where special agrarian tribunals were given exclusive jurisdiction over land reform cases, the courts tended to favour the landowners and the forces of conservatism. Thus it was only when the central government was politically committed to reform, and deliberately built up strong peasant organisations as political support against conservative landowner interests, that major land distribution occurred (this was the case in Chile, Peru, and to a lesser extent Colombia in the late 1960's and early 1970's).

By the mid 1970's the distributive phase of these land reforms from above had ground to a halt throughout Latin America. In Central America, where military governments staunchly defended the interests of the large commercial farmers producing for the export market, land reforms never got off the ground throughout this period. In Brazil, land reform terminated after the military coup of 1968, in Chile likewise in 1973. By 1979, the participants at the seminar on "Human Rights in the Rural Andes" organised by the International Commission of Jurists noted that "agrarian reform has been abandoned throughout the Andean region". Since that time many peasant organisations which were once promoted by the reform-minded governments themselves (such as ANUC in Colombia, or the CNA in Peru) have been subject to severe repression. Throughout Latin America - whether in Brazil, Central America, or the Andes - similar tales are told daily of the harassment, imprisonment, torture, and murder of peasant leaders fighting to gain or defend the right to subsistence lands.

In some cases the reformist initiatives were terminated through violent military intervention. In other cases they ended less dramatically. But in structural terms, the reasons why this spate of reforms began, why they did, and ended when they did are basically similar. They began with a certain amount of consensus among reformist politicians, a large sector of the agrarian bourgeoisie, the US government and sectors of the military, all of whom wished to break down the feudal remnants of rural society and make increasing use of wage labour. Peasant militancy, and growing demands for the enforcement of labour legislation, minimum wage and tenancy agreements, certainly played a part in the reforms. Eventually, the militant demands of landless peasants for the land far outstripped the concessions that the agrarian bourgeoisie was willing to make. Moreover, the reforms often released additional labour onto the market. Not only did the landless tend not to benefit from these limited reforms: landowners tended to expel *colonos* and tied labourers from their land, particularly when the agrarian reform programmes had "land for the tiller" elements that aimed to convert sharecroppers and tenant farmers into owners.

We now return to food production, and the question of the right to food. Ironically it was these land reform programmes, which proclaimed the aims of social justice by terminating semi-feudal systems, that contributed to the food scarcity that plagues Latin America today. Under the old hacienda system, *colonos* might have to provide labour and part of their crop to the landowner, but they enjoyed a measure of food security. Capitalist farmers, who bring more of their lands under direct production, have no further use for the old *colono* system. As the labour surplus increases, depressing rural wages, it proves more profitable to use outside labour than to keep a small parcel of land more or less permanently out of production for the market through the *colono* system. Essentially, the *colono* tends to be another victim of the boom in export-oriented commercial agriculture. When there is a sharp rise in the price of such cash-crops as coffee, cotton, and sugar on the world market, the commercial farmer aims to bring more and more of his land area under cash-crop cultivation and to evict the traditional squatters. This phenomenon - the eviction of traditional squatters from their subsistence parcels on the fringes of large estates - has been a source of acute conflict in recent years, most notably in Brazil and such Central American Republics as El Salvador and Guatemala.

And then there is the problem of seasonality of employment. As subsistence farming gives way to export agriculture, as the frontiers of commercial agriculture expand and push untitled squatters off their traditional lands, the number of absolutely landless rural workers reaches alarming proportions. In Colombia it has been estimated at over two million. In El Salvador it was up from 12 per cent of the labour force in 1960 to an estimated 60 per cent by 1975. In Brazil, most of the 24 million people in the drought-ridden areas of the north-east are now said to be landless. And in export agriculture the bulk of employment is seasonal, usually for some three or four months per year. A small percentage of the labour force is guaranteed year-round employment: it is this minority which tends to be unionised, they enjoy a minimum wage, and the schooling, health care and pensions which have to be provided by employer to employee under the corporatist Latin American models (in which welfare obligations fall not on the State but on the individual landowner and employee). The majority has no permanent contract, no guaranteed employment or wage, and no legal claim against any entity for food and other necessities in the long period of scarcity. This is the new and burgeoning proletariat, tens of millions strong throughout Latin America, to be found on the edge of the commercial plantations or in the shanty towns that now proliferate in the major Latin American cities.

4. Concluding Comments

One can end with a few general observations on the nature of those economic and social rights which make up the "bundle of rights" involving the right to food, within the framework of this Latin American analysis. That land rights, labour rights, and the right to food are conceptually and pragmatically linked is a fairly obvious point. As food is generally produced on the land, access to the land or its produce is a prerequisite for survival. In a food surplus situation, or in an advanced welfare state, the access does not have to be direct. Some of the least equitable land tenure systems, in which agricultural land is concentrated in a few hands, may meet the nutritional needs of all the national population at a readily accessible price, and perhaps even leave a substantial exportable surplus. Access to food can be guaranteed in a multiplicity of ways - through food subsidies and cheap food policies, through social security or unemployment benefits, through family and child benefits, and the other mechanisms that may be taken more or less for granted by the citizens of the modern welfare state.

In the above situation, it is seen as the duty of the State to ensure the existence of the right to food for all citizens. Property as such is not directly tampered with, except through fiscal measures that guarantee some redistribution of the produce, and subsidies that affect the decision of the farmer to produce one commodity rather than another. In Latin America, as has been seen, State welfare mechanisms tend to be non-existent, in particular for the rural poor. But legislation in the area of economic and social rights does two

200

basic things. First, at least in the letter of the law, it provides for the redistribution of property which does not fulfil its social function; second, it places a large number of welfare obligations on the individual landowner. The battle is then to have the existing law enforced. When peasant movements were strong, and received some support from reform-minded governments who were determined to enforce the law even when it represented the interests of the peasants rather than the landowning elite, this led to some redistribution of agrarian property and resources. But as the rigid enforcement of social laws already on the statute would necessarily entail quite drastic redistribution, one of two things had to happen. **Either** the reform movement would become increasingly radicalised, leading to the whole- scale transformation of economic and political structures in the countryside. **Or** the governments themselves would resort to increasing repression against those peasant movements who demanded the enforcement of existing law. Except when there has been a *de facto* political upheaval (as in Cuba 25 years ago, or Nicaragua today), the latter has tended to happen. Peasant movements have been dismantled, rural repression has escalated, and in some cases the legislation in the area of economic and social rights has been amended through national security legislation restricting freedom of movement.

Nevertheless, there is no doubt that peasant leaders, progressive lawyers, and religious personnel have in the past made extensive use of existing law to support demands for radical social change. But, today the Latin American labour, agrarian reform laws provide for a complex and interlocking system of rights and obligations, which are in theory justiciable in municipal law. However, rights claims under this system can only be made against a landowner with whom the peasant or rural worker has some kind of contractual relationship. Such laws can be invoked to demand a minimum wage, genuine freedom to organise and bargain collectively, housing, health care, food, the abolition of peonage, fairer contracts for tenant farmers and share-croppers, etc. This was all well and good for the traditional estate labourer, or the salaried plantation employee, who could use such law to his advantage. For the floating landless labourer today, with no contractual relationship with any landowner, such legal remedies are useless. In many cases the only remedy is direct action, through land invasion and occupation in the search for a subsistence plot. And if that fails or meets with military or police repression, the only remedies left are far less peaceful ones.

Notes

1. Statistics taken from World Bank country report on Guatemala, 1980
2. See de Janvry, The Agrarian Question and Reformism in Latin America, (1981).
3. See OXFAM publications, An Unnatural Disaster: Drought in North East Brazil, (1984).
4. ILO Convention 107, "The Protection and Integration of Tribal and Indigenous Populations", 1957.
5. See Alston, Making and Breaking Human Rights, Anti-Slavery Society, (1979).

6. From: Redistribution with Growth, Joint Study by the World Bank's Development Research Center and the Institute of Development Studies at the University of Sussex, (1974).
7. See: Tribal Peoples and Economic Development: Human Ecologic Considerations, International Bank for Reconstruction and Development, (May 1982).
8. From: Loveman, Struggle in the Countryside, (1976).

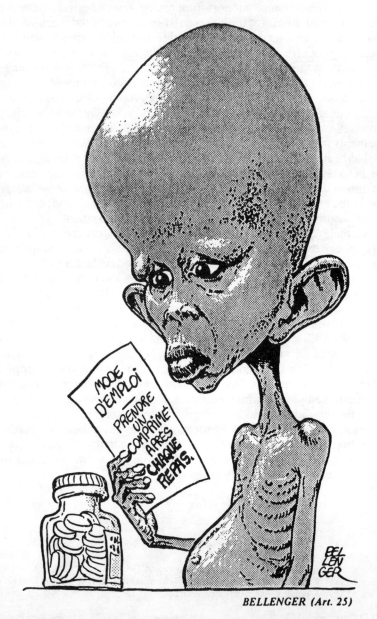

BELLENGER (Art. 25)

Reprinted with permission from 'Dessine-moi un droit de l'homme'
EIP-ISBN 2-88137-000-4

202

Developing the Human Right to Food as a Legal Resource for the Rural Poor. Some Strategies for NGOs

by
Clarence Dias and
James Paul

1. Developing Human Rights: A Participatory Approach

If human rights are to prove meaningful to those who most need them (namely the victims of human rights' deprivations), it is vital to adopt a "participatory approach" to the development of human rights and their enforcement. Thus, for example, in the development of a Human Right to Food, it is vital that groups of the rural poor presently confronted with hunger and malnutrition (and other support and action groups working with them) articulate **their** concerns and needs in regard to deteriorating food situations and formulate **their** strategies to develop and enforce a body of law to secure **their** right to food.

The essence of any human right is the power to command the protections promised by the right. The participatory approach is designed to help victims of human rights deprivations gain that power. The participatory approach is based on three underlying propositions:

1. Law is a resource which can be used both defensively and assertively by the rural poor in their struggles against conditions which produce impoverishment, deprivation, and oppression.

2. Human rights are very important "legal resources", because they empower the rural poor to participate in these struggles and demand protection of their basic interests.

3. Non governmental organizations (NGOs) of various kinds (from "grassroots" to international groups) have vital roles to play in these struggles.

Law as a Resource for the Rural Poor

It is notorious that in many third world countries (and elsewhere, too) law is used (and abused) to maintain social relations and patterns of "development" which produce economic impoverishment, physical deprivation, and political impotence. Thus, law (or, often, only the pretext of law) may be used to control access to vital resources (e.g., credit and basic services) or impose oppressive relations (e.g., in employment, land tenure, indebtedness) or to immunize public officials who abuse powers from accountability for their lawless behavior.

203

Paradoxically, just as law can be used to sustain practices which maintain impoverishment and impotence, so it can be used (both defensively and assertively) in organized struggles to change these terms and initiate a process of development by and for the rural poor.

In this approach law means more than simply official State law. There are other kinds of law which people, working together, can also use to help identify and redress wrongs, to protect and advance shared interests. These bodies of law include indigenous, customary (people-made) law and traditional concepts of fairness and justice; international law, notably the UN Covenants and other sources which declare universal human rights' law. All of these sources of law can be used (and have been used) by self-reliant, participatory groups of the rural poor to address many shared, pressing, social problems.

International Human Rights as Sources of Empowerment

Human rights laws can be used as very important resources by victims of oppression and deprivation. Particularly important are two bodies of "human rights" laws which are solemnly declared to be "universal" by the UN Declaration and UN Covenants on Human Rights (and by numerous other international legal instruments). These are:

1. the right of people to participate in political affairs, notably through their own organizations; and

2. the right of people to enjoy access to food, health, and education.

These two bodies of rights have a symbiotic relationship with each other; and they can be used to empower countless victim groups of people throughout the world who presently lack power and whose lives are presently threatened by hunger, disease, and lack of knowledge of ways to confront these essentially man-made (or man-condoned) conditions. Through self-reliant, organized efforts, victim groups can exercise the rights to:

(a) participate in processes designed to develop specific content to rights to food, health, and education by identifying specific remediable practices which threaten or deny these basic needs;

(b) impose accountability on officials and other power wielders who engage in, or condone, these wrongful practices; and

(c) undertake self-help activities to identify basic needs in relation to food, health, and education and to protect access to resources and promote activities to satisfy these needs.

The development of any new right enabling people to realize their basic needs is a process which usually entails a conjuncture of efforts by concerned specialists and progressive elites on the one hand to secure a declaration of the right and its implications, and grassroots' efforts by people to secure measures to interpret, apply, and enforce that right in particular contexts. This process often requires the generation and dissemination of new knowledge (including knowledge of law) creating new popular awareness, and then mobilization and demands by those who need specific legal protections

204

in order to realize their basic rights. Perhaps the most important chapters in the history of struggles for human rights are those which depict the efforts of wronged peoples to gain knowledge of their basic rights, and then assert particular rights which they deem essential to protect those basic rights.

The Crucial Role of NGOs

The term "non governmental" organization often connotes a rather neuter meaning in UN and related circles. But, in fact, governmental groups (including international agencies) are often neuter groups when it comes to sensitivity and political will to develop human rights. NGOs are often essential to enable people's participation in struggles to gain the power to realize rights which the world community has promised.

Those who most need the protections and entitlements contained in rights to food, health and education (*i.e.*, the rural poor), can least afford to be left dependent on governmental organizations for development of these rights. Rather they must create and use their own organizations to demand feasible measures necessary to realize their rights; and these "grassroots" organizations must usually be helped, in turn, by other kinds of NGOs. Indeed, the participation of at least several kinds of NGOs may be essential in developing and giving specific content to human rights' law; and in asserting, realizing, monitoring compliance and enforcing specific human rights.

By NGOs, we mean and refer to a variety of groups:

1. grassroots, participatory organizations of the rural poor;
2. social-action groups, which work with and for the victim groups;
3. legal and other specialized support groups which facilitate these struggles by providing technical knowledge and skills to the activist groups, and publicity and advocacy for their claims;
4. international groups which provide similar support to the other three.

The importance of developing networks and coalitions of these kinds of groups to enable victim peoples to realize their rights can hardly be overstated. Of course a central role must be played by grassroots groups, for their power to identify and enforce their rights must be the main object; if the poor are, in fact, to enjoy their rights. But all of these different kinds and levels of group activities may be essential if victim groups are to be formed and gain the resources they need to press claims for protection of their rights; if they are to gain the power to realize rights which the world community has promised.

2. Developing the Human Right to Food: Some Strategies for NGOs.

The participatory approach differs from conventional efforts to elaborate a right to food; efforts which assume that the content of the right must be developed "top-down" by UN agencies and by the work of cadres of "expert" officials, "eminent persons", "scholars", and other elites. Of course that

205

work is important. But, in our view, the right to food, like all other essential rights, must also be developed by those who most urgently need it. If the right is, indeed, to be a right of people, it must be used as a source of power by people; it must enable the victims of practices which demonstrably create food shortages to seek appropriate redress. Unless the law built around the right to food is developed in this way, the right will be meaningless for those who most need its protection, no matter how elegantly it is described by international elites.

Securing recognition of the right to food as a right of people capable of enforcement by people is, perhaps, the first challenge.

It is all too commonly claimed that there really is no human right to food, because:

1. The UN Covenants and other international declarations which proclaim the existence of a "right to food" only call for the assumption of "moral" obligations by governments; they create no entitlements which people can claim and enforce.

2. Even if these declarations do imply that people do have "a right to food", that proposition is legally meaningless because the "right" has no content.

3. Even if the right could be infused with some content, there can be no way of enforcing the entitlements promised.

In our view, these kinds of propositions ignore the plain meaning of the UN Covenants, the symbolic relationships between basic human rights and basic human needs, and the historic role of popular participation in struggles of peoples to realize human rights in order to satisfy essential needs. In different times and places people have mobilized and won recognition of those particular rights which were necessary to secure needs deemed essential.

Recognition of a right to food, like recognition of the right to life and physical security, should be a basic commitment of any government worthy of legitimacy. While the right to food may be less developed in countries where most people enjoy adequate access to food, articulation and enforcement of that right becomes a matter of the utmost importance in places where many people are confronted with declining production and other man-made threats to the availability of the food on which they rely for their very survival.

Article 11 of the UN Covenant on Social, Economic and Cultural Rights (commonly thought to be a primary source of the right to food) was drafted with precisely those concerns in mind; the plight of peoples in (mostly third world) countries who face deteriorating food systems.

A large part of the text of Article 11 does indeed set out (in rather vague terms) obligations to be assumed by governments. Those obligations are designed to protect those systems of production or distribution which secure the existence of food to all sectors of a country. But these general undertakings are indicative, not definitive, of a more basic underlying obligation. The Covenant calls upon governments to "recognize the right of everyone" to "adequate food" (Section 1) and, again (Section 2), to recognize "the fundamental right of everyone to be free from hunger." Thus, the particular gov-

ernmental tasks prescribed are founded on a more basic undertaking to recognize the underlying right of the people. By acknowledging food as a
"fundamental" human right, governments recognize their accountability
to people to secure the right; for the essence of a human right is the empow-
erment of people to insist that the right be enforced by measures appropriate
to the circumstances.

Thus, the existence of a right to food enables people to demand that governmental (and other) bodies address practices which threaten the production, distribution or preservation of food sources on which they rely. The
right provides an essential commitment to develop protective measures
geared to the country's needs; and people can demand their rights by the im-
position of accountability of those who fail to create or enforce these measures. The right enables people to participate in shaping policies and obligations designed to protect themselves from these ravages, which are all too
often inflicted by public or private actors under the pretext of promoting
"development".

Like all declarations of "fundamental" human rights, the right to food
must be seen as a bundle of rights, and these component rights must be developed locally to address a wide variety of problems in different social and
physical environments.

Identifying Component Rights which, together, make up people's basic
right to food is the second challenge. The task is to work with affected
groups, in different settings, to identify those particular practices which
threaten or presently impose intolerable deprivations in regard to food.

It is notorious that rural communities are the first and major victims of
food shortages; and it is equally notorious that these shortages are produced
by some combination of practices, such as the following (and these are only
illustrative):

- degradation of food-producing physical environments;
- withdrawal of productive land from food production under circumstances which threaten the food supplies of people;
- unfair terms of trade and/or lack of other incentives to producers (notably small-scale ones);
- interventions which enable governments (and sometimes private actors,
acting like feudal landlords) to siphon off food in one area to create surplus
supplies in others, thus exposing more vulnerable groups to the risk of famine;
- lack of facilities for local storage of crops, and for transport and marketing;
- lack of credit, extension, and inputs to small farmer producers; and
- lack of basic agricultural research directed towards their needs.

Where these and/or other practices demonstrably threaten the needs of
the rural poor in regard to food and nutrition, they can be remedied by various kinds of corrective legal measures. Through organization, deliberation,
and interaction with concerned specialists, people can come to understand
that they have rights to protect sources and systems of producing and distributing foods. Through interaction, they can identify those practices of gov-

ernmental or other bodies which significantly impair these basic rights; they can identify appropriate legal measures to prevent these wrongful practices; and they can assert their rights to demand these legal protections in order to vindicate their basic right to food.

Strategies to demand recognition and protection of Component Rights are a third set of tasks.

Once people begin to identify legal measures needed to vindicate their right to food, they can use a variety of strategies to demand them. Of course the particular strategies developed in any country must be determined through the collaboration of concerned groups and geared to the specific conditions and available resources and other factors which define food problems in that country. But it is possible to suggest, here, some illustrative lines of action, which NGOs, working together, can undertake.

These conditions might form a national working group to focus attention on "the right to food" and on ways to enforce it through more explicit legal protections.

The working group might undertake activities such as the following:

1. Promotional activities to familiarize people with their rights. Each group might prepare appropriate materials calling attention to the human right to food and to other human rights law, international and national, which bears on the rights of people to participate in activities to secure their right to food, and particularly the right of victim groups to participate in these processes.

2. Critiques of national policies and practices bearing on food production and distribution. Each group might prepare documents identifying practices which are clearly harming or threatening particular communities or sectors of the population, e.g. documents exposing discriminations in the allocation of resources by officials to small-scale food producers; or exposing activities which degrade food-producing environments; or expropriations of lands or water or forest resources on which people depend for food as well as livelihood.

3. Invocation of the right to food in national and international forums. Some practices may be susceptible of challenge in the courts in new test cases designed to implicate the right to food. Others could be challenged before administrative or legislative bodies. Protests might be lodged with international agencies such as FAO. A basic purpose is to dramatize demands for legal measures to protect food systems.

4. National charters of food rights might be developed, setting out in detail some of the component rights claimed and the ways by which these rights can be protected and steps people can take to demand protective measures.

5. Codes of Conduct. Each group, as necessary, might draft and publicize codes directed at people in agencies and firms which should be particularly sensitized to food issues by virtue of the power they wield over systems of production or distribution.

6. Critiques of national compliance reports required by signatories of human rights conventions. Under the UN Covenant, States Parties are required to report to the Secretary-General (according to guidelines issued by

ECOSOC) their efforts to discharge various obligations toward food production and distribution set out in the Covenant. Working groups might try to catalyze efforts at national level to subject these governmental reports to closer scrutiny and also to develop "alternative" non governmental reports; a strategy which, generally, may help put pressure on governments to take these rights more seriously.

Again we stress that the action strategies outlined here are only illustrative. The basic problem for concerned NGOs is to help initiate action by people to protect their rights.

3. Generating, Sharing, and Using New Knowledge to Secure the Right to Food.

NGOs concerned with using human rights to mobilize action against threats of hunger must obviously go beyond general pronouncements on the subject. The harder tasks are to work within specific (but differing) country environments to create knowledge which helps people in the country:

1. understand their right to food and how they can develop and use it;
2. take appropriate steps to realize that right.

The task may be difficult because, in most settings, there is an absence of an effective interdisciplinary network of human rights activists, scientists, social scientists, and jurists; an absence of combined efforts by grassroots" workers and different kinds of specialists to create the particular kinds of functional knowledge needed in that particular country to develop the human right to food. For example, the relevant scientific communities may have knowledge of important components of food problems and needs, and they may subscribe to the values underlying human rights and the priorities they imply. But these, often indispensable, experts may fail to appreciate their potential role as human rights activists because they have yet to perceive the way in which their knowledge can be used by other activists and specialists to develop legal measures to protect human rights; notably rights to food, health care, and education (*i.e.* access to essential knowledge). Similarly, lawyers may fail to see how the human right to food can be "operationalized" because they fail to see how specific bodies of scientific (and other "non-legal") knowledge can be used as bases for legal claims. Finally, people immediately threatened by food shortages may have indispensable perspectives on their needs and problems, but they may not understand how other practices and conditions affect their situation, and they may lack knowledge of their rights. Strategies to demand recognition and protection of component rights to food require efforts to fuse the knowledge of scientists, social scientists, lawyers, and the surrogates of grassroots groups.

Generating Needed Knowledge

Within countries threatened with food shortages there may already be im-

209

portant activities which are producing, or which can produce, different components of the knowledge needed to catalyze combined efforts by NGOs to demand protections for the right to food.

At grassroots levels there should be existing, or inchoate, organizations of victim people (*e.g.* peasants, agrarian laborers, fishermen, women food producers). These groups can contribute first-hand knowledge of practices which threaten sources of food production, of distribution, on which they depend. They need knowledge of their rights and means of enforcing them.

At national levels there may be groups of scientists, environmentalists, consumers, and others who also understand how particular practices (*e.g.* pesticides, crop displacement, food pricing, and distribution structures) are contributing to food deprivation. They, too, may need to know how this knowledge can be used to establish component rights and protections of the right to food.

At international levels there are, of course, many groups which are generating important components of knowledge which can be used in particular countries (*e.g.* knowledge of new technologies). But to be effective, international NGOs must be linked to and informed by national and grassroots groups.

At all of these levels there are social activists and (potentially at least) human rights lawyers who can identify ways of developing legal and other measures targeted against those responsible for wrongful practices, once such practices have been identified.

These existing bodies of knowledge can be marshalled and used to initiate periodic national reviews which would:

(a) identify violators of rights to food, *e.g.* apathetic bureaucracies which fail in their obligations to the rural poor; planners who ignore food problems; transnationals which destroy food environments; wealthy elites whose lifestyles are only sustainable through the perpetuation of hunger and exploitation of others;

(b) to identify victim groups, *e.g.* children, women, landless laborers, subsistence farmers;

(c) to identify institutions of research and action which could be drawn into a network for human rights activism around issues relating to the right to food; and

(d) to identify remedial measures to protect people's right to food in the particular setting.

Sharing and Using Knowledge

National reviews or similar efforts can be used by journalists, innovative advocates, teachers, and other publicists in campaigns to educate and dramatize needs to recognize people's right to food and ways of protecting it. There are many forums which may be used:
- the "media" (including schools and adult education programs);
- governmental bodies (*e.g.* ministries of agriculture, agencies which are

supposed to enforce environmental protection laws);

- the courts (*e.g.* civil suits brought by victim groups against persons or firms who negligently destroy productive resources such as land or crops, suits against distributors of dangerous pesticides, polluters of fishing waters, and other degraders of food-producing environments) and

- reform commissions and ombudsman-type agencies (*e.g.* demands for reforms in the administration of services (extension) or in the practices of relevant state enterprises (commodity boards)).

International and other forums outside of a particular country can be used by surrogates of victim groups. For example, international NGOs can help local social-action groups bring grievances before:

- international organizations which are charged with monitoring human rights enforcement, or international organizations which provide assistance to "development disaster" projects (such as dam building, which produces only displacement, poverty, and famine for the "victims" of the project);

- the foreign media to expose practices of TNCs which harm food-producing environments, or policies of international donors which ignore the needs of threatened peoples, or which produce crop displacements and other kinds of food problems; and

- foreign courts (e.g. tort suits against producers and exporters of products which are foreseeably dangerous to food producers or consumers in third world environments).

There are other roles which concerned international NGOs can play in efforts to secure protection of people's right to food. These NGOs may have far easier access to some of the essential knowledge, and to important advocates and forums. For example, they can make special contributions in helping to:

- promote understanding of the nature of the universal human right to food in international organizations, notably UN agencies and in some of the conventional NGO human rights organizations which, regrettably, have paid little attention to the right to food;

- help expose violations of this right by transnational actors (TNCs and international agencies);

- develop needed scientific research which can be used by victim groups (e.g. to improve production; to evaluate the impact of new technologies).

Hopefully, all this demonstrates the importance of developing working coalitions and effective networks among NGOs in order to combine bodies of knowledge and skills necessary to protect peoples' right to food in different parts of the world.

Strategic Action Campaigns

One way of catalyzing needed coalitions of NGOs, sympathetic specialists, and victim groups is to mobilize around campaigns to deal with a visible disaster which:

(i) can be alleviated by combined efforts to produce remedial measures, and which

211

(ii) quite clearly dramatizes the importance of the participatory approach to the development of the human right to food.

For example, a recent issue of India Today (February 29, 1984) provides this report:

"One out of every 20 children born in 11 populous districts of the sub-Himalayan belt in eastern Uttar Pradesh and northern Bihar is virtually retarded with no hope of recovery. This happens because the mother's body lacked an adequate supply of iodine. This discovery has been made by a group of researchers in the capital's All India Institute of Medical Sciences (AIIMS), who say they are shocked at what they have found. So is the international scientific community.

The new findings have busted the decades-old myth that iodine deficiency - which is common in large parts of India, China, Indonesia, Nepal, Vietnam, and some other regions of the world - caused just goitre, an ugly swelling of the thyroid gland in the neck which is, however, no more than a cosmetic problem.

The AIIMS researchers have conclusively proved that iodine deficiency in these areas, inhabited by over 125 million people in India alone, has resulted in widespread feeble-mindedness. Says Dr. N. Kochupillai, the leader of the AIIMS team: "In the villages we have surveyed so far, 4 to 15 percent of the babies are born with thyroxine deficiency that will prevent them from realizing their full mental potential".

The scientists have, however, not stopped at just discovering a problem of such wide-ranging consequences. Last fortnight they submitted to the Union Health Ministry the report of their experiment on a program to arrest the decay by injecting all the women in the region with iodine. This would not only give babies born in the future enough iodine for brain development at the foetal stage, but will also maintain sufficient quantities of breast milk for three to four years.

The findings have already been presented at international forums including the Asian Congress of Nutrition at Bangkok in November 1983, where participant nations - Australia, China, Indonesia, Thailand, Vietnam, and India - adopted a joint resolution to fight the problem together and to make eradication of iodine deficiency a major component of the "Health for All by 2000 A.D." program.

Ideally, medical experts say, the way out is a complete ban on the sale of uniodized salt. But since that requires building of technical infrastructure for iodization and a distribution network in far-flung areas, the ICMR-AIIMS group has come up with an alternative to "buy time" till a breakthrough is achieved.

In fact, UNICEF had initiated India's National Goitre Control Programme (NGCP) by donating as many as 12 salt iodization plants. But the scheme has functioned in fits and starts because of the apathy of the State Governments. Says Dr. Pandav: "Of the plants given by the UNICEF, two were installed at Gauhati and they never started functioning. Now UNICEF is offering more plants, but we are not in a position to take these as we have

212

not even been able to decide where to install them.

A consequence of this administrative failure has been a spurt in the quack business. In regions with a high rate of deficiency, hundreds of small-time clinics peddle iodine paint as a magic cure for the problem.

Medical experts [also] explain that with increased deforestation and flooding, iodine is being washed away from the topsoil in increasingly large regions of the country and unless steps are taken now, there will be no way of preventing the birth of an increasing number of retarded children."

This report of a terrible tragedy suggests a number of points which we have stressed here:

(1) the need for a variety of NGOs to join together to address the problem, particularly victim-group organizations whose rights will only be protected when they understand their problem and when they are able to command food supplies with the requisite iodine;

(2) the need for concerned experts and NGOs (including international NGOs) to convert what WHO and medical groups perceive to be a "nutritional" problem into a most urgent "human right" problem; a problem of empowering gravely threatened people to demand remedial measures;

(3) the need for concerned people to recognize that protection of these rights goes far beyond the "stop-gap" measure proposal (e.g. injections); the "bill of component rights" of the women, children (and children-to-be) in Uttar Pradesh and Bihar includes rights to: remedy government failures to produce iodized salt and hold apathetic officials accountable; popular instruction on alternative methods to correct dietary deficiencies; enforcement of existing environmental conservation laws (and enactment of new ones where necessary), and these are only illustrative measures; and

(4) the need for different kinds of NGO groups, activists, and specialists to combine their knowledge to help those threatened to protect themselves.

The "iodine tragedy" exemplifies a type of shocking scenario which is regularly discovered in one or another part of the world today (e.g. tragedies caused by the exportation of dangerous pests and pesticides). These "discoveries" can, at least, be utilized by human rights' activists to mobilize requisite knowledge and skills so that the victims of events can secure redress as a matter of right rather than grace and charity.

We have sketched a participatory approach to the development of the human right to food as a means of empowering victim groups (and social-action groups working with and for them) to identify and demand protections against man-made practices which produce food shortages, hunger, and malnutrition. In this approach, the development of the right to food and measures to protect it is an ongoing process. It will require continuing efforts to generate and fuse different kinds of knowledge and skills, continuing efforts to forge concerted action by different kinds of NGOs, and continuing efforts by jurists and others to review existing bodies of law and develop new kinds of legal protections to redress harmful practices and secure those component rights which impart substance to the right to food.

Part V:
Annexes

SIM Right to Food Conference:
A Synthesis of the Discussion

prepared by
Rene Guldenmund

Legal assistant at the Europa Institute of the University of Utrecht.

SIM CONFERENCE

From 6 to 9 June 1984 the international conference on "The Right to Food, from Soft to Hard Law", was held at the conference centre "Woudschoten" near Utrecht. The SIM * project on the right to food (see SIM Newsletters nos. 4 and 6) culminated in this conference, which was co-organized by the Norwegian Human Rights Project and the Christian Michelsen Institute. There were 42 lawyers, nutritionists, and development experts, from all parts of the world, and from both non-governmental and intergovernmental organizations. The conference provided a forum where lawyers and non-lawyers could discuss the various aspects pertaining to the right to food. Working papers were prepared by 15 participants. The morning sessions were plenary sessions, the afternoon sessions were divided into working groups.

Pieter van Dijk, chairman of the board of SIM, presided over the opening session. The keynote speaker was Philip Alston (Harvard Law School), and introductions were given by Hans Thoolen, Director of SIM, and Asbjørn Eide of the Norwegian Human Rights Project.

There were working groups on Food Needs and Food Policies, chaired by Tony Jackson (OXFAM) with introductions by Adolfo Mascarenhas (BRALUP, Tanzania) and Wenche Barth Eide (Institute for Nutrition Research, Norway); on the Right to Food and Existing Law, chaired by Ramendra Trivedi (Human Rights Institute, Lucknow, India) with introductions by Roger Plant (researcher, England) and Fried van Hoof (University of Utrecht); on the topic of Human Needs, Human Rights, and the Role of Law in Development, chaired by Henry Shue (University of Maryland, USA), with introductions given by Clarence Dias (Centre for Law in Development, New York), Lim Teck Ghee (CAP, Malaysia), Pierre Spitz (UNRISD, Geneva), and Peter Weiss (Centre for Constitutional Rights, New York).

Other working groups considered IGO Responses to Food Needs, chaired by Rup Hingorani (Patna University, India) with introductions by José Antonio Viera-Gallo (FLACS, Chile), Gert Westerveen (SIM), and Katarina Tomasevski (University of Zagreb, Yugoslavia); and NGO Responses to Food Needs, chaired by Dinah Shelton (University of Santa Clara, California, USA), with introductions by Rolf Künnemann (Food First International Action Network) and Robin Sharp (WFA, England). Theo van Boven presided over the closing session.

1. Food needs

The estimation of food needs is the first issue to be addressed, whether in a "political" or a "technical" approach, to implementation of the right to food. It is often stated that there is a lack of data on the hungry, but this assertion was rejected during the Conference in favour of the view that there is a lack of *information* rather than of data. It was emphasized that the two things should not be confused. There are plenty of data available as a result of which policy makers have a wide choice from which to select. Data might be false, partial, misleading or irrelevant, particularly with respect to the right to food. For example, the annual production figures for basic foodstuffs do not reflect seasonal variations which can be crucial for meeting basic food needs. The available data thus have to be analysed and interpreted in the light of other relevant information. Despite this crucial difference between data and information, it was concluded that there was a frustrating lack of such integrated analyses, as a result of which a distorted picture of reality is perpetuated.

The existing data bases for the assessment and reporting of food needs were discussed extensively. From a human rights viewpoint, it is a particularly significant issue, since decisions based on inappropriate data can affect the fate of millions of the people. *Participation* was emphasized as the key too effective decision-making and as an indispensable element for defining and realizing the right to food.

As to information needs, it was frequently stated that the data used do not reflect closely enough the actual conditions. On this ground the rejection of the term "hunger" was even proposed, implying the abolition of data on the extent of the realization of calorie/ protein norms which are currently being used to determine the existence of hunger. It was also suggested that quantitative information should be supplemented by *qualitative* analyses.

Yet, while there was a high degree of consensus on the need for utmost caution in the design and use of quantitative information, it was emphasized that people need all the information they can get, if they are to be able to assert their right to food in a meaningful way.

2. The concept of "food" in the context of the human right to food

A dialogue between lawyers and specialists from other right to food related disciplines (nutritionists, agriculturalists, developmentalists, economists, political scientists) raised the crucial issue of how the concept of "food" is to be defined if it is to be meaningful in the human rights context. A lot of criticism was addressed to the traditional concern with "calorie requirements" as the criterion for determining the satisfaction or otherwise of peoples' food needs. This led to the assertion that people are often treated as machines as if "fuel" (calories) is needed to keep up the "engine". Alternative approaches were discussed, focusing particularly on the need to define food in a wider sense, taking account of human and social factors and lowering the level of analysis to the local level. It was underlined that food has to be defined in terms of requirements for a culturally satisfactory food pattern.

Discussions of *world hunger,* a popular topic of international political and expert meetings, were criticized for frequently over-simplifying the problems on the agenda. If "hunger" is simply defined in terms of calorie/ protein requirements, quantitative averages may be the appropriate criteria for defining the nature and scope of the problem. But if hunger is defined in terms of economic, social, political, cultural and other structural factors, which deprive some people of access to land, work and food, then the range of issues to be addressed is much wider (including land tenure, access to work and food, etc.) and is oriented towards the causes of hunger, rather than its manifestations. The discussions during the Conference reflected the latter approach.

3. Food strategies and food policies

The concept of food strategies, as recently promoted by international food agencies, was a frequent topic of discussion during the Conference. It was noted that, while the newness of the concept precluded making any definitive evaluations, the promises implied in the relevant documents advocating food strategies do not seem to have been fulfilled. In some respects it seems that, while implying a new approach to solving food problems, food strategies are often used merely as a slogan. There has been little attempt to understand how food systems function in practice and a lack of analysis of food problems in a specific time and space context. There was little or no participation in the formulation of food strategies by the local people, other than governmental officials. The issue of *who* will shape food strategies was considered extremely important. Additionally, the belief that international agencies know what are the needs of particular countries was questioned.

Again, the lowering of the level of analysis and planning was considered necessary. It was asserted that concern for food security should not be confined to the national average, but analysed at the local and household level.

The controversy over whether to seek to impose stronger obligations upon governments was also discussed in that context. The essential approach of the majority of lawyers is to elaborate governmental obligations relating to the realization of the human right to food. However, imposing obligations upon governments strengthens the role of the state and removes the focus of activities from the people themselves to the authorities. The example of Tanzania was given: in former times, it was customary for households to have food reserves in granaries, but that idea is dying out now, and instead people look towards the government for assistance in conditions of food shortages. The contrary approach of Switzerland was cited, where the legislation requires every household to have food reserves for at least 15 days.

4. The right to food and international law

The international law approach to the human right to food was the overall

217

focus of the Conference. Extensive discussions dealt with the interpretation of the existing sources if international law, primarily international human rights law, but also international monetary law as applied by the IMF (the International Monetary Fund), the law governing international development assistance, the legal regimes of food aid, and the lack of international legal regulation of property issues.

An issue attracting a lot of attention during the discussions was the impact of economic and monetary measures on the enjoyment of human rights, and on the right to food in particular. The need to clarify the human rights implications of such measures was emphasized particularly since such consideration is completely lacking at present.

The distinction between "soft" and "hard" law was analysed from various perspectives, including the one focusing on human rights as a whole being treated as "soft" law. The orientation suggested by the very title of the Conference, *from soft to hard law* implied both the translation of human rights norms into "hard" law and the integration of human rights norms into other existing areas of "hard" law.

It was also recognized that the undue proliferation of new human rights leads to the weakening of the normative strength of the overall concept and of its appeal to public opinion, thereby diminishing the support for human rights movements. It was frequently emphasized that the human right to freedom from hunger, as the first stage in the realization of the right to food, has been singled out in the Covenant as a "fundamental" human right - the only economic, social or cultural right to achieve such recognition. While there was no support for any hierarchies of human rights voiced at the Conference, it was frequently emphasized that the right to food has not acquired the priority accorded to it by the relevant sources of international law and policy-documents of the relevant international agencies.

Discussions on the significance of the right to food as a *fundamental* human right brought up questions of the interpretation of basic international law provisions. It was stressed that the relevant sources spoke about the fundamental right to freedom from hunger. The discussions on fundamentality and universality resulted in proposals to structure the right to food in terms of different levels of obligation in order to facilitate its progressive realization. Freedom from hunger was suggested as the minimum norm, which should immediately be realized for everybody; the right to food, which should take account of both the quantity and quality of food, would be the intermediary norm; and the right to adequate food, as the full norm, would include the requirement of a culturally satisfactory food pattern, while affirming the full enjoyment of human rights in its proclamation and realization.

ILA RIGHT TO FOOD COMMITTEE

Several members of the International Law Association's Committee on the Right to Food, chaired by Asbjørn Eide, who is also the UN Subcommission's rapporteur for a study on the right to food, participated in the conference and benefited from the comments by other participants. The ILA Committee, which is studying the possibility of strengthening the right to food through a more elaborate international instrument, also used the occasion of the conference to meet several times in private.

On the basis of these discussions the Committee submitted a preliminary report to the ILA General Conference in Paris in August 1984. The Committee will send its final report to the next General Conference, in 1986.

5. The right to food and municipal law

A general approach to the right to food was suggested by the widely recognized need to increase the use of law to affirm, uphold and protect human rights. It was pointed out that local conditions were a critical factor in determining whether "soft" or "hard" law approaches were more appropriate. Numerous examples were given of well formulated laws being completely ignored and of instances in which "soft" law had proved to be eminently workable in practice. Additionally, it was asserted that there are many ways of using law to promote respect for human rights without needing to resort to human rights legislation in the narrow sense.

Within the discussions on the right to food and municipal law, particular attention was paid to case studies of India and of land rights in Latin America.

The Indian Constitution does not refer to the right to food, but it does embody the basic guarantees envisaged by the Universal Declaration of Human Rights. The right to food is covered by interpretations of the directive principles of the Constitution, dealing with the right to work and the protection of employees, the right to adequate means of livelihood, the right to education, and the duty of the State to raise nutritional levels and to improve public health. The practice of the Indian Supreme Court was cited as an example of making traditionally non-justiciable rights enforceable by creative interpretation of the law.

Issues of access to land in Latin America were analysed from human rights perspectives, and the attention of the participants focused on the impact of export-oriented agriculture on the enjoyment of the right to food. Interlinkages between land rights and the right to food were discussed specifically by using examples of extensive land-reform programmes.

The introductory question of "soft" and "hard" law as options for the promotion of the right to food was further developed through discussions of the border-lines between laws and policies on the one hand, and between food laws and human rights laws on the other hand.

6. International Actors and the right to food

The discussion of the impact of existing international organizations on the

219

promotion of the right to food was divided into an analysis of inter-governmental organizations (IGOs) and of non-governmental ones (NGOs). Yet, this division was not underlined in the discussions, since there are many reciprocal influences which bring the work of the two types of organizations closer together.

Discussions focusing on the IGOs culminated in the assertion that the extent of a given agency's emphasis on the right to food is in negative proportion to its power: thus the most powerful IGOs do not seriously advocate the right to food, while human rights bodies which do, have no power. It was particularly emphasized that some of the UN agencies which have a significant impact on access to food for millions of people, such as the IMF, avoid any reference to human rights. Additionally, it was emphasized that the FAO promotes legislation on many topics related to the human right to food, but not on the right to food. Again, the fact of "technical" laws regulating "technical" issues and "soft" law dealing with human rights came up. It was considered significant that the FAO has largely ignored the legal aspects of the right to food.

A principal issue discussed was the role of IGOs in monitoring the satisfaction of food needs. After lengthy discussions, three suggestions were advanced: to set up an international monitoring system through co-operation among the relevant UN bodies; to redesign the reporting system under the Covenant; and to set up an NGO monitoring scheme which would employ an Amnesty International-type approach involving the "mobilization of shame".

Proposals for monitoring schemes were evaluated against the necessity of defining a precise focus for any such scheme. It was emphasized that the right to food was too vague, too broad and too far-reaching; a priority task for researchers was therefore to specify its contents, so that operational components could be identified and monitored.

The need to give precise content to the right to food at the same time as initiating action on a variety of levels by and for those deprived of food was stressed. The need for popular solidarity where violations occur was identified as a priority and the "urgent action" model of Amnesty International was suggested as a possible approach.

Constraints and difficulties faced by NGOs were noted with concern, especially government harassment and pressure in many countries, lack of funding and personnel, and the frequent existence of mutual suspicion among NGOs.

Because of, and to some extent in spite of, these difficulties, it was generally concluded that the greatest need is a network of support by and among NGOs which would include the mobilization of other private sector groups such as professional organizations of lawyers and doctors and churches in the fight against hunger. This network could strengthen existing NGOs, building and using human rights law and developing a concrete, realistic program of action on the right to food. It was unanimously asserted that in all such efforts, the interdependence and inseparability of all human rights must be recognized and reaffirmed.

220

Specific proposals for action which were discussed during the Conference, included NGO investigation and fact-finding of specific cases of food deprivation. The need for a constant dialogue between human rights lawyers and NGO activists was emphasized, wherein the latter may identify concrete examples of violations of the right to food for remedial action.

Also mentioned were proposals for:
- building grassroots support for victims of violations of the right to food, through educating and mobilizing public opinion;
- using legal strategies such as national and international test cases;
- adopting mechanisms such as boycotts to dramatize and influence particular issues.

It was concluded that these and other actions could be undertaken by a co-operative network of NGO's which would then contribute to efforts underway in intergovernmental organizations to elaborate and implement a right to food strategy.

NGO FOLLOW-UP

A number of non-governmental organizations and networks also had an informal meeting, in which the non-governmental follow-up was the central theme. It was agreed to continue to seek ways and means to exert pressure on IGOs and governments to give substance to the existing right to food and to underscore this right to food approach in their actions. At the World Food Assembly, a meeting to be held in November 1984 in Rome, the question of NGO action will be discussed further.

It was agreed that Rolf Künnemann of FIAN would take the lead in preparing the follow-up, including the possibility of an annual report written and published by non-governmental organizations and individual researchers with the aim of focusing attention on the real causes of continuing world hunger.

* Netherlands Institute of Human Rights (SIM).

Index

Authors' notes

ALSTON, Philip, LL.M, B. Comm. (Melbourne), LL.M, J.S.D. (Berkeley) is Lecturer on Law, Harvard Law School, 1984-85. He is on leave from the United Nations Centre for Human Rights in Geneva where he has worked since 1978. In 1974-75 he was Principal Private Secretary to a Cabinet Minister in the Australian Government. Among other publications, he is the editor of the English version of The International Dimensions of Human Rights (2 vols., UNESCO, 1982).

DIAS, Clarence J., is a legal aid lawyer from Bombay, India. He has taught law at the post-graduate faculty of law of the University of Bombay and at Boston College Law School. He is currently president of the International Center for Law in Development, New York.

GOODWIN-GILL, Guy S., M.A., D. Phil. (Oxon), Barrister-at-law, has worked as a Legal Adviser in the Office of the United Nations High Commissioner for Refugees since 1976, prior to which he taught law in London. His publications include International Law and the Movement of Persons Between States (1978) and The Refugee in International Law (1983).

HOOF, Godfried van, is at present Senior Lecturer at the Europa Institute of the University of Utrecht in the Netherlands. He received his LL.M in 1974 and his J.S.D. in 1983 from the University of Utrecht. He has published extensively on the theory of international law, international economic law and human rights. His publications include the book Rethinking the Sources of International Law (1983).

PAUL, James C.N., in addition to his work at the International Center for Law in Development, currently is Professor at the law school of Rutgers University and is an Adjunct Professor of Law at Columbia University. He was earlier academic vice-president at Haile Selassie University, Addis Ababa, Ethiopia.

PLANT, Roger, is an independent writer and consultant based in London, specializing in human rights and rural development issues in Latin America and South East Asia. He is the author of Guatemala: Unnatural Disaster (1978) and Sugar and Modern Slavery (forthcoming, 1984). He has been a consultant to the UN, ILO and several international NGO's.

SHUE, Henry, is a Senior Research Associate at the Center for Philosophy and Public Policy of the University of Maryland. His publications include the book Basic Rights: Subsistence, Affluence and U.S. Foreign Policy (1980).

225

SPITZ, Pierre, is a French agronomist, economist and sociologist. His home institution is the French National Institute of Agricultural Research (INRA), Department of Economics. On leave from INRA since 1977, he has been directing at the United Nations Research Institute for Social Development (UNRISD, in Geneva) an interdisciplinary research project on food security (Food Systems and Society).

TOMASEVSKI, Katarina, is a Scientific Associate of the Institute for Social Research of the University of Zagreb, Yugoslavia. She received the LL.M from Harvard Law School in 1977 and the J.S.D. from Zagreb University in 1981. Her publications include The Challenge of Terrorism (1982) and Measurability of the Realization of Human Rights (1983).

WESTERVEEN, Gert, is a legal researcher at the Netherlands Institute of Human Rights (SIM). In 1981 he took a masters degree in public international law and in Dutch constitutional law at the University of Amsterdam. He wrote earlier on the right to food in a Dutch publication Voor Spek en Bonen (Be present on sufferance).

Contents

227

AMARTYA, Sen, is Drummond Professor of Political Economy at Oxford University and Fellow of All Souls College. He has been Professor of Economics at the London School of Economics, at Jadavupur University, Calcutta, and at Delhi University, as well as Visiting Professor at the Massachusetts Institute of Technology, the University of California at Berkeley, Stanford University and Harvard University.

His publications include: Poverty and Famines: an essay on entitlement and deprivation (1981).